DECOLONIZING ETHICS

PENN STATE SERIES IN CRITICAL THEORY

Eduardo Mendieta, General Editor

The Penn State Series in Critical Theory showcases the work of contemporary critical theorists who are building upon and expanding the canon of the Frankfurt School. Based on a series of symposia held at Penn State University, each volume in the series contains an original essay by an internationally renowned critical theorist, followed by a set of critical essays from a number of authors as well as the theorist's response to these essays. Books in the series will focus especially on topics that have been previously neglected by the Frankfurt tradition, including colonialism and imperialism, racism, sexism, and ethnocentrism. They offer analyses and readings that show the continuing relevance of one of the most innovative intellectual traditions of the last century.

Other books in the series:

Amy Allen and Eduardo Mendieta, eds., *From Alienation to Forms of Life: The Critical Theory of Rahel Jaeggi*

Amy Allen and Eduardo Mendieta, eds., *Justification and Emancipation: The Critical Theory of Rainer Forst*

Decolonizing Ethics

The Critical Theory of Enrique Dussel

EDITED BY AMY ALLEN AND EDUARDO MENDIETA

The Pennsylvania State University Press
University Park, Pennsylvania

Portions of chapter 3 previously appeared in Linda
Alcoff, "The Hegel of Coyoacán," in *boundary 2*
45, no. 4 (2018): 183–202. Copyright, 2018, Duke
University Press. All rights reserved. Republished
by permission of the copyright holder, Duke
University Press. www.dukeupress.edu

Library of Congress Cataloging-in-Publication Data

Names: Allen, Amy, 1970– editor. | Mendieta,
    Eduardo, editor.
Title: Decolonizing ethics : the critical theory
    of Enrique Dussel / edited by Amy Allen and
    Eduardo Mendieta.
Other titles: Penn State series in critical theory.
Description: University Park, Pennsylvania :
    The Pennsylvania State University Press, [2021] |
    Series: Penn State series in critical theory | Includes
    bibliographical references and index.
Summary: "A collection of essays on the work of
    Latin American philosopher Enrique Dussel,
    focusing on his ethics of liberation"—Provided by
    publisher.
Identifiers: LCCN 2020058278 | ISBN 9780271089553
    (paperback)
Subjects: LCSH: Dussel, Enrique D. | Ethics—
    Philosophy. | Philosophy of liberation.
Classification: LCC B1034.D874 D43 2021 |
    DDC 170—dc23
LC record available at https://lccn.loc.gov/2020058278

The Pennsylvania State University Press is a member
of the Association of University Presses.

It is the policy of The Pennsylvania State University
Press to use acid-free paper. Publications on
uncoated stock satisfy the minimum requirements
of American National Standard for Information
Sciences—Permanence of Paper for Printed Library
Material, ANSI Z39.48-1992.

CONTENTS

ACKNOWLEDGMENTS

First and foremost, we want to express our deepest gratitude to Enrique Dussel, who agreed to be the subject of our symposium and submit his work to the critical scrutiny of many colleagues who have been studying him for decades. Dussel came to the symposium despite some recent severe health issues, which fortunately he has overcome. Then he provided us with his epilogue, notwithstanding his busy schedule as the recently appointed secretary of educational and political training of the new Mexican left party MORENA (Movimiento de Regeneración Nacional). As secretary, he has undertaken three lines of action: the development of proposals for a decolonial education, the training of young politicians with an ethical sense, and the implementation of study circles on politics in marginalized neighborhoods (barrios). We mention this just to underscore the character of Dussel's commitment and engagement. He is not only a first-class philosopher but also an organic intellectual and a teacher of the people. We also want to thank our contributors, who revised two and three times their essays and who patiently have waited for the publication of this book, which was delayed by all sorts of misfortunes. We are deeply thankful to them for their outstanding contributions. We want to thank our graduate students who presented our speakers and chaired sessions at the symposium: Brooklyn Leonhardt, Benjamin Randolph, Alberto Bejarano Romo, and Nicole Yokum. Special thanks go to our colleague Mariana Ortega, who was a participant in the symposium and hosted a wonderful reception for all the participants. We also want to express our gratitude to the following units at Penn State for their generous financial and intellectual support: the Philosophy Department, the Rock Ethics Institute, the Latinx Studies Program, and the Latin American Studies Program. Eduardo would like to express his gratitude to Matthias Lutz-Bachmann and Thomas Schmidt for their invitation to be a research fellow at the Forschungskolleg Humanwissenschaften of Goethe University in Bad Homburg, Germany, where this volume was finalized. We want to also express our deepest gratitude to Emily

Ann Slimak, who coordinated all the details of the symposium, from travel, hotels, and visas to meals, poster designs, and programs. It was a delight to work with her. Finally, we want to thank Kendra Boileau, our editor at Penn State University Press, for her enthusiasm, support, and patience. We are excited to see the growth of our productive partnership come to fruition. Last but not least, we want to also express our gratitude to Alex Vose, who has diligently, efficiently, and professionally overseen the production of all the volumes in this series.

viii

Amy Allen and Eduardo Mendieta
STATE COLLEGE, PENNSYLVANIA

CHAPTER 1

Introduction

Amy Allen and Eduardo Mendieta

1. ENRIQUE DUSSEL'S WORK IN CONTEXT

The aim of this book series is to chart an agenda for contemporary critical theory. Although the intellectual orientation of the series is rooted in the Frankfurt School tradition of critical theory, as reflected in the focus of our first two volumes, we also seek to engage the work of prominent critical theorists—in the catholic sense of this term—whose thinking expands this field of vision. Almost a century after the Frankfurt School was founded in 1923, the task of rethinking the project of critical theory from a global perspective, one that is responsive to the pernicious ongoing legacies of colonialism and imperialism, could not be more pressing. In this context, we are delighted to focus our attention in this volume on the work of Enrique Dussel. Dussel is not only a towering critical theorist in his own right; his ethics of liberation also engages critically and productively with Frankfurt School thinkers such as Karl-Otto Apel, Jürgen Habermas, Theodor W. Adorno, Max Horkheimer, and Walter Benjamin. Although Dussel undoubtedly pursues his own distinctive critical-ethical vision, he does so in conversation with the tradition of Frankfurt School critical theory, alongside other traditions, including hermeneutics, phenomenology, Marxism, world-systems theory, and decolonial thought. By challenging the residual Eurocentrism, developmentalism, and formalism of Habermasian critical theory and by offering his own materialist and liberatory ethics, Dussel offers an ambitious and expansive agenda for critical theory for the twenty-first century.

Enrique Dussel is without question the most important Latin American philosopher of the last century. His work is extensive, massive, encyclopedic, interdisciplinary, and widely impactful, even if this impact is measured superficially by the translations and pirated editions of his works. A search of the philosophy, theology, and ethics dissertations written in English, German, French, and Spanish will reveal that he is the most studied Latin American philosopher of the last half century. He is now very well known for his elaboration of a philosophy, an ethics, and a politics of liberation. He has also produced major works on the history of the Latin American church, world history, Marxiology, history of Latin American philosophy, ethical theory, and political philosophy.[1] His work embodies the synthesis of several currents and traditions of thinking in Latin America as well as the creative reception of twentieth-century hermeneutics, phenomenology, existentialism, philosophical anthropology, and in the last two decades in particular, the work of the Frankfurt School.[2] His work was nourished by the 1960s and 1970s debates around whether "there existed a Latin American philosophy." On the one hand, these debates brought together figures such as Leopoldo Zea (representing a very important tradition known as Latinamericanism), Augusto Salazar Bondy, Juan Carlos Scannone, and Arturo Andrés Roig, to name some of the most prominent figures, resulting in what then became known as the *philosophy of liberation*; on the other, we have the then contemporaneously emergent tradition of the *theology of liberation*, with figures such as Gustavo Gutiérrez, Ernesto Cardenal, Leonardo Boff, Juan Luis Segundo, and José Míguez Bonino, among many others.[3] Both of these movements emerged in conversation with the political-economic theory of *development of underdevelopment*. Among the articulators of this theory, we find the works of Andre Gunder Frank, Enzo Faletto, Celso Furtado, and Fernando Henrique Cardoso. The work of these political economists would influence and interlink with the work of what then became known as world-systems analysis, as is today best represented in the work of Immanuel Wallerstein. World-systems analysis and the development of underdevelopment became very important for Dussel's own view of world history and Latin America's place within it. Two additional currents that nourished the work of Dussel were the *pedagogy of liberation*, best articulated by Paulo Freire but also advanced by thinkers such as Ernesto Cardenal, and the *sociology of liberation*, best articulated in the work of Orlando Fals Borda.[4] All of these thinkers, currents, schools, and traditions were engaged in what we could call "disciplinary insubordination."[5] That is to say, they all agreed that the "traditional" and inherited modes of producing knowledge about Latin American social reality were either inadequate to this reality, at best, or in fact misleading, obfuscating, and falsifying, at worst. The modes of producing knowledge thus had to be reclaimed, refashioned, and rebuilt so that the knowledge they generated could be useful for projects of social liberation. This project entailed developing new historiographies of Latin American thought, engaging with hitherto neglected social agents, critiquing the project of the nation-state, and challenging the notion of development that undergirds the neoimperial economic and political projects of the United States and Europe.

Here it must be emphasized that a key point of convergence for all these movements and thinkers of "disciplinary insubordination" was the critique of the dominant—read Eurocentric—idea of progress, or what was called *desarrollismo* (developmentalism). Developmentalism was the ruling capitalist, liberal, Eurocentric ideology that entailed setting Latin America on a distinct historical trajectory already traced and paved by Europe and the United States. Developmentalism was, and is, in fact an entire philosophy of history, with both its prophets and its theodicies. This is an important point to underscore because all of these acts of epistemic and disciplinary insubordination pointed to a crisis, an anomaly, of traditional ways of thinking: if entering the Parthenon of modernity meant trekking the road of development, why was it that Latin America not only seemed to always trail back but actually seemed to be going backward? Additionally, why were large sectors of Latin American society—especially the many Indigenous peoples spread out through Latin America—not to be found on this allegedly well-traveled road to modernity? While African, Southeast Asian, and Indian nations were engaged in projects of decolonization and the subsequent pronouncement of their entry into a postcolonial chamber of history, Latin American thinkers recognized that such projects and pronouncements were not simply premature but also misleading and inaccurate. The development of underdevelopment, or what were called pejoratively the *dependistas*, recognized that Euro-American hegemony was predicated on a mythology: that history moved in stages, from archaic, to primitive, to premodern, to modern; that earlier stages would be left behind; and, additionally, that this trajectory could be discerned and calculated by economic algorithms, formulas, and indexes. What these unsubordinated thinkers recognized is that colonialism, neocolonialism, imperialism, and neoimperialism had configured a world-system of economic, political, social, and epistemic subordinations and dependencies.

Enrique Dussel's published "selected works" include thirty books, ranging from the history of Latin American philosophy, to the development of Marx's critique of capitalism, to the articulation of an ethics of liberation, to his three volumes of a politics of liberation.[6] Volume 29 of these selected works is tellingly titled *Filosofías del Sur: Descolonización y Transmodernidad.*[7] We also now have the anthology of his most recent essays, titled *Anti-Cartesian Meditations and Transmodernity: From the Perspective of Philosophy of Liberation.*[8] We refer to these recent titles in particular because they allow us to call attention to the fact that Dussel has, since his earliest works,[9] embraced the project of thinking from the Global South, aiming to decolonize thinking by tracing a different version of history, one that dispenses with vanguards, winners and losers, and, of course, theodicies and that recognizes that there are multiple modernities or different ways of being "modern." Furthermore, by focusing on Dussel's encyclopedic and extensive work, we have sought to highlight how his version of the "decolonial turn" emerged from a major "disciplinary insubordination" that heralded a true epistemological revolution in Latin America and the Americas at large.[10]

2. FROM THE "DE-STRUCTION" TO THE "DECOLONIZATION" OF (THE HISTORY OF) ETHICS

Dussel's epilogue at the end of the present volume offers an autobiographical trajectory of his thinking. Yet what remains implicit in his account is how consistently, doggedly, searchingly, and one may say obsessively and in an insomniac way (to use that most apropos Levinasian expression) Dussel has thought and written about ethics. Notwithstanding the breadth of his work, at the core of it is the "ethical question," the "ethical demand and interpellation" of the victim, the poor, the orphan, the destitute, the refugee, the "Indian," the gay person, the rape victim. While Levinas argued that ethics is *prima philosophia*, Dussel argues that *ethics* is the very source and elaboration of any critical thinking. Dussel has written five ethics, each one bearing the stigmata of a distinct method and orientation.[11] Yet these distinct approaches are united in the ethical imperative to attend to the victims of every ethos and social system. These five ethics, it can be argued, correspond to five stages of Dussel's philosophical itinerary.

The first, which extends from the late 1950s through the early 1970s, could be called the *hermeneutical stage*. Dussel's philosophical production begins with the analysis of two ethical worldviews and their corresponding "ethical-mythical nucleus" (an expression that he takes over from Paul Ricoeur): the Semitic and the Greek. His *Humanismo Helénico* (1963) and *Humanismo Semita* (1964) set out to elucidate the life-worlds from which two contrasting but encompassing cosmovisions (*Weltanschauungen*) gave rise to two different conceptions of the human, with their contrasting views on the relationships among the body, the soul, community, and God/gods. The operative idea in Dussel's first two books was the Ricoeurian one of mythopoesis—that is, the idea that different cultures are rendered distinctly coherent by their unique myths, rituals, religions, allegories, and metaphors. It is against this background that Dussel set out to think about the uniqueness and distinctness of Latin America. Thus we could say that these two books exemplified a *hermeneutical ethics*.

A second stage, extending from the mid-1960s through the early 1970s, could be called *ontological*.[12] During this stage, in particular as he takes up his teaching position in Argentina in 1969, he undertook what he will call a "de-struction" of the history of philosophical anthropology and of ethics in order to develop an ethics of liberation for Latin America. Thus volume 3 of his selected works is made up of his *Lecciones de antropología filosófica* (1969) and *Para una de-strucción de la historia de la ética* (1970). The former is a set of lectures in which he argued that philosophy properly thought is philosophical anthropology and that philosophical anthropology properly thought is in turn fundamental ontology. But the being of the human is a historical being; its being is historical. The human being is not in history but is history—that is to say, the being of the human is temporality. The noteworthy pivot of the lectures is that to understand properly the being of the human, we must undertake a *de-strucción* of the history of philosophical anthropology and thus of ontology. This project is taken up in the 1970 lectures, but now, the *de-strucción* of the history of philosophical anthropology and ontology becomes the *de-strucción* of the history of ethics. As Dussel makes clear when introducing the lectures on the history of ethics from 1970, *de-strucción* is not a destructive but a critical—that is, positive—task. He writes, "*Struo* in Latin speaks of joining, stacking, accumulating, piling. For this reason de-constructing means untying, unstacking, sifting through, but not simply to ruin."[13] The positive aim of this "de-struction," however, is to elucidate what in 1970 he calls an "ontological ethics" or "ethica perennis."[14] We could then say that these two courses set out to elaborate an *ontological ethics*.

A third stage, which we can call *analectical*, begins with Dussel's discovery of the work of Emmanuel Levinas in the early 1970s through the mid-1980s. As was noted, Dussel had been lecturing on the "destruction" of the history of ethics, but with a positive aim: to develop an ethics for and of the Latin American life-world and history. What were originally lectures, however, became a three-volume work on ethics—namely, *Para una ética de la liberación Latinoamericana*.[15] The first two volumes are framed by the thought of Ricoeur and Heidegger, expanding the work Dussel had done in his lectures from the 1960s.

However, in 1971, when Dussel is introduced to Levinas's *Totality and Infinity*, the project of the de-struction of the history of ethics becomes the project of developing an ethics of liberation framed by Levinas's concept of the absolute otherness of the other. In this stage, Dussel's method is no longer hermeneutical or ontological but "metaphysical." In order to think about the alterity of the other, we need not dialectics but analectics—that is to say, we need to think not from the difference that is tethered to the logic of the totality, of the same, but rather from the "distinctness" or irreducible nonassimilable otherness of the other. It should be noted that while it is tempting to think of the discovery of Levinas as catalyzing a break, a rift between ontology and metaphysics, a turn from Heidegger toward the thinker of infinity and the face of the other, this would be misleading. A close reading of the texts from the late 1960s reveals how Dussel was thinking with and against both Ricoeur and Heidegger. As we saw, the "de-struction" of philosophical anthropology at the service of a de-struction of ontology aimed to serve as a prolegomenon to a de-struction of the history of ethics with the very specific aim to develop an ethics for what would be more explicitly called "an ethics of Latin American liberation."

The work that is most emblematic of this stage is *Philosophy of Liberation*, written in the early 1980s in Mexico, as Dussel begins his exile.[16] The operative ideas during this period are Levinasian notions of totality and exteriority. Here it is important to note that in volume 3 of the trilogy *Towards an Ethics of Latin American Liberation*, Hegel and Marx appear as thinkers of the totality. In the *Philosophy of Liberation*, Marx once again appears as a thinker of Being, of the totality, of the "same" and "one" (Hegel's *Geist* and Marx's *Das Kapital*) that closes itself off to the alterity of the other. In the writings from this period, in fact, dialectics is juxtaposed to analectics. Dialectics is the logic of the thinking that grounds itself out of itself and that assimilates everything to itself without leaving a remainder. Analectics is the thought that thinks from the distinctness of the other without assimilating the alterity of the other to mere difference. Analectical logic opens itself to the radical otherness of the other in such a way that it can never ground itself. This thinking thus is without ground. It is this analectical logic that becomes the deconstructive method of Dussel's philosophy of liberation during the mid-1970s. Then we could argue that this ethics from the early 1970s is an *analectical ethics* or an *ethics of alterity*.

8   A fourth, *Marxist* stage emerges in the mid-1980s, as Dussel began to read Marx differently, and lasts until the early 1990s. As was noted at the outset, during the 1970s, Dussel was engaged in debates within the then vibrant theology of liberation. A central point of contention in these debates concerned the role that Marx could or should play within the theology of liberation. Related to this was a debate over how to understand "el pueblo" and "the poor" both biblically and theologically—that is, were the poor the same as Marx's proletariat, those who only have their labor power to sell? Dussel's intervention in these debates culminates in his 1986 *Ética communitaria*, which was translated into English in 1988 under the title of *Ethics and Community*.[17] This *Ethics* must be read in conjunction with the works on Marx that Dussel undertook during the late 1970s and 1980s. Dussel's first work on Marx during this period is his 1977 book, *Filosofía de la producción*, which is made up of a translation of Marx's notebooks on technology and an extended analysis of the text.[18] The book was expanded in 1984.[19] This book was followed by three volumes on the genealogy of Marx's *Das Kapital* through a close reading of the different drafts that Marx wrote before he settled on the published version of volume 1 of *Das Kapital: La producción teórica de Marx: Un comentario a los "Grundrisse"* (Marx's theoretical production: A commentary on the *Grundrisse*, 1985); *Hacia un Marx desconocido: Un comentario de los manuscritos del 61–63* (Toward an unknown Marx: A commentary on the manuscript from 61–63, 1988); and *El último Marx (1863–1882) y la liberación Latinoamericana* (The last Marx [1863–1882] and Latin American liberation, 1990).[20] This trilogy on *Das Kapital* was complemented by *Las metáforas teológicas de Marx* (The theological metaphors of Marx, 1993).[21] The 1980s and early 1990s were Dussel's decade and a half of an in-depth study of Marx.

At the center of Dussel's detailed reconstruction of the genesis of *Das Kapital* is the discovery of the centrality of the concept of *lebendige Arbeit* (living labor) for Marx's critique of capital. In Dussel's reading, Marx emerges not as a thinker of the totality and the dialectics of the self-positing and self-grounding of being but as the thinker of the exteriority of capital: the exteriority of living labor to both the market and the expropriation and accumulation of surplus value. Instead of a dialectical and Hegelian Marx, what Dussel presents us with is an analogical (analectical) and Schellingian Marx. This rereading of Marx allows Dussel to give concreteness to the Levinasian other, which is no longer simply a metaphysical other but a concrete, material, embodied, historical other: the poor, the wretched of the world, of history, of global capitalism. While Dussel traces carefully the evolution of Marx's economic-political thinking, he also foregrounds the specifically *ethical* dimension of Marx's critique of capitalism. Centering the category of *lebendige Arbeit* reveals a Marx who is interested not simply in the "logic" of capital but also and perhaps most centrally in the unethical, immoral character of a system that expropriates the "life" of workers, turning them into fungible commodities. In Dussel's hands, then, Marx becomes one of the great ethical thinkers of the West. We are amply justified, then, in claiming that this fourth stage in Dussel's intellectual itinerary can be called Marxist, or, more generally, a historical materialist stage. If we are attentive to the third volume of Dussel's trilogy on the genesis of *Das Kapital*, with its focus on living labor and the ethical critique of capitalism, and read it in tandem with *Las metáforas teológicas de Marx*, we can think of these works as the elaboration of a Marxist ethics. Then we could argue that the ethics from the decade and a half of the 1980s and early 1990s is a *Marxist ethics*.

A fifth and final stage, which we can call *ethical critique*, at least for the moment, begins in 1989, when through the mediation of Raúl Fornet-Betancourt, Dussel enters into a decade-long dialogue and debate with Karl-Otto Apel, culminating with the publication of Dussel's *Ethics of Liberation: In the Age of Globalization and Exclusion* in 1998. Dussel insists that this ethics is now a proper *ethics of liberation* because it brings together the material, intersubjective validity, and feasibility dimensions into a comprehensive ethical system. In other words, this "critical" liberatory ethics is both material and formal. To this extent, then, we suggest that this period be called ethical critique. Here we can only foreground two key moments in the debate with Apel that, arguably, show why Dussel left behind the Levinasian ethics of alterity and the metaphysics of radical otherness. One moment has to do with the priority of the community of life to the community of communication (*Kommunikationsgemeinschaft*). There is no communication if subjects are not able to live—that is, a condition of possibility of discourse is that the other be alive. Apel, whose work aimed to advance Peirce's agenda of linguistifying Kant, took the primacy of the communication community as the point of departure for his version of discourse ethics. Dussel, by contrast, taking the suffering corporeality of the ethical subjects and the expropriation of their lives through the labor market as his point of departure, argued for the primacy of the community of life as a material precondition for the communication community. In other words, there can be no community of communication if that community has not first secured its material survival and sustenance. The second moment has to do with the Apelian-Habermasian bifurcation of the *Begründung* and *Anwendung*—that is, the justification (or grounding) and application of ethics. Apel talked about levels A and B of ethics, where A refers to the justification of ethical norms and level B refers to the application of those norms. For Apel, the key function of ethical theory is precisely the adjudication and elucidation of the moral norms that enable humans to coexist in community. As an approach to moral theory, discourse ethics prioritizes intersubjective validity over substantive ethical values. For Dussel, however, moral validity is empty if it does not refer to the material moment of ethics. Ethics must address the material life of ethical subjects who must secure their dignity and integrity in concrete conditions of privation and injurability, to use Judith Butler's most apropos term. Apel retorted that questions of survival and distribution are part of what he calls an ethics of responsibility, which is subordinate to the formal ethics of intersubjective validity, or the formal ethics of discourse. In fact, Apel claimed that Dussel's ethics of liberation is but a version of an ethics of responsibility that aims to address the issues attendant to the application of moral norms and to this extent belong to what he called part B of ethics. Apel's argument, then, was that Dussel's ethics of liberation is concerned merely with questions of application, not justification.

From this decade-long but productive dialogue with Apel, Dussel acquires a new set of philosophical tools that enables him to reformulate his ethics of liberation on a new philosophical basis.[22] A quick overview of the structure of the 1998 *Ethics of Liberation* allows us to see how Dussel's ethics of liberation has moved beyond Levinasian phenomenology. This massive and impressive ethics has three major sections, though Dussel himself divided it into two major parts. The first part consists of a "World History of Ethical Systems"—in Spanish, *eticidades*. The second is called "Foundations of Ethics," and the third, "Critical Ethics, Antihegemonic Validity, and the Praxis of Liberation." The "Foundations of Ethics" part is itself divided into three parts: First, we have the material moment of ethics, or what he calls the moment of the practical truth of ethics. Ethics is grounded in the corporeality of living ethical beings, and it must address their lives. Then we have the moment of intersubjective validity, or what Dussel calls formal morality. Finally, we have the moment of ethical feasibility—that is, that a valid moral norm is one that can actually be enacted. In order for an ethics to be meaningful, it must be enforceable. For Dussel, these three moments are equally primordial. To focus on one at the exclusion of the others, or even to give one primacy over the others, is to fall into reductivism. The third part, the critical ethics, mirrors, but now critically or negatively, foundational ethics; thus we have ethical critique, antihegemonic validity, and the praxis of liberation—what Dussel calls the principle of liberation. Every system for the production and reproduction of life cannot but produce victims, specific victims—namely, the victims it generates by the very means through which that system seeks to perpetuate itself. These victims challenge the ruling system by articulating a counterhegemonic validity. Any ethics worthy of the name must articulate an ethical critique from the perspective of what Dussel calls the "negativity of the victims" of that system. The community of life, which is prior to the community of communication, turns into the community of victims that articulate the negation of the negation of the ruling system. Here it becomes clear why Dussel must begin with a "world history of ethical systems." The history of ethics is the history of the critique of ethical systems that produced their own victims and consequently the articulation of their own respective antihegemonic validity. For Dussel, there is no ethics without the history of ethics and thus without the history of the ethical critique of the victims of history. Therefore, what Dussel had called earlier the "de-struction" of the history of ethics has turned into the history of ethics that is deconstructed from the standpoint of the victims of history.

A major shift has taken place. The Levinasian other, which was transformed into the "poor" and the "pueblo" in the Marxist ethics of the fourth stage, has now become the victim and the community of victims of the ruling system. We need to underscore that this victim is no longer thought of in terms of Levinasian alterity, the *otredad del otro*, the otherness of the other. The victim is always a specific victim, the victim of a given mode of production and its correlative system of the circulation of commodities. We ascended from metaphysics to historical concreteness, from the indeterminate nature of the other to the historical indexicality of their destitution and precarity. Dussel thinks, furthermore, that the history of ethical systems narrated in terms of the emergence and coalescing of interregional systems (that for a long time remained delinked and nonsubordinate to each other or to one) underwent a major shift, beginning in 1492 with the discovery and/ or invention of America. The "invention" of the Americas, the "discovery" of the New World, became the catalyzing event that led to the integration of the hitherto interregional system into a world-system, under the subordination of Spanish and Portuguese dominion (launching the hegemony of Europe). To summarize, Dussel's post-1998 *Ethics of Liberation* and his *Politics of Liberation* have three elements that are antithetical or allergic to radical alterity: First, both foundational and critical ethics require intersubjective validity—that is, a justification of moral norms and ethical values that require, if not the consensus, at least the validation of all those affected by the application of those norms. Radical alterity cannot enter into this process of adjudication and justification. Second, what could be called the *long durée* of the ethics of liberation aims to recover and valorize the lessons learned from past victims of now anachronistic or defunct ethical systems, which have been rendered both immoral and illegitimate by the specific critiques of the victims they created and rendered invisible. Third, the community of victims refers to a corporeal vulnerability and injurability of ethical subjects that are explicitly historically indexed. In Dussel's fifth ethics, *ethical agency is grounded in the corporeality of the ethical agent*—that is, being-alive as a condition of the possibility of ethical agency. For this reason, we should think of ethical agency as ethical flesh, ethical corporeality. But this flesh is thoroughly historical. This means, then, that our *ethical flesh is riveted to history*. We all suffer our flesh, but in different forms in accordance with the affordance of material circumstances. Dussel's ethics of liberation is therefore at the same time an archeology of ethopoesis, the ethical creativity of those who challenge the ruling *ethos* expanding the horizon of those to whom we respond. To paraphrase Adorno, there is a direct lineage between the slingshot and the atom bomb but not one between barbarism and the response to the suffering of our victims. This is why ethics must always be prefaced by a global history of ethical systems—the memory of the vanquished and victims in and of history. It could be argued, then, that the ethics of 1998 forward is *an ethics of liberation of the community of life*.

In the preface to his 1998 *Ethics of Liberation*, Dussel notes that this "new" ethics is a second "step" compared to the early 1970s *Para una ética de la liberación Latinoamericana*. Indeed, it is a major step. But the fundamental focus remains the same: the poor, the victim, the excluded ones, the other of and in history. Dussel offers four clarifications as to how this ethics differs from the prior "four" that he wrote, as we tried to argue in this introduction. First, Dussel notes, this ethics is no longer a prolegomena, a preparatory ethics; it is an ethics "sin más"—an ethics *simpliciter*, as such, without further qualification. Second, whereas the early ethics were framed in terms of Latin American "liberation," now the horizon is planetary, global, world "liberation." The poor and victims are not only in Latin America. Third, while the prior ethics is framed by an engagement with the works of Gadamer, Heidegger, Levinas, and Ricoeur, this latest ethics is marked by an engagement with a whole host of contemporary ethical thinkers: Apel, Habermas, Hinkelammert, Honneth, Rorty, Rawls, Taylor, Vattimo, Walzer, and so on. Fourth, Dussel is poignantly aware that he writes in the late 1990s, in the shadow of the collapse of the Soviet Union and, putatively, the triumph of Western liberal capitalism over socialism. He very consciously writes against the background of both cynicism and defeatism of those movements that were the voice of the poor and the victim. Nonetheless, it is precisely against this so-called end of history that Dussel affirms the imperative to develop an ethics, now from the perspective of the immense part of humanity that is systematically excluded, exploited, and expropriated from the benefits of "globalization."[23] The ethics of liberation, then, is simultaneously an *ethics of globalization from below.*

The question remains, In what sense can we understand the *Decolonizing Ethics,* which is the title of the present book as well as the thrust of Dussel's work, as we have argued thus far? The overall trajectory and evolution of Dussel's work have been from the de-struction of ontology to the de-struction of the history of ethics to now a positive project: decolonizing ethics by rethinking it from the standpoint of the ethics demanded by the poor and victims of globalization. While in the introduction to his 1998 *Ethics,* the project of a "decolonial" turn or a "decolonization of ethics" remained implicit, in the introduction to the *Politics of Liberation,* an expansion of the ethics of liberation into the field of politics, the turn becomes explicit. In that introduction, in fact, Dussel declares, "The 'decolonizing turn' is a global historical-philosophical challenge."[24] This sentence comes after Dussel has identified *seven limits* that must be "deconstructed" in order to develop both an ethics and a politics of liberation. The first limit is *Hellenocentrism,* which claims that all modern Enlightenment culture comes from Greece and that the Europeans are the direct inheritors of this tradition, to the exclusion or neglect of the contributions of other ancient civilizations, such as the Egyptian, the Mesopotamian, the Phoenician, and the entire Semitic world, which are antecedent and sources of Greek culture. The second limit is the *Westernization* or *Europeanization* of modern ethical and political theory that pretends that the West and Europe are not internally heterogeneous or dependent on the contributions of the Eastern Roman Empire, Byzantium, and the incredibly important role that Constantinople plays in linking the ancients to medieval and Renaissance Europe. The third limit is *Eurocentrism,* which cripples our ability to understand the contributions of other cultures as well as the way in which "Europe" is an idea, an ideal that emerged from an intercultural dialogue, of religions, cultures, traditions, and institutional challenges. A fourth limit is the invidious and self-serving *periodization* of world history that temporalizes, or creates, a specific narrative, relegating some cultures to a prehistoric past while placing the West at the forefront of history—that is, the latest moderns of the most modern. The fact is that world history looks very different when traced from the Middle East, India, China, or pre-Colombian Turtle Island (the Indigenous name for the so-called New World). A fifth limit is the *secularism* of philosophy and political theory, whereby Dussel understands "secularism" as an ideology that masks not only the "West's" own "not yet secularized" status but also the ways in which other cultures are secular and also on the way to secularization. Secularism is an ideology, and secularization is an ongoing process that will continue so long as societies meet the challenges of organizing their interactions and making sense of the world on different conceptual frameworks. A sixth limit is what Dussel calls the theoretical and conceptual *colonialism* of philosophy tout court in developing countries and societies that ignore, neglect, demean, and subordinate their own philosophical traditions to those of the colonial metropolises (Europe and the United States). The seventh limit is that of the failure to understand or even acknowledge the entanglements of the so-called discovery of the "New World" and the "project" of modernity. The limit here signals the failure to understand the epochal character of the "invention of the Americas," to use the title of Dussel's 1992 Frankfurt lectures.[25] Modernity, argues Dussel, does not begin with the Reformation, or the French Revolution, or the French Enlightenment; rather, modernity begins with the question, Are these peoples of the New World human, and should they be evangelized, colonized, and enslaved? It is the "invention" of the Americas that will enable Europe to become the pivot of a now interlinked world-system that up through 1492 had been delinked regional systems.[26]

To summarize, then, the task of decolonizing ethics means orienting ourselves by the recognition of these seven limits, which gravitate around three key imperatives: first, we must deconstruct the history of ethics; second, we need to develop an ethics with a global perspective in mind, an ethics for the large majority of humanity that is excluded from the gains of "modernity"; and third, the imperative to recognize the plurality of cultures—that is, of ethopoetic cores and semantic reservoirs that are not liabilities but resources for ethical perspectives and ways of being with one another in justice. There is a fourth imperative that is not readily legible from the seven limits traced by Dussel but that can be read in his other works, in particular in his 1992 Frankfurt lecture alluded to earlier, and that is the imperative to decolonize the "ethical self." We can and must read Dussel's work as a *decolonial genealogy of the ethical subject and ethical agent* in two ways. First, his work relocates the "sources of the modern self" to the sixteenth century with the colonization of the "New World." Modern subjectivity is informed by the European colonial project that is launched with the "discovery" of the New World, which in Dussel's argument is its material condition of possibility.[27] Second, as Dussel insists, the trajectory of the modern ethical subject does not simply go from late antiquity through the medieval, Renaissance, and Enlightenment periods of European history; it also includes ancient China, Mesopotamia, Egypt, and the Semitic worlds. These traditions gave expression to different conceptions of the ethical subject that were more attentive to the corporeality, injurability, and vulnerability of the "living" subject. Decolonizing ethics thus also means attending to different sources of ethical agency.

3. OVERVIEW OF THE VOLUME

Our volume opens with a contribution from Enrique Dussel that lays out some of the major stakes of his ethics of liberation. In "Are Many Modernities Possible? A South-South Dialogue," Dussel argues against notions of multiple and alternative modernities, insisting that modernity is a contingent, concrete, singular, and nonrepeatable event of world history that cannot be replicated in alternative contexts. Moreover, it is an event that is indelibly linked to colonial domination. Thus for non-European countries to attempt to follow the same path Europe took to modernity can only lead them to colonial misery. Dussel insists that we should think instead of overcoming modernity in the direction of transmodernity. Fulfilling this task begins with fostering a dialogue among the cultures of the south that includes not only a critique of modernity but also a willingness to incorporate the best of modernity. The end result of this process would not be a universal culture—because univocal universality is necessarily dominating—but rather a cultural pluriversality that is open to the specificity and alterity of different traditions.

The next seven chapters in this volume explore various themes in Dussel's work. The first four of these chapters address aspects of Dussel's ethics, with a shared focus on his materialist principle. Linda Martín Alcoff's chapter, "The Hegel of Coyoacán," presents Dussel as a kind of renegade Hegelian: a thinker as attentive as Hegel was to the geography and historicity of philosophy and as committed to an immanent, dialectical style of argument who nonetheless breaks radically with Hegel's developmentalism and with his focus on an abstract idea of freedom as the driving force of history. For Alcoff, the materialist principle at the core of Dussel's ethics, a materialism that must be understood as pragmatist rather than reductive, leads him to focus less on abstract notions of freedom and more on the concrete struggles of victims for liberation from existing systems of oppression. Whereas Alcoff offers a largely sympathetic reconstruction of Dussel's ethics, Mario Sáenz Rovner's chapter, "Ideality and Intersubjectivity: Dialectics and Analectics in a Philosophy of Liberation," takes a more critical approach. While acknowledging the tremendous value of Dussel's decolonization of key Marxist concepts and his emphasis on the relationships among capitalism, colonialism, and imperialism, Sáenz Rovner is critical of Dussel's reading of Marx's concept of living labor, which he finds insufficiently immanent. Unlike Dussel, who turns to Levinasian analectics to rethink living labor, Sáenz Rovner argues that Hegelian dialectical logic can be rescued from its sexism, racism, and Eurocentrism. Like Alcoff, Don Deere focuses on the materialist principle of Dussel's ethics in his chapter, "The Upsurge of the Living: Critical Ethics and the Materiality of the Community of Life." Deere demonstrates in detail how Dussel's materialism moves beyond alternative materialist approaches to ethics such as utilitarianism and also beyond the ethical formalism of liberalism. Although Dussel's ethics combines materialist and formalist aspects, Deere insists that it is best understood as a materialist ethics that incorporates a formalist moment (not vice versa). For Deere, contrary to Sáenz Rovner, the analectical material moment in Dussel's thought that refers to the concrete suffering of excluded victims is also the original critical moment. Continuing the thread of focusing on Dussel's ethics, Jorge Zúñiga M. focuses on the north-south debate between Dussel and Apel in his chapter, "Ethics of Liberation and Discourse Ethics: On Grounding the Material Principle of Life." Although he praises Dussel for his ability to subsume key aspects of Apel's discourse ethics within the ethics of liberation, he is also critical of Dussel's ethics inasmuch as it fails to grapple fully with the problem of how the materialist principle at its core is grounded. As such, Dussel's ethics has not yet fully risen to Apel's challenge. In the final section of his chapter, Zúñiga offers as a friendly amendment or supplement to Dussel's ethics two possible strategies for grounding the materialist principle, each of which aims to demonstrate the non-circumventability of life for ethics.

The next three chapters discuss broader issues in value theory, including aesthetics and philosophy of history, in relation to Dussel's work. In "On the Apophatic Urgency of Now: A Future for the Philosophy of Liberation," Oscar Guardiola-Rivera argues for an aesthetic turn in Dussel's work. Guardiola-Rivera seeks to excavate and build on this aesthetic turn, viewing this as the complement to Dussel's earlier project of de-struction of the history of ethics. Linking Dussel to Jewish thinkers such as Walter Benjamin, Ernst Bloch, and Emmanuel Levinas, Guardiola-Rivera reads Dussel's work as an interrogation into one of the oldest questions in philosophy, the relationship between ethics and aesthetics, and interprets him as an aesthetic-critical interpreter of the philosophy of history. Alejandro Vallega's chapter, "An Introduction to Liberatory Decolonial Aesthetic Thought: A South-South Path, from Indigenous and Popular Thought in América and from the Sense of *Xu* in Chinese Painting," explores further the aesthetic dimension of Dussel's thought. He begins by arguing that Dussel's materialist ethical principle has an aesthetic basis, specifically an account of sensibility. He goes on to develop this insight into a sketch of a decolonial aesthetics of liberation through a "south-south" dialogue between Rodolfo Kusch and Chinese traditional painting. Amy Allen's chapter, "The Ethics and Politics of Progress: Dussel and the Frankfurt School," explores further the philosophy of history strand identified by Guardiola-Rivera. Allen articulates the complex and ambivalent conception of progress that runs through Dussel's ethics and reveals some points of concordance between Dussel's work and the Frankfurt School, in particular the work of Theodor Adorno.

19

Our volume ends with Enrique Dussel's "Epilogue," which offers a rich and fascinating intellectual autobiography in which the author situates his own work in its existential, geographical, cultural, and historical context and charts his own self-understanding of the various shifts his work has taken over the last fifty years.

NOTES

1. See the translator and editor's introduction to Enrique Dussel, *The Underside of Modernity: Apel, Ricoeur, Rorty, Taylor and the Philosophy of Liberation*, trans. and ed. Eduardo Mendieta (Atlantic Highlands, N.J.: Humanities, 1996), xiii–xxxi. See also the introduction to Linda Martín Alcoff and Eduardo Mendieta, eds., *Thinking from the Underside of History: Enrique Dussel's Philosophy of Liberation* (Lanham, Md.: Rowman & Littlefield, 2000), 1–26; and the introduction to Enrique Dussel, *Beyond Philosophy: Ethics, History, Marxism and Liberation Theology*, ed. Eduardo Mendieta (Lanham, Md.: Rowman & Littlefield, 2003), 1–18. See also Frederick B. Mills, *Enrique Dussel's Ethics of Liberation: An Introduction* (Switzerland: Palgrave Macmillan, 2018), 1–20.

2. For a more extensive treatment, see Eduardo Mendieta, "Critique of Decolonial Reason: On the Philosophy of the Calibans," *Graduate Faculty Philosophy Journal* 41, no. 1 (forthcoming).

3. For an excellent overview of this constellation and debate, see Gustavo Leyva, *La filosofía en México en el siglo XX: Un ensayo de reconstrucción histórico-sistemática* (Mexico City: Fondo de Cultural Economica y Secretaría de Cultura, 2018), chap. 6, 423–500. See also *The Stanford Encyclopedia of Philosophy*, ed. Edward N. Zalta, 2016 ed., s.v. "Philosophy of Liberation," by Eduardo Mendieta, January 28, 2016, https://plato.stanford.edu/archives/win2016/entries/liberation/.

4. We are fortunate that we now have in English a work by Dussel that brings together these two currents in an exemplary fashion. See Enrique Dussel, *Pedagogics of Liberation: A Latin American Philosophy of Education*, trans. David I. Backer and Cecilia Diego (Goleta, Calif.: Punctum Books, 2019).

5. Here we are drawing on some ideas developed in the introduction to Santiago Castro-Gómez and Eduardo Mendieta, eds., *Teorías sin disciplina: Latinoamericanismo, postcolonialidad y globaización en debate* (Mexico City: Miguel Àngel de Porrua, 1998), 5–30.

6. They can be found here: https://www.enriquedussel.com/Libros_OSelectas.html.

7. Enrique Dussel, *Filosofías del Sur: Descolonización y Transmodernidad* (Mexico City: Akal, 2015).

8. Enrique Dussel, *Anti-Cartesian Meditations and Transmodernity: From the Perspective of Philosophy of Liberation*, ed. Alejandro A. Vallega and Ramón Grosfoguel (The Hague: Amrit, 2018).

9. It needs to be noted that already in works from 1963 to 1964, Dussel had called for thinking from and out of the Latin American life world and history. In the early 1960s, Dussel was calling for a provincializing of Europe, on the one hand, and placing Latin American history in a world context, on the other.

10. See Nelson Maldonado-Torres, "Enrique Dussel's Liberation Thought in the Decolonial Turn," *TRANSMODERNITY: Journal of Peripheral Cultural Production of the Luso-Hispanic World* 1, no. 1 (2011), https://escholarship.org/uc/item/5hg8t7cj.

11. Arguably Dussel has written six, if we take his recent *14 tesis de ética: Hacia la esencia del pensamiento crítico* (Madrid: Editorial Trotta, 2016). However, the basic ideas in this text were all elaborated in the 1998 *Ethics of Liberation*. This last text clarifies and expands on what is developed in this major ethics.

12. The "ontological" work that Dussel was developing during this time was also heavily *philosophical anthropological* along the lines of Max Scheler, Helmut Plessner, Arnold Gehlen, and the young Habermas, who inflected philosophical anthropology with epistemology.

13. Enrique Dussel, *Lecciones de antropología filosófica, Para una de-strucción de la historia de la Ética*, Obras selectas 3 (Buenos Aires: Docencia, 2012), 20.

14. Ibid., 201.

15. Enrique Dussel, *Para una ética de la liberación Latinoamericana*, Obras selectas 8 (Buenos Aires: Docencia, 2012).

16. Enrique Dussel, *Philosophy of Liberation*, trans. Aquilina Martinez and Christine Morkovsky (Maryknoll, N.Y.: Orbis Books, 1985).

17. Enrique Dussel, *Ethics and Community*, trans. Robert R. Barr (Maryknoll, N.Y.: Orbis Books, 1988).

18. Incidentally, this text was produced in collaboration with his son, Enrique Dussel Peters, who has meanwhile become an important Mexican economist.

19. Enrique Dussel, *Filosofía de la producción* (Bogotá: Editorial Nueva América, 1984).

20. Enrique Dussel, *La producción teórica de Marx: Un comentario a los "Grundrisse"* (Mexico City: Siglo XXI, 1985); Dussel, *Hacia un Marx desconocido: Un comentario de los manuscritos del 61–63* (Mexico City: Siglo XXI, 1988), which was edited and translated as *Towards an Unknown Marx: A Commentary on the "Manuscripts of 1861–63,"* trans. Yolanda Angulo, ed. Fred Moseley (New York: Routledge, 2001); and Enrique Dussel, *El último Marx (1863–1882) y la liberación Latinoamericana* (Mexico City: Siglo XXI, 1990).

21. Enrique Dussel, *Las metáforas teológicas de Marx* (Estella, Navarra: Editorial Verbo Divino, 1993).

22. A collection of the texts written for these encounters has been published; see Karl-Otto Apel and Enrique Dussel, *Ética del discurso y ética de la liberación* (Madrid: Editorial Trotta, 2005).

23. Enrique Dussel, *Ética de la liberación en la edad de la globalización y la exclusión* (Madrid: Editorial Trotta, 1998), 14–15.

24. Enrique Dussel, *Politics of Liberation: A Critical World History*, trans. Thia Cooper (2007; repr., London: SCM, 2011), xvii.

25. Enrique Dussel, *The Invention of the Americas: Eclipse of "the Other" and the Myth of Modernity*, trans. Michael D. Barber (New York: Continuum, 1995).

26. The essays are collected in Dussel, *Beyond Philosophy*, and further expand on each one of these limits.

27. See Dussel, *Underside of Modernity*, in particular the chapter on Charles Taylor; and Dussel, *Invention of the Americas*, in particular part 1, "From the European Ego: The Covering Over."

CHAPTER 2

Are Many Modernities Possible?

A South-South Dialogue

Enrique Dussel

The following is the thesis of this chapter:

It is not possible to imitate, apply, or develop the *existing modernity* to other cultures given that modernity is a nonrepeatable fact of world history. For this reason, we will have to dialogue about the meaning of a *spirit of modernity* if we take into account that modernity is not merely a concept but also a historical fact that is singular and nonrepeatable and that cannot realize itself as an essence that could reemerge or once again in a renewed way arise in future alternative modernities departing from other cultural traditions (such as the Islamic Arab, the Latin American, the African Bantu, the Hindustani, and so on). For this reason, we will have to develop together a discourse on the possibility of *overcoming radically* modernity, *subsuming its technological and scientific* advancements that would be in accord with the ethical, ontological, and political structures of the cultures of the south in order to thus converge, without dissolving them, in a new humanity, in a new historical age, culturally and civilizationally *transmodern* (that is to say, no longer modern but instead as *another age* of the world history of cultures).

It is necessary to find *another place* in order to reformulate a mode 23 of existence, a complete attitude toward life, toward human life, that would allow the launching a new world, a new history, an age of humanity that would be grounded on a new basis, on another foundation, on another intersubjective project and objective of humanity than that of European modernity.[1] It is not a matter of modernizing an existence that is not sufficiently modern, whether it be backward or traditional (in the eyes of the modern interpretation), but instead of departing from *other* ontological, historical, anthropological, and ethical-political *horizons*, from the most authentic traditions of each culture toward a better, more just world, one that is more adequate to the ecological demands of nature. The historical tradition of each culture is not a substantive entelechy that is given once and for all but a historical, ontological structure that is qualitatively growing, which adapts coherently with its past to the new authentic exigencies that enable the survival of this culture with other cultures in a pluriversal, analogical worldhood and not as a univocal, homogeneous, excluding universality that would be the fetishized product of only one culture.

The great Moroccan philosopher Taha Abdurrahman (born in 1944 in El Jadida, Morocco), who is well known for his studies in logic, the philosophy of language, and science, agrees with the fundamental positions of the philosophy of liberation in the sense that modernity created a formalist philosophy that distanced itself from a humanistic ethics of life, conceiving reason principally and exclusively as theoretical, abstract, and formal. For this reason, he proposes to reformulate an ethics that coheres with the Islamic philosophical tradition, which also criticizes European modernity as an expression of Western civilization.[2] Today all of this is an object of debate. I believe that our dialogue ought to begin with the conception of modernity itself.

Abdurrahman proposes the thesis of thinking as necessary not to European modernity but instead to "multiple modernities," thus negating the European claim to exclude other cultures from the possibility of creating their respective modernities. This is to say, the project would consist in constructing "an Ethical Islamic theory that is capable of confronting the un-Ethical position of Western civilization."[3] In order to achieve this, he proposes "to found an Arabic Modernity instead of trying to replicate Western Modernity."[4] In addition, "we should take *another route* that is based upon our way of life."[5] The problem to discuss is precisely what this other route consists of, what its inspiration and its origin are, how it can be traced, and where it may lead. This would entail having a clear concept of modernity itself.

Abdurrahman sets out from a certain description of the concept of the "spirit of modernity," as we are told by Sirin Adlbi Sibai,[6] a "spirit" that could be described because of its semantic components that then are applied to its different historical actualizations. The methodological path is a descent from identity to its differences. Our Moroccan philosopher describes the general moments or determinations of modernity in three principles: the principle of majority, the principle of critique, and the principle of universality.[7] Let us give the word to our great philosopher:

> The . . . observation turns around the need to consider modernity as an internal and not external *application*. The postulate according to which there would be two types of modernities, one *interior* and the other *exterior*, is completely wrong. *Real* modernity cannot be achieved but through the direct *application* of *the spirit of modernity* supported by the three principles already mentioned (principle of majority, principle of critique, and principle of universality). Thus, a direct *application* cannot but be an *interior* modernity, while what others call an *exterior* modernity, alluding to the experience of non-Western countries, can barely be considered a modernity in the proper sense.[8]

I want to consider first, logically, the object of the dialogue. What are we talking about when we use the term *modernity*? Are we talking about (1) an a priori (in the order of reality) as an *abstract* universal concept that could be *applied a posteriori* on a *real* concrete historical level or

(2) an *a priori* concrete historical reality (in the order of knowledge) of which its ontologically constitutive moments could be described *a posteriori* in order to have knowledge of its *particularity*? If modernity is an a priori universal concept in the order of reality (1), then it can be *applied* to singular cases (movement of the univocal universal by descent toward the being or thing in which said universality is applied). This would amount to the movement of universality (*Allgemenheit*) toward singularity. But if modernity were the name or word (2) that names a *period in the history of a culture* that is singular (*Einzelheit*), there would be no such possible *application* (*applicatio* or *Anwendung*); instead, it would be an imitation, reduplication, or falsification.

25

It would seem that Abdurrahman's thesis would be that of considering the "spirit of modernity" as a concept that would have to be described a priori (1), from which are deduced the possibilities of its multiple applications in the *differential* modernities, so long as cultures fulfill the three formulated principles (of majority, of critique, of universality).

In the philosophy of liberation, we consider modernity as a real, concrete, singular, unique event (2) about which we have to discover its fundamental ontological structure, which pretends to impose itself as universal. This is the claim of domination itself. The universality of modernity, I assert, is an illusory claim that in the real historical process defined things in such a way that the supposed application to other cultures would be a falsification because of imitation. In this consists precisely the coloniality of knowledge—namely, in the intent to apply an assumed universality that is an inimitable singularity by another culture outside Europe. Because modernity was the alleged product of a *unique* process of Europe itself and was constructed conceptually on an inapplicable utopia (equality, liberty, fraternity, which were neither realized nor possible to apply) and because it was predicated on the exploitation, domination, and alienation of the other *colonial* cultures that were part of its own definition, it could not be and should not be universalized.

We should also dialogue about the claim that there exist an interior and an exterior modernity or, said differently, that there is a modernity developed only by Europe (the *interior*) and globalized in other cultures (the *exterior*). This aspect of the discussion is a necessary dimension of the reflection about the decolonization of cultures and their knowledges. This is so because modernity, which is unique, historical, concrete, and inimitable (and thus inapplicable), places itself as the *center* (and not merely as the *interior*) of the other cultures that are the exploitable *periphery* (and not merely *exterior*, because they do not cease being *interior to the global market* that is dominated by said center). This is to say that modernity is already a singular period of *Europe* (which has as an *ex quo* reference its feudal medieval period) but at the same time is the reference of a period of *world history* in which Europe learned to manage or make use of its "centrality" in order to dominate that imperial/colonial modernity, extracting many products from its colonies and, thanks to its political-military domination, subsuming those products within its own cultural structure to its exclusive benefit. In other words, many civilizational components of other cultures called exterior to Europe, its "colonies," are constitutive moments that are passed off as modern discoveries (think here, at the technological level, of steel, paper, the printing press, paper money, the compass, gunpowder, the discovery of America, the Industrial Revolution—all moments of the history of Chinese technology and not European[9]). For this reason, the issue is to discover the "spirit of modernity" interpreted as a concrete, ontological, anthropological, ethical, political structure of domination, which using the *creations of all the other dominated cultures* (of the Islamic Arab, its mathematics and astronomy, among many of its knowledges) developed them creatively but at the same time made them pass as if they had been its exclusively proper inventions through an immoral recourse to the concealment of their sources.[10] Only a decolonized vision of the unique and inimitable modernity (because it is constructed from and with the human and natural wealth of its colonial periphery, said periphery will not be able to have its own future periphery) can disaggregate theoretically these apparent oppositions. Let us look at some of them.

European modernity is not only a European fact but also a world fact, as we have already claimed. In my book *1492: El encubrimiento del otro: Hacia el origen del mito de la modernidad*[11] (published under the English translation *The Invention of the Americas: Eclipse of "the Other" and the*

Myth of Modernity[12]), I attempted to show that there is a Eurocentric view of modernity that defines it as an exclusively European fact. It is for this reason that this Eurocentric view attempts to argue that its origins lie in the Italian Renaissance, the German Lutheran Reformation, the English political revolution, and the French Enlightenment (as it can be seen, it is an entirely Eurocentric interpretation). My goal during the last fifty years has been to show that the *opening of the* underdeveloped *Europe*, peripheral, dependent, blocked, and besieged by the Islamic-Arab world (later the Ottoman Empire), one that in turn was the *center* of the Eurasian continent (although beyond the caliphate of Baghdad, with China and India as productive economic and cultural poles of this continent)—this is to say, the opening up of Europe to the *Atlantic Ocean* and from there the Pacific Ocean (through Mexico in the west and in the east through Africa to the Indian Ocean)—was the origin of the *unique and inimitable modernity*.

This change of the *geopolitical center* of world history at the end of the fifteenth century (1492), brought about in the south of Europe (by Portugal and Spain, the most cultured and advanced nations in Europe due to their centuries-long contact with the Islamic-Arab Caliphate of Cordoba), was a European and simultaneously a world event.

Europe (especially after the eighteenth century in the north of Europe) acquired the capacity to *inform* itself about all the knowledges of cultures frequently disconnected among themselves. Today this is done with computers and the World Wide Web. This capacity to *read* the *archives* of other great cultures, which at the moment were more developed than Europe (and henceforth they would function as peripheral cultures), enabled the assimilation and appropriation of their dispersed knowledges, sciences, and technologies. This capacity was made possible by the *management* of this new centrality (now global, which included America and not only the Eurasian continent), first by linking hitherto *delinked* knowledge archives, concealing their *origins* later, and then ultimately by judging them *negatively*, because they had originated in what were now considered colonial cultures. Those discoveries were now derided and dismissed and were evaluated as primitive and backward. Of course, it should be acknowledged that there were true novelties proper to Europe, some of them great, such as those of Isaac

Newton. Nonetheless, it was in this *management* of this centrality that the myth of "Europe's superiority" (as Eurocentrism, whiteness, patriarchy, etc.) and the ideology of "Oriental despotism" emerged. This is all an ideological management of knowledges and of practical, military, political, and economic domination (also epistemological colonialism) that passes unnoted in the abstract description of the "spirit of modernity." A thesis that would have to be debated would be the acceptance or rejection of whether *coloniality is the essential element of the definition of modernity*. Thus are born bipolar concepts that can be understood as ideological tricks of modernity itself—for example, the contradiction of "modernity/tradition," which can be considered "modern" because "modernity" is presented as the dominating civilizational development that places "tradition" as being made up of backward, ancient, and superseded customs. Were this opposition to be accepted, one would be playing the game of modernity (as Santiago Castro-Gómez thought in his *Crítica de la razón latinoamericana*[13]). If we set out from modernity in opposition to the nonmodern, the latter is defined as negativity, as the primitive, the anachronistic, the superseded.

If, however, the point of departure is inverted, and we talk instead of "tradition/modernity," the sense of the question changes. This is to say, taking "tradition" as the permanence of the practices and theories of a culture in history, one cannot but recognize that modernity itself had a homogenous growth with its own medieval European "tradition," including its economy, morality, science, and technology. Let me illustrate. Let us take a steam engine in the eighteenth century (an engine that was inspired by the engines produced by the Chinese technological revolution that was prior to the one that took place in England),[14] which was meant to move with velocity and precision, and the *traditional* medieval English loom. Here we set out from the "tradition," which was not rejected; an innovation took place and for this reason remained "traditionally" English (it was a new stage in the living British tradition). The English Industrial Revolution was then "traditional" (since *tradition* is not static but instead evolves in history) with respect to *European* technical production, implementing some variations (in large part taken or inspired, as I already indicated, by the industrial revolution of Chinese capitalism, which was prior to that of England), which was not presented as an opposition or contradiction between *tradition* and *modernity*; on the contrary, modernity was a *technological* growth of a prior homogeneous *artisanal* tradition. What takes place later (with the exception of China because of its great scientific and technological advancement from 400 C.E. until the 1800s, but it entered into a crisis for internal geopolitical reasons) is that other cultures (now colonial, dominated, and exploited because of their resources) had to abandon their traditional artisanal techniques (which were annihilated), imposing upon them from without the new modern European technology. Modernity, using its periphery, exploits and dominates, prostrating these now peripheral cultures, putting them in disadvantageous situations worse than those in which they found themselves before the beginning of colonization. That modernity, then, is not an abstract structure that can be applied to other concrete historical-cultural situations (this was already called in the 1960s in Latin America the "theory of development," "developmentalism" [*desarrollismo*], or "the developmentalist fallacy," the ideological moment of epistemological, technical, and economic domination by the colonial intellectual elites of the Eurocentric, metropolitan, and colonialist modernity). This fallacy consists, exactly as Taha Abdurrahman indicates, in wanting to use the *same path or route* that modern, colonialist Europe traversed. If a dependent colony, postcolony, nation, or culture attempts to follow the same European path, it will never arrive at modernity but instead will increase its colonial misery and dependency. It is concerned precisely with taking "another route," but not the European *modern* route, whose growth entailed the de-struction of the path so that other cultures could arrive at the same modern ends because it destroyed the very same conditions that made possible their origin and growth. Indeed, it is necessary to take *another route*, but one that is radically other than and distinct from that of European modernity. Its pretend *imitators* will remain neocolonial or dependent countries of modernity, which is now North American–European, which nonetheless begins its twilight and entangles in its inevitable crisis its supposed imitators or those that attempt to apply its already transited path.

It is for this reason that the theoretical-philosophical, ethical, and political theme that we have to face is that of showing the way out of

29

the present situation of the cultures and countries of the south that were colonies. If repeating modernity in a new way could show itself as impossible—that is to say, that it would not be a process of partial or total "modernization"—then what other path opens up as a possibility? Over the last five decades, I have thought about this problem from within the movements of the philosophy of liberation, dependency theory, and the history of the world-system and more recently under the denomination of epistemological decolonization—namely, the problem of showing an alternative path toward different future modernities.

This would be a position that (1) opposes a certain *fundamentalism* that rejects in whole all the components of modernity or (2) accepts a *modernization* that would apply the essential elements of modernity, taking into account the differences (be they cultural, religious, political, economic, historical, etc.).[15] Both oppositions would continue to reject or affirm modernity. It is overcoming that threshold in order to situate the question beyond the horizon of modernity but subsuming valuable aspects that should not be undervalued but inserted within a different structure that then changes their nature.

If we take as a partial hypothesis that proposed by Paul Ricoeur, my professor in the Sorbonne since 1961, in his book *Historie et verité*,[16] who suggests we speak of a "noyau éthico-mythique" (ethical-mythical core, which for him is the traditional essence of "culture" and its fundamental "ethos") that gives meaning to human existence and that teaches the use of technological, scientific, and economic tools and so on (which Ricoeur denominates as "civilization"), we could thus make a distinction between the national *culture* of a people and the civilizational moment that this people could share with other peoples, this being a more abstract aspect that would be located at the world level (such as was the case with bronze during the Bronze Age or iron, which was used first by the so-called Indo-Europeans in the Neolithic). In any event, we would have to introduce some modifications to this proposal, because as it is, it retains some problems that we have already criticized in other works,[17] but let us accept it for the moment so that we can advance our description.

The essence of cultures (the Islamic Arab, the Latin American, the Chinese, the Indian, the African Bantu, etc.) has as a foundation of

Schema 1

From modernity to its application in multiple modernities

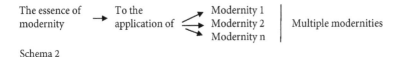

Schema 2

From the age of the only modernity to the new transmodern cultural age

From the modern age of the   a new age of humanity
only colonial/modernity   toward➞   in the cultural transmodern pluriversality

their world a certain interpretation and global practice of the natural and human reality (what Ricoeur calls "noyau éthico-mythique," which we could translate as "ethical-ontological") in which modernity itself is included. In other words, modernity had (and has in its contemporary crisis) its own and different "noyau éthico-ontologique" to those of all existing cultures. It is that "noyau" (core) that we frequently criticize because it is *nonethical* according to the point of view of the cultures of the south. It should be considered, however, that it had its own *modern morality* since the end of the fifteenth century, beginning with Ginés de Sepúlveda, a moralist Spanish philosopher of the sixteenth century, and passing through Hobbes in the seventeenth, Kant in the eighteenth, Nietzsche in the nineteenth, and Friedrich August von Hayek in the twentieth, the Viennese formulator of neoliberalism, which justifies the coloniality, capitalism, and liberalism that are imposed on peripheral cultures.

It is thus that in this twilight of European modernity, we ought to debate the way to define our future. Will it be merely to return to the essence of modernity and to apply it as a whole later, departing from the experiences of the postcolonial cultures? Or will it be instead leaving aside modernity's *noyau éthico-ontologique* (its cultural essence) and selecting, without modern, capitalist, or liberal criteria, what would count as the qualitative growth (and not merely quantitative growth) that is necessary for technology, science, economy, politics, aesthetics, and so on in accordance with the *noyau éthico-ontologique* of each culture of the south (the Islamic Arab, the Latin American, the Chinese, the Indian, the Hindustani, the African Bantu, etc.). This would not be the attitude of Mahatma Gandhi, who opted politically to practice the artisanal techniques of India against the European modern ones (which counted as symbolic but is not a realistic mode of resistance). Rather, the task would be to opt for one's proper cultural attitude (the already indicated *noyau éthico-ontologique* of each great culture of the south)—namely, to elect, select, and bring about with autonomy and responsibility the *subsumption* (*subsumptio* in Latin, *Aufhebung* in German, which means neither obeying an external imposition nor mimetically applying modernity without ethical principles) of that science, technology, economy, and so on of modernity that would be coherent with its own *noyau éthico-ontologique*. For this reason, this subsumption would discard, for instance, the antiecological technologies that destroy life in general and human life in particular (with the side consequences of poverty, inequality, suffering, etc.) or a capitalism that bases itself in the criteria of the growth in the rate of capital gain as the origin of rationality and efficacy. Those criteria are opposed to the millennial Semitic ethic, from the Code of Hammurabi from 3,700 years ago, to the ethic of the Palestinians and the prophets of Israel, to the good message to the poor by the founder of Christianity, to the Prophet Muhammad as is given expression in the Koran.

At the beginning of the philosophical dialogue of the cultures of the south, there ought to be a discussion about the critique of modernity as part of the project of a recovery of the ethical foundations of their own cultures. This may entail criticizing deviations that centuries of colonialism and imperialism have inflicted in the most authentic interpretation of the most primal and originary message of each one of them. This may open up a path to recover the valorization of their own traditions and, from this valorization, opening up a dialogue with the alleged only possible modernity, which is the European one. This could lead to discoveries and inventions that do not contradict ethically our respective traditions. In this way, we may accomplish not a "modernization" but a subsumption of the best inventions of modernity from our respective places of origin, from the distinct ethical-ontological cores of our cultures.

The next step would be a fecund dialogue among these revalorized cultures of the south, each one having recovered a valuable interpretation of its past, opened up and made creative through the act of subsuming the best of modernity (but from other ethical-political, ontological, anthropological bases: the already named *noyau éthico-mythique*), opening to the cultural works of the south in order to learn mutually that process, assimilating the internal values (and not through the extrinsic application of another dominating culture).

In this way, we would advance in the following centuries toward a situation not of a universal culture (where one would refuse the right of others and impose its singularity as universality, which was modernity's claim) but instead of being respectful of the alterity of other positions. This is to say that humanity would traverse a period of centuries of cultural pluriversality (and not of a homogeneous, singular, and imposed universality)[18] toward a globality (*mundialidad*) with an analogical similarity.

I will not name this new age of humanity—in which cultures respect themselves as equals and in which humanity would survive the inevitable ecological crisis caused by capitalism and modernity[19]—as the age of the *multiple modernities* of different cultures. Instead, it is a new global age where the *pluri*versality (in place of the *uni*versality claimed theoretically but refuted in reality by modernity) of a necessary long and enduring south-south dialogue would allow the emergence of a new global civilization, thus far unsuspected and not imagined in the present as diverse. For this reason, I want to call this new age of humanity *transmodernity* (but opposing the critical proposal of some intellectuals of the north that they call *postmodernity*).[20]

APPENDIX 1

Five Moments in the Development of the Critical Consciousness of Eurocentrism and the Birth of Epistemological Decolonization

The critique of Hellenocentrism in philosophy and the general critique of Eurocentrism by the philosophy of liberation (1969) and the critique of Orientalism (1976), and later taking into account the more relevant historical studies, will arrive at a fifth moment, which today we name the epistemological decolonization of the academic and intellectual world, as much in the center as in the global periphery. The process is open and is full of new discoveries.

34

It is to be noted that there are five generations of thinkers that we must take into account. The first generation was that of great historians at the beginning of the twentieth century (Nikolay Danilevsky, Alfred and Max Weber, Pitirim Sorokin, Karl Jaspers, Werner Sombart, Oswald Spengler, Arnold Toynbee, Leopoldo Zea, etc.).[21] The methods, thinking, and theories of these thinkers were appropriated in Latin America in the following ways: within the economy by the theory of dependence since 1963 (with the work done in Brazil and later in Chile) and in the philosophy of liberation by those departing from the questions "Is there a philosophy of our America?" as was asked by Augusto Salazar Bondy and other philosophers in Argentina, who emerged around 1969. These thinkers articulated some initial intuitions that were to be explored in the next decades.

The second generation places Europe in world history critically (Fernand Braudel, Immanuel Wallerstein, Giovanni Arrighi, Samir Amin, etc.),[22] which is already explicitly critical of Eurocentrism. This generation introduced economic-political arguments that included the Muslim world (thus contributing to the critique of Hellenocentrism thanks to the work of Samir Amin and Martin Bernal). Edward Said's critique of Orientalism in 1976 should be placed within this generation.

A third generation of anti-Eurocentric criticism is accomplished when the "China factor" is included (the civilizational development accomplished between 400 and 1800 C.E.), in which we see the unfolding of science and mathematics, from Baghdad to India to China, as central moments in the history of the civilizations of the Eurasian continent (with the contributions of Joseph Needham,[23] Andre Gunder Frank,[24] Kenneth Pomeranz,[25] etc.).[26]

The fourth anti-Eurocentric generation takes a step forward and criticizes the residual Eurocentrism of the third generation. John M. Hobson showed the influence of the Chinese revolution, and of Asia in general, in instruments, machines, and industrial procedures that went on to influence England. This is all presented in his work *The Eastern Origins of Western Civilization.*[27] Jack Goody, a professor in Cambridge, England, belongs to the fourth generation with his works *The Theft of History* and *The Eurasian Miracle.*[28]

The fifth generation, named "epistemological decolonization," includes Latin American authors such as Aníbal Quijano,[29] Walter Mignolo,[30] and Ramón Grosfoguel;[31] thinkers in the tradition of the philosophy of liberation;[32] and many others well described in José Gandarilla's anthology *La crítica en el margen: Hacia una cartografía conceptual para rediscutir la Modernidad*[33] or by Sirin Adlbi Sibai in her book *La cárcel del feminismo: Hacia un pensamiento islámico decolonial,*[34] both of which situate the critique at the level of social science, philosophy, and the natural sciences and technology, to which we would have to refer in order to undertake our dialogue about modernity.

35

APPENDIX 2

"Univocal Universality" or "Analogical Pluriversality"
of the Future Age of Humanity (Which I Call
Tentatively Transmodernity), Beyond Modernity

Two diagrams should suffice, in the style of Charles Sanders Peirce, in order to illustrate the diversity between a possible future universal culture defined according to the logical expression of univocity (which contains identity and difference) and analogy (which instead consists of analogical similarity[35] and distinction).

Diagram 2.1

Univocal universality that excludes and expands
"the same" (from out of its identity)

In this case, the *truth claim* (Jürgen Habermas's *Wahrheit Anspruch* in German) is imposed by force on the other dialogue partners, given that whoever makes this claim assumes a priori that they "possess" all of truth. There is no space for anything else but domination through force (and in the last instance, war), without any possible learning on the part

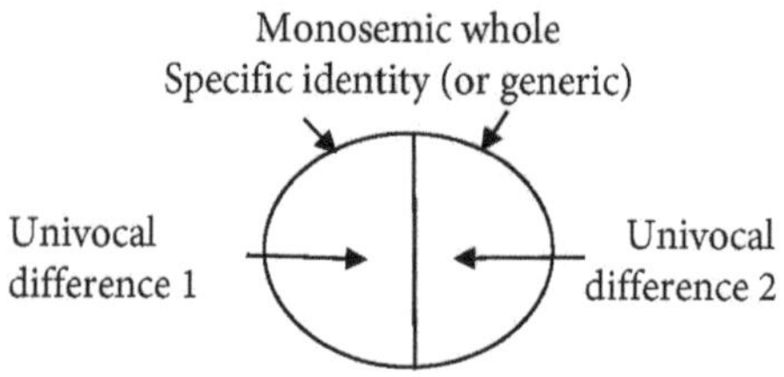

Monosemic whole
Specific identity (or generic)

Univocal
difference 1

Univocal
difference 2

of the other, the simple universal expansion of "my/our truth." Dialogue here is superfluous, and the violence of arms is valid inasmuch as it imposes truth on those who ignore it. It is taken to be irrational insofar as it takes from the other their genuine freedom of arguing, of not accepting the arguments, or of accepting them responsibly and freely as their own. Univocal universality is necessarily dominating.

Diagram 2.2

Cultural dialogue ought to have as its ethical principle the attitude of respect of the "analogical pluriversality" that enables the progressive understanding of the truth of others in analogous aspects of growing "similarity" (neither univocal nor identical).[36]

The *logical* diversity between the universalist univocity (of identity/diversity) and the pluriversality of analogy (of similarity/distinction) allows from the beginning of the process of honest and ethical human dialogue that each interlocutor can have their "truth claim," which presupposes that it be "valid" for the other members of the community of discussion. It is only when the whole community agrees by means of consensus on the same truth "validity"[37] that the goal of its "truth claim" will have reached its "validity claim." If this consensus is not entirely agreed on, nonetheless there will be an advancement in a mutually enriching understanding. It is not a matter of skepticism of many truths but rather of a distinction among different similar interpretations that are not identical in the face of the incommensurable plenitude of reality itself in relation to the cognitive finitude of the human being.

Translated by Eduardo Mendieta

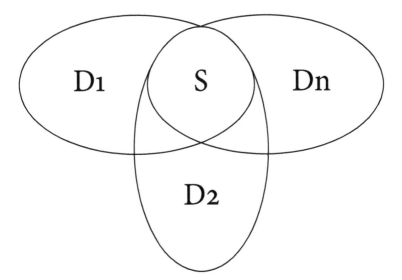

Note: S: similarity; D1: analogical distinction 1; D2: analogical distinction 2; Dn: other analogical distinctions. In mathematical notations of sets, one could express "similarity" or what is *common* and the coincidence of the distinction of the analogous in the following way: *Similarity* = analogical *distinction* 1 **n** analogical *distinction* 2 **n**. To the extent that the dialogue grows, "S" also increases, without there being a loss of the "analogical distinction" of each interlocutor, of each culture in the intercultural dialogue.

NOTES

1. To write "Europe" is tautological because there has not been and there will not be another modernity, as I will argue in this chapter.

2. In Enrique Dussel, *Ethics of Liberation: In the Age of Globalization and Exclusion*, trans. Eduardo Mendieta, Camilo Pérez Bustillo, Yolanda Angulo, and Nelson Maldonado-Torres, ed. Alejandro A. Vallega (Durham, N.C.: Duke University Press, 2013), and in many other works (see https://www.enriquedussel.com/works .html), I, in turn, think similarly that we have to develop a critical ethics of life, of consensus and feasibility that have their practical and theoretical grounding in the existential experience of the Semitic peoples (Mesopotamian, Egyptian, Palestinian, Jewish, Christian, and Islamic), a horizon that could be a point of departure in a very relevant dialogue in our time.

3. As an initial reference, see Samir Abuzaid, "Professor Taha Abdurrahman," *Philosophers of the Arabs*, http://www.arabphilosophers.com/English/philosophers /contemporary/contemporary-names/Taha_Abdulrahman/English_Article_Taha _Abdulrahamn/English_Abdulrahamn.htm.

4. Ibid.

5. Taha Abdurrahman, *The Question of Ethics*, 195–96. Cited by Abuzaid, "Professor Taha Abdurrahman."

6. Sirin Adlbi Sibai, *La cárcel del feminismo: Hacia un pensamiento decolonial* (Mexico City: Edicionesakal, 2016), 92.

7. Ibid., 92–93. Sibai is here quoting and translating into Spanish from the Arab from Taha Abdurrahman, *El espíritu de la Modernidad: Introducción para la fundación de una modernidad islámica* (Casablanca: Al-Markaz Al-Zaqafi Al-'Arabi, 2006).

8. Sibai, *Cárcel del feminismo*, 92–93, citing Abdurrahman, *Espíritu de la Modernidad*, 33–35; emphasis added.

9. See Needham in appendix 1.

10. This is what Jack Goody calls *The Theft of History* (Cambridge: Cambridge University Press, 2008); see appendix 1.

11. All of my works can be found at http://www.enriquedussel.com.

12. Enrique Dussel, *The Invention of the Americas: Eclipse of "the Other" and the Myth of Modernity*, trans. Michael D. Barber (New York: Continuum, 1995).

13. Santiago Castro-Gómez, *Crítica de la razón latinoamericana* (Bogotá: Universidad Javeriana, 1996).

14. See references cited under appendix 1 in this chapter.

15. This could be denominated as an altermodernity, another noncapitalist modernity, multiple modernities, and so on, but always modern.

16. Paul Ricoeur, *Historie et verité* (Paris: Editions du Seuil, 1955).

17. What happens is that a civilizing instrument inevitably produces some variations on the level of the "noyau éthico-mythique." Arnold Toynbee himself showed that an English hospital in Cairo in the nineteenth century would change the traditional interpretation of illness, the role of women as nurses, and so on. It produced "cultural" effects (in Ricoeur's hypothesis).

18. In *Cárcel del feminismo*, Sibai writes on page 269, "I do not opt to use the Dusselian concept of *pluriversality*, but rather from the *Tawheed* I reaffirm *universality*, which is the universality *of the heterogeneous* . . . a universality that unites, that philiates [*hermana*] in difference [I would have written 'in the distinction'] and *plurality* [this plurality is expressed in the word *pluriversality*] of the multiple expressions of existence, which are nothing but the manifestation of the infinite beauty of Alah." As can be seen, it would seem that *pluriversality* is a juxtaposition of *equivocal* positions (where each distinction is irreconcilable and incommunicable with the others). This would be a skeptical pluriversality containing juxtaposed and contradictory positions. Sibai speaks, instead, of a "universality *of the heterogeneous*." What happens is that this heterogeneity refers to a "similarity" (that is not a univocal "identity") that is the "common" of different positions with the "analogical distinction" of each participant (be it at the level of the arguer, culture, or religion) and that universality (that is neither univocal nor excluding) ought to be named a "pluriversality with analogical similarity of its parts." What we are speaking of is an analogical "pluriversality" where there are many "similar" moments ("common" but not "identical") and nonetheless analogical distinctions (which are not merely the specific differences of the univocal identity). This would seem like a superficial question of words and not of concepts. However, it is not so. The identity/difference of Hegelian difference has to be superseded by an analogical rationality of the

similarity/distinction of pluriversality that allows for respectful and fecund dialogue, without dogmatisms or exclusions, and that also does not allow the affirmation of a unique universality for all without the mediation of honest, sincere, and tolerant discussion that is respectful of the alterity of the other—that is to say, an ethical discussion. I think this is what is expressed in authentic tolerance (neither that of John Locke nor the modern version), and this is what I agree with. Otherwise, we would fall into the fanaticism of dominating universality. Here then I am in complete agreement with our author with respect to the *semantic content of Tawheed*, but I believe that the choice of an ambiguous word such as *heterogenous universality* creates confusion. It would be a matter of clarifying semantically the terms used.

39

19. It is important to indicate that the pretend technological "creativity" of European modernity (which was an imitation of the *anterior* Chinese technological revolution; here, see Joseph Needham, *Science and Civilization in China*, 7 vols. [Cambridge: Cambridge University Press, 1954–2004]; Kenneth Pomeranz, *The Great Divergence: China, Europe and the Making of the Modern World Economy* [Princeton: Princeton University Press, 2000]) was the result of a market mechanism. Each corporation had to produce a commodity with the lowest value/price in the market, because in *competition* (*concurrencia* in other languages), it could sell its commodities and thus destroy its competitors (who offered the same commodities at a *higher price* because they had worse technology). As in eighteenth-century England, there was a need to invent a better technology that would allow in the *short term* to decrease the price of the commodities, and this propelled, for the first time in human history, the explosion of inventions and the creators of a new technology. The background ethical problem consists in that the criteria of the invention and subsumption of technology in the process of production are not for the sake of improving the positive qualities of human life or the use value of the commodity but rather to increase the gain of capital—that is, solely to its exchange value. If we had to use nonrenewable energy (such as petroleum) and to burn it (knowing of its immense qualitative value and its imminent exhaustion in addition to the negative effect on the environment and other negativities against life), its immorality was of no concern (if life were the fundamental criteria of life and not the gain of capital because of the death of nature and humanity's suicide). However, at the beginning of the twentieth century, no company could attempt to produce a solar energy–fueled automobile because its development would have required *the long term* of dozens of years; meanwhile, the company would have been excluded from competition in the market. This company would have run out of resources to produce because it had not sold anything in the market. This is to say that the pretend *creativity* (one of the principles of modernity), now modernity's technological creativity under the criteria of the gain of capital, is noxious and nonethical for humanity (and China is already suffering its consequences). We will have to identify another motivation and ethical criterion for creative invention of technology that is neither capitalist nor modern. In this way, we can dismantle one by one the supposed positive and creative values of modernity. To repeat or apply them, even in multiple modernities of diverse cultures, would be, in any event, humanity's suicide.

20. See Linda Martín Alcoff, "Enrique Dussel's Transmodernism," *TRANS-MODERNITY: Journal of Peripheral Cultural Production of the Luso-Hispanic World* 1, no. 3 (Spring 2012): 60–68, https://escholarship.org/uc/ssha_transmodernity /1/3.

21. In Enrique Dussel, *Hipótesis para el estudio de Latinoamérica en la Historia Universal*, Obras selectas 2 (Buenos Aires: Docencia, 2012); I initially remained within this type of interpretation.

22. See my interpretation of this generation in the introduction to *Ethics of Liberation*, 1–52, paras. 1–55; or in my *Politics of Liberation: A Critical World History* (London: SCM, 2011).

23. Needham, *Science and Civilization in China*.

24. Andre Gunder Frank, *ReOrient: The Global Economy in the Asian Age* (Berkeley: University of California Press, 1998).

25. Pomeranz, *Great Divergence*.

26. On this topic, see some of my most recent works, such as "Transmodernity and Interculturality: An Interpretation from the Perspective of Philosophy of Liberation," *TRANSMODERNITY: Journal of Peripheral Cultural Production of the Luso-Hispanic World* 1, no. 3 (Spring 2012): 28–58, https://escholarship.org/uc/item /6591j76r.

27. John M. Hobson, *The Eastern Origins of Western Civilization* (Cambridge: Cambridge University Press, 2004). Hobson is a professor at the University of Sheffield, and he remembers that in his city, the first European factory for the production of steel was built, which was set up by Chinese technicians (who had discovered the metal in the second century of the common era).

28. Goody, *Theft of History*; Jack Goody, *The Eurasian Miracle* (Cambridge: Polity, 2010).

29. Aníbal Quijano, *Cuestiones y horizontes: Antología esencial: De la independencia histórico-estructural a la colonialidad/descolonialidad del poder* (Buenos Aires: CLACSO, 2014).

30. Walter Mignolo, *Habitar la frontera: Sentir y pensar la descolonialidad (Antología 1999–2015)* (Barcelona: CIBO-UACJ, 2016).

31. Wikipedia, s.v. "Ramón Grosfoguel," https://en.wikipedia.org/wiki/Ram%C3 %B3n_Grosfoguel.

32. Toward the end of the decade of the 1960s, I already began to critique European centrality and the discovery of a philosophy that would be critical from the perspective of the periphery. See the theme in https://www.enriquedussel.com/works.html.

33. José Gandarilla, ed., *La crítica en el margen: Hacia una cartografía conceptual para rediscutir la Modernidad* (Madrid: Akal, 2016).

34. Sirin Adlbi Sibai, *La cárcel del feminismo: Hacia un pensamiento islámico decolonial* (Madrid: Akal, 2016).

35. *Similitudo* in Latin, *resemblance* in French, *similarity* in English, *Ähnlichkeit* in German, and *semejanza* in Spanish.

36. This growth of understanding, if it can capture the cultural originality of the other, is Hans-Georg Gadamer's "fusion of horizons"; see Hans-Georg Gadamer, *Verdad y Método*, vol. 2 (Salamanca: Editorial Sígueme, 1988), ii, 4, 9, 379. "Fusion of horizons" "increases" what both spheres have in "similar" as the dialogue continues through time: "For what do we mean by 'transposing ourselves'? Certainly not just

disregarding ourselves. This is necessary, of course, insofar as we must imagine the other situation. But into this other situation we must bring, precisely, ourselves. Only this is the full meaning of 'transposing ourselves.' If we put ourselves in someone else's shoes, for example, then we will understand him—i.e. become aware of the otherness [*alterity* in the Spanish translation], the indissoluble individuality of the other person—by putting *ourselves* in his position. . . . Transposing ourselves consists neither in the empathy of one individual for another nor in subordinating another person to our own standards; rather, it always involves rising a higher universality that overcomes not only our own particularity but also that of the other"; Hans-Georg Gadamer, *Truth and Method*, 2nd rev. ed., trans. Joel Weinsheimer and Donald G. Marshall (New York: Continuum, 2011), 304. It is precisely the role of analogy and not of univocal universality that demands the submission of the other to the identity of the statement of the *ego* that expands its identity (*mismidad*) as internal difference to the other in the world of the I itself (*si mismo*).

37. *Validity* (*Gültigkeit* in German, *validité* in French) is not the same as *truth* (Wahrheit, verité). *Truth* is the reference (*Bezug* in German, *référance* in French) of subjectivity to reality; *validity* is the reference of a member of a community of communication to that very community and its acceptance or rejection by other members of the community regarding the argument that is being presented for its acceptance or rejection, for its validation (to validate it) or invalidation (invalidation is not *falsification*; this term is being taken in its Popperian sense). The *truth claim* is not the same as the "validity claim." The *time of dialogue*, of honest discussion, is the time in which, although each member of the dialoguing community raises a truth claim while the arguments that are put forward have not yet been accepted by others, it has not yet reached the validity claim because such a compliance is only reached if the opponents have accepted the truth judgment of the first. In the global horizon of the interphilosophical, intercultural, or interreligious dialogue, it is the time of "pluriversality" of each culture of the whole of humanity that has a "similar" horizon (S) but not of identity. There is an acceptance of heterogeneous or distinct aspects that are increasingly "similar." This situation can develop over centuries.

CHAPTER 3

The Hegel of Coyoacán

Linda Martín Alcoff

Reading through Enrique Dussel's recently translated magnum opus, *Ethics of Liberation: In the Age of Globalization and Exclusion*, one can be forgiven for conjuring up the image of a certain other philosopher who famously preferred working with big canvases. Like Hegel, Dussel is an impossibly large thinker, a theorist who reaches back through the entirety of recorded history and philosophy to account for the current impasses in our thinking and to chart a way forward. Also like Hegel, at least the Hegel of *Phenomenology of Spirit*, Dussel develops his argument with a patiently dialectical progression of analysis and critique. This new liberation ethics is put forward as a comparative advance, building on—indeed, subsuming—all that is useful from what is past (or still influential) normative thought. And despite their heavily historicist readings of philosophical ideas emphasizing their location of origin, both Hegel and Dussel aim to develop an ethics with a universal reach.

Here, perhaps, the comparison ends. Hegel wrote from what he took to be the intellectual center of the then world-system of capitalism and colonialism and global commerce, referring to "the German Spirit" as the "spirit of the New World."[1] He viewed the cultures and societies of the distant colonies as just so much Paleolithic data about what the species has been able to overcome. Dussel rectifies Hegel's mistaken thinking about where the European center of the world-system in 1806 (the date of the publication of the *Phenomenology*) actually was; in truth, it was a bit west of Jena in that period. But more importantly, Dussel points out that the colonies were a central, causal, and constitutive feature of modernity, including the European Enlightenment, and that the colonized parts of the world actually had some intellectual and political advantages over the myopic tendencies of the Europeans.[2]

43

Turning the tables on Hegel's assessment of the "backward" parts of the world, Dussel presents Hegel's errors—his rush to judgment about peoples and cultures he knows nothing about and his grandiose representation of the German epistemological standpoint—as prime evidence that Hegel's own geographical location in fact presented epistemological obstacles, a classic case of what some call the epistemology of ignorance. But Dussel does not in any way absolve Hegel on the grounds of these contextual considerations: Hegel's willful ignorance and his invention of developmental modernism served to justify a lack of investigation. Hegel assumed without attempting to make any serious investigation that there was nothing to learn from the Chinese, Indian, Aztec, Incan, Yoruban, or Ashanti cultures other than negative lessons from their demise. They had been conquered, superseded, and outstripped, not to mention ransacked, proving, he thought, their inferiority and inadequate capacity to adapt and grow. What is most interesting about this familiar colonial attitude, however, is the way in which Hegel's richly contextual and historicist philosophical viewpoint manifested a contradictory position in this regard: one could surmise a philosopher's worth, he thought, from the particularity of their geographical origin, thus indicating that the origin is a relevant consideration in judgment, and yet the particularity of Hegel's own contextual origin revealed not its limitations but its status as the universal. The relevance of history and culture for Hegel led not to relativism but to an absolutist justification of his own epistemological standpoint. It was only because Hegel wrote *from* Europe that he could write *of* Man.[3] A major task of Dussel's *Ethics* is to show how this idea has been maintained even in Western-influenced critical philosophies, from Weber through Habermas.

In contrast, Dussel acknowledges the nonuniversal nature of his own context of enunciation. Like every other Latin American philosopher since El Inca Garcilaso de la Vega, Dussel has been forced to contemplate how this context is situated with respect to the regime of European truth. Hegel's teleology of history offered a rare justification of Eurocentrism: most others just took it for granted. Hegel's developmentalist justification remains with us today in assumptions about which societies are "ahead" and which are "behind," who can lead the world "forward" and who is dragging us, as a species, "backward." Those writing in the "backward" regions have long had to credential their arguments in relation to the vanguard. After half a millennium of colonialism, this has not yet changed.

Dussel is not writing an ethics of liberation for Latin America but "a critical philosophy born in the periphery . . . which has the intention of being relevant on a global scale."[4] How is this possible? Interestingly, his explanation owes something to Hegel's amalgamation of historicism and universalism without being a simple reversal (where the colonized world becomes the most advanced). Consider again Hegel's account, which explains away the contradiction between a universalist aspiration emerging out of a consciously articulated historical and geographical location. For Hegel, philosophy is the successful leaving behind of not the material world but its manifestation in thought. As such, philosophy plays a crucial role in helping the universal spirit gain self-understanding, bringing the spirit to consciousness.[5] The location of philosophical thought, then, has a role to play in philosophy itself and in some cases can assist in the production of self-understanding and hence the development of the universal. For Hegel, in other words, philosophy is not the transcendence of history but conditioned by history. Further, philosophy is the condition for the production of history insofar as history is a development of autonomy through enhanced self-understanding.

Dussel's own account accepts Hegel's view about the relevance of location and the necessity of reading the history of philosophy in light of the history of the world. Hence historical location is inevitably a part of philosophical thought, and philosophical thought is advanced via a dialectic. And he suggests that the contrast of his own location from Hegel's is not coincidental to their thought. Their geographical divergence is in fact related to their philosophical differences. Hegel soon moved from Jena to become a professor in Berlin, a city with a long history at the center of the Austro-Hungarian Empire that hosted the infamous conference in 1884, organized by Germany's first chancellor, Otto von Bismarck, in which the European powers met to "divide Africa." There is little doubt that Hegel's dismissive treatment of African cultures contributed to the hubris such a project required. In contrast, Coyoacán is the Nahuatl name for the neighborhood in Mexico City where Dussel sought refuge after the Argentine military dictatorship bombed his apartment in 1975. As a municipality, Coyoacán began as a village on the southern shore of Lake Texcoco, survived the Spanish conquest to become the first capital of New Spain in 1521, and eventually became incorporated into Mexico City as the effect of urban sprawl. Both places, then, were embroiled in colonial histories but from opposite ends.

Dussel shares Hegel's attentiveness to the geography of philosophy, but crucially, he drops Hegel's developmentalism and redefines the local in a more global frame. Europeans largely denied that European modernity was dependent on the transnational flows of ideas and goods that colonialism intensified and instead characterized their Enlightenment as "self-caused," to mimic Aquinas's characterization of God. In contrast, Dussel maintains that modernity has always been a decentralized, transnational, and relational phenomenon.[6] As a result, there is no local that can proclaim itself to be the vanguard: there is only domination and a plethora of global victims. Dussel replaces the Hegelian perspectivism grounded in an imagined developmentalist trajectory of time with a materialist perspectivism grounded in the geography of place, both literal and structural: the world looks different depending on who is doing the looking.

From his own spatial location in the Global South, Dussel deconstructs not only Hegel's colonial developmentalism but also his central thesis: that the story of human history is the story of the advancement of freedom. Dussel rejects Hegel's notion of freedom as the central criterion that establishes whether progress has been achieved, and he does so in a way that looks to be noncoincidentally connected to their diverse

45

geographical genealogies. For Hegel, freedom is the central concept for both history and philosophy, since it alone drives the dialectic and explains historical ruptures and motivates the cunning of reason and the ongoing growth of human understanding—the freedom to move, to grow, to expand, to create the conditions for autonomy, and also, we might silently think, the freedom to vanquish anyone who stands in the way. For Hegel, freedom is the story of human history; the development of freedom countermands every other consideration, ethical or otherwise. In contrast, for Dussel, the central concept is life, material life. The ultimate ethical criterion is not freedom but the "reproduction or development of the life of each human subject in the community."[7] Systems—whether philosophical, political, or economic—that thwart and inhibit the reproduction or development of material life are invalid. Dussel makes use of new versions of naturalism to argue that this value trumps all others, even freedom.[8] Yet in a sense, to value life is to value the creative capacity: human beings being what they are, the nature of life can never coexist with stasis or the cessation of movement and development. Citing the Chilean biologist and philosopher Humberto Maturana, Dussel puts this as follows: "We are a moment of autopoietic life."[9] Hence the protection of life will nurture the capacity to continue the open-ended movements of history. Hegelian freedom, at least in some of its iterations, has served as an alibi for the de-struction of life, even whole cultural communities. For Dussel, Hegel does not understand freedom; by making freedom more important than material life, he in fact diminishes freedom. In Dussel's rendering, the protection of material life will maximize the creative capacity of the species.

Although Dussel's *Ethics of Liberation: In the Age of Globalization and Exclusion* is nominally divided into two parts, it has three principal sections: a historical reconstruction and comparative analysis of global "ethical systems" and their core intuitions; a development of Dussel's account of what must be the foundational principles of ethics, including intersubjective validity (or the discursive), the question of material effects, and the requirement of feasibility; and lastly, an elaboration of how to achieve an antihegemonic validity among the community of victims as well as a praxis of liberation. There is a constitutive relationship, in his view, between the critical and the positive aspects of ethics. Critique of existing systems is a process of judging from the standpoint of the victims that every dominant system has generated, where "victim" is defined simply as all those excluded from the very ability to maintain and secure their lives, to be discussed later, while the positive reconstruction is guided by what the liberation of victims calls upon us to do.

At one point, Dussel suggests that the struggle of victims is to discover nontruth, nonvalidity, and nonefficacy. Echoing Adorno here, Dussel holds that to make sense of the fact that the impoverishment of the majority of the world's people and the imminent danger of ecosuicide are not on the agenda of dominant systems of thought, we need to venture beyond, and cultivate a skepticism toward, the intelligible, the valid, and the true: "The system of domination *is not* 'true,' 'valid,' or 'efficacious' in regard to the life or the dignity of the victims. The critic, both the victim and the organic intellectual, becomes a skeptic who is critical of the truth and validity of the system."[10] Only through discovering the fundamental lack in currently dominant systems, processes, and values can the community of victims reach toward creative, reconstructive formulations. This is the task Dussel defines as the agenda of a philosophy of liberation: to provide a diagnosis of why the global material challenges to life remain unaddressed in social theory and to fashion an ethics that will put these challenges at the center.

Yet to seek out nontruth, invalidity, and nonefficacy is to risk becoming unintelligible, marginal, and invalid. To think from the perspective of what has been necessarily excluded is to venture beyond what Foucault aptly called the regime of truth. Such has been the fate of Dussel's own work within the Western agora itself. This is not to say that every criticism of Dussel is on the side of domination but that the relative inattention his work receives reflects the Eurocentric frames in place. Who else today is attempting to develop a critical materialist and globally relevant ethics? However many limitations Dussel's philosophy of liberation may have, how can it be summarily ignored?

Dussel has been publishing for more than half a century scores of highly original and erudite books analyzing and disputing the dominant ethical systems of the West. He has engaged in lengthy exchanges with the likes of Habermas, Ricoeur, Rorty, Apel, and others; produced a multivolume study of Marx with innovative interpretations; and written extensively on Levinas, Christianity, and the conquest of the Americas. The *Ethics* synthesizes many of these earlier analyses, but here his goal is more systematic: to generate a new metaethics or starting place for ethical thought and practice. He engages broadly with the Western philosophical tradition from Plato to Foucault, assessing strengths and weaknesses, criticizing but also crediting the useful, legitimate, and important developments to be incorporated into his own system. From this sweeping comprehension of the whole, patterns of exclusion by this tradition begin to emerge. Most starkly, nowhere is the material condition of the laboring victims given a full focus—those who die early deaths due to malnutrition—an estimated billion and a half people in our own present time.

Marx is a notable exception, and from Marx, Dussel extracts significant theoretical value for liberatory thought. For example, the concept of *living labor* as the "essential mediation of capital" was a critical idea developed in Dussel's five-volume interpretative study of Marx published in the 1980s.[11] Labor under capitalism, as Marx famously argued, has been commodified and alienated so much that it little resembles the creative and communal laboring activities that define the special manner of life for the species *Homo sapiens*. Mostly when Marx talks about labor, he is referring to a condition in which human agency has been deadened in forms of work that render men and women as machines. But there are other moments when Marx gestures toward another conceptualization of labor, not in its deadened commodity form but in its exteriority to capitalism, as it exists apart from the wage machine. The concept of living labor, then, makes it possible for Dussel to introduce the agential productive practices of Indigenous groups that operate off the grid, outside of commodification, and provide a glimpse of labor as it once was and still is in the exteriority of capital and that might one day flourish again in its living state. The concept of living labor thus allows Dussel to turn our focus toward a form of labor and of praxis that exists outside the Eurocentric frame. In Latin America, Indigenous peoples make up an ever-present alternative form of life not fully assimilated to the wage-work model.[12] Marxists should look here, not for the vestiges of primitive accumulation Marx took to be the historical forbear of capital but as a contemporary sphere of possibilities that can expand our conception of the feasible.

More startlingly, Dussel reads Marx as fundamentally a theorist of ethics. This argument is more prominent in the new *Ethics* and provides a key part of his running argument against what he refers to as the "so-called naturalistic fallacy," or G. E. Moore's claim that "is" can never lead to "ought."[13] Many of Marx's interpreters—not just those who won state power—rendered Marx into a descriptive social scientist who shied away from value claims and normative proposals. They argued that even if his editorial tone sometimes suggested otherwise, Marx was aiming to explain and predict more than morally condemn. Dussel takes this positivist rendering of Marx to be simply false and rejects the idea that "from judgments of fact, normative judgments cannot be deduced by means of a logical-analytical derivation."[14] The normative implications of Marx's critique of capitalism are not *applications* of his critical analysis or a secondary stage of argument but preconditions of his fact-laden critique. It's not that Marx is simply revealing laws and structures while leaving the values debate to others. Rather, Marx is *showing* us that workers are getting *robbed*, that wages are a form of *theft*.

In this way, Dussel uses Marx to shore up one of the central tenets of *Ethics*: that judgments of fact are in a continuous loop with judgments of value. For example, to identify a potential food as poison is to identify it as a danger to be avoided by human beings. The descriptor "poison" contains this imperative. Dussel makes use of the pragmatist traditions as developed by William James and Hilary Putnam to drive home this point: that the determination of facts is always an operation in a particular place by a person or persons with a particular set of ends. These ends should be subject to revision in the process of inquiry itself if it is found they will not lead to truth, but this does not make them irrelevant or secondary to the work of description. "Poison" denotes a substance that is harmful to or for a given species, threatening its survival. There is no secondary ethical argument needed. The "is" leads directly to an "ought." Dussel argues further that just as we cannot pursue scientific inquiry in a way that transcends all interests, all points of view, we cannot engage in debates over values autonomously impervious to factual concerns. In this way, Dussel makes his case that Marx was an ethicist: he was revealing the structural mechanisms that diminish the capacity of capitalist societies to meet human needs—in other words, a poison.

50

At the same time that he repudiates the hard distinction between facts and values, in this book, Dussel expands the naturalistic grounding of his ethical approach. He begins part 1 with an embrace of recent work in the neurosciences that purports to show that the cerebral functions of the brain perform a continuous loop of description/ascription. Dussel takes this as a further argument against the naturalistic fallacy, since brain function itself merges descriptive and evaluative operations. He concludes that we need to find a different way to explain what we are doing when we are doing ethics that will not rely on or assume a neat and clean fact/value division.

Although his turn to naturalism and the neurosciences will be anathema to some readers, Dussel is making a serious attempt here to connect the sort of practical rationality he is calling for with recent work on the biology of brain function that demonstrates the flexibility and holism of nonintentional cognitive operations, in which "feeling states" are nonnegotiable players: "In order to construct its object, the process of categorization requires 'passage' through the 'evaluative-affective system.'"[15] Like some others in this literature, Dussel seems to form evaluative conclusions about the apparent self-regulations of the brain, but he is also making the naturalized epistemology move to argue that our normative ideals of theoretical practice need to be in line with the realities of cognition. I am as skeptical as the next social theorist toward the inflationary claims some make about neurophilosophy, and especially toward the reductive nature of functionalist explanations advanced in this genre, most notably about religious belief. Dussel's efforts here may also look like an opportunistic attempt to cash in on the panache of the latest scientific theories. But as a theorist long committed to materialism, it makes sense that Dussel will be interested in its newer iterations now gaining traction in philosophy. Hence I understand Dussel's turn to the neurosciences to be primarily motivated by his materialism. Human beings have bodies, and the needs and vulnerabilities of these bodies provide the ultimate basis of social critique as well as the conditions for a potential universalism across diversity. As our understanding of bodily processes grows, this can helpfully amplify the material grounds of normative thought. And it can provide further ways to criticize the abstractions of formalism that would make mate- 51 rial considerations secondary to deliberative process, as if the latter were not a material practice itself.

The most original and distinctive element of Dussel's ethics of liberation has been its "material principle," and he has long justified this principle with a naturalistic argument appealing to universal human need. For Dussel, the material principle is something that one recognizes or not; its ethical significance does not actually require an ethical argument. Dussel does not much care for the word *naturalism*, associating this term with the hubris of early positivists who believed they could describe an unmediated world. I am importing the term here both as a way to characterize his focus on human need and as a means to place these in relation to a naturalistic turn that is currently, along with the new materialism, sweeping philosophy. But it is important to underscore that for Dussel, the sphere of the natural is not separable from the sphere of value, and thus his is a more sophisticated naturalism that understands the articulation of need, via the Hegelian and Marxist tradition, as always already mediated, located, and interested. And via Weber, Dussel sees human inquiry as a constituting act. But the circumstances of these constitutions (or social constructions, if you prefer) can be charted in their material specificity: there are conditions in which we find ourselves facing a reality that poses challenges to our lives and to human life in general.

The tradition of American pragmatism, a truly hemispheric trend, as Gregory Pappas's new book decisively shows, is Dussel's main way of fending off the tendency of all forms of materialism toward reductive explanation.[16] He shows how this tradition takes aim at the way in which the naturalistic fallacy has been used to render ethics and morality an obfuscating tangent to the quest for philosophical truth. Determinations of fact lead to practical action not because the "is" determines the "ought" as a secondary step or an implication under logical closure but because the determination of the "is" works within a material sphere of particularity always already mediated, indeed saturated, with value-laden orientations. Dussel could have made better use of recent work in feminist epistemology to develop these arguments, to show the social context of rationality as well as the epistemic productivity of values in science.[17] The pragmatist arguments work at an abstract level to theoretically elaborate a way to relate facts and values, while the work in feminist and social epistemologies takes, in a sense, the next step: to trace the epistemic role of values in cognition, both institutional and individual. One hesitates to criticize Dussel for not engaging with more sources given the incredibly broad array he addresses, more than almost any existing social theorist, and yet in these sections on the relations between materialism and cognition, he really could have made use of the feminist work.

In Dussel's view, if the central concept of a materialist ethics is life itself, the concept of need cannot be far behind. This marks a contrast with other trends toward revising a form of vitalism that views life as fundamentally an unfettered motility. For Dussel, the idea of life is far from an abstract conception of unbounded motion, as it is in the Deleuzian approach—for example, where it signifies a "plane of immanence" or a Spinozist-like open-textured substance. Deleuze's way of engaging in speculative ontologies has a creative virtue, no doubt, but it takes us so far from the concrete conditions of material realities that one has to do quite a bit of work to apply his ideas in ways that lead to specific normative directions for action. For Deleuze, life is something of a metaphorical rendition for the existence of a form of unstoppable movement that underlies the most basic strata of the universe, and in this sense life and death share the plane of immanence and are each contingent accidents of desire, his most primordial term.[18] And desire is famously cast adrift of need in Deleuze's account of first things: unmoored by either the Freudian/Lacanian category of lack or the Marxist category of need, desire for Deleuze is first and foremost a creative motion, free in form, capable of attaching, or not, to any conceivable object. In this way, Deleuze's philosophy appears to align with that other Hegelian tradition that makes freedom fundamental as both the most basic condition of life as well as its goal.

When Dussel speaks of life, by contrast, he means to invoke realities more at the visible surface than the abstractions we might imagine to

exist beyond the phenomenal domain. Dussel insists that ethics begin
to consider the obvious rather than the arcane. The sphere of the obvious and the clearly visible includes poverty, malnutrition, war, and a
systematic assault on the ability for more than a billion of the earth's   53
human inhabitants to sustain their lives, not to mention the jeopardy
of the earth's nonhuman inhabitants and the sustainability of the earth
itself. Life itself, outside the metaphorical sphere, is in peril. To understand this requires coming to terms with need: the need for a means
of sustenance, both in the immediate present and in a more long-term
sense. Thus for Dussel, the concept of life signifies need more than it
points toward freedom.

So what of ethics? If there is a running argument throughout this
book against the is/ought distinction, Dussel has an equal concern with
formalism in ethics with its concomitant minimalism and proceduralism. More particularly, Dussel's concern is the formalism that empties
ethics of all substantive content by rendering its own operations on a
metalevel or prior to considerations of substance. Formalisms of this
sort separate questions of the good from questions of what is valid, rendering the debate over substantive ends as posterior to the debate over
decision procedures. Hence instead of focusing on material challenges
such as global poverty, formalists retreat to process questions about the
conditions in which ethical decision-making occurs. Although Dussel
agrees that such questions are vitally important, he suggests that the
trend toward formalism in the twentieth century has been motivated
in no small part by a dawning awareness about how colonialism and
ethnocentrism distorted debates over the good. Formalism provided a
way to avoid organizing diverse cultural notions of the good into hierarchies of value, such as what we find in Hegel. Debating contrary
notions of the good requires the philosopher from formerly colonizing
countries to face the issue of colonialism; retreating to formal questions
of process allows the same philosopher to reassert his capacity for an
abstract approach that legitimates a claim to have universal reach.

As a result of the turn to formalism, Dussel allows that there have
been important advances in ethical work on communication and
decision procedures. But the methodology of abstraction is a serious
problem: "What is important in our reading is to consider with attention

how, having once denied the material aspect of ethics as a point of departure (the inevitable problem of all formalisms), we are required to construct irresolvable hypothetical scenes, which will then always have to be corrected in order to attempt to recuperate step by step but never adequately, the materiality denied at the outset."[19] Moreover, formalist approaches and their abstract criteria of proceduralism can undermine the very social movements that create new and effective responses to crises by launching criticisms if they fail to live up to ideal procedures. Validity then becomes an obstacle to the good. An ethics of liberation pursues validity as part of an overall approach that espouses goodness claims as well as a feasibility component. Validity has no prior claim to these other two considerations.

At the risk of simplification, let me offer a characterization of Dussel's approach vis-à-vis the other major approaches to ethics currently under discussion in the Global North as a way of clarifying the distinctiveness of his contribution. What are the main ethical approaches on offer? John Rawls's theory of justice takes as a criterion of good policy that it produces an advantage for the least well off among us; this serves as the criterion of justice. Yet this mandate is too weak to launch a decisive challenge to global capitalism. Taxes could be insistently progressive, labor regulations might be fashioned with teeth, and so on, and yet these incremental changes leave private capital in place. Liberalism in its classical formulations advances certain specific principles of institutional formation and conduct—universal suffrage, individual liberty, freedom of speech and assembly—as the measure of just societies, no matter how else they may operate or what other outcomes they may produce. Hence liberalism refrains from putting the basic question of property and labor on the table for normative debate. Dussel claims that neither Rawlsians nor classical liberalism can generate effective responses to the material crisis.

Utilitarians offer a way to prioritize available goods without a way to reframe the notion of "utility" itself or to question the conditions by which goods are made available. Equating ethics with maximizing preferences is an approach uncomfortably isomorphic with the consumer capitalist emphasis on choice. Proceduralists such as Habermas, Dussel's closest ally, emphasize the need for inclusive processes of judgment such that all who are affected by an issue have an uncoerced say in the relevant policy determination, another important but insufficient approach. The poor may be at the table, but if the discussion has been framed in such a way that their living conditions are not up for debate, there can be no transformative change. Habermas puts the commitment to procedures over substantive commitments to human needs. Communitarians are realistic about the cultural foundations of value judgments and want states and individuals to recognize the legitimacy of cultural forms of life, but they reduce moral reason to the opaque plane of culture, beyond which there is no appeal. Hence they leave ethicists impotent to address oppression promulgated in the name of culture or religion.

55

These approaches often harbor contrasting notions about the metaphysical conditions of human existence and social life. Dussel finds positive elements in all of them and attempts to incorporate the insights he finds useful. But none have the capacity to bring the ongoing material deprivation of the world's peoples center stage or to produce feasible remedies. None takes the material threat to life as its central charge.

Dussel groups most of these approaches (except for communitarianism) within the category of formalism, and he argues that formalism has an intractable limitation because it makes it impossible to take "the material aspect of ethics as a point of departure."[20] Formalisms start with abstract representations of processes and decision procedures and then attempt an application to specific contexts. But "this intention is impossible to fulfill. A merely formal position can never enunciate material principles" in a specific real-world domain.[21] Hence moral validity cannot be reduced to or defined as a question of process apart from outcomes or content; this is exactly how the starvation of millions can come to attain "validity." The fundamental problem is that ethics cannot be developed outside of the real, outside of life, apart from the actual history of social movements, and from any materialist analysis. Strict proceduralism can never provide answers to the concrete and specific questions that must be answered before procedures can be set up: Who must be included in this particular case? How are groups to be defined? What are the frames of debate? It is common practice for political agents to use proceduralism against democratic movements by characterizing actors as terrorists or uncooperative or disobedient of preset rules. Every activist knows that the first line of attack against social movements by defenders of power is always on procedural grounds.

Discourse ethics begins with abstract notions of community and then attempts to apply these to concrete contexts. In contrast, the ethics of liberation starts with the social movements of the excluded that require attending to global and local structures operating in the here and now. As such, the ethics of liberation starts with unjust and undeserved inequalities underlying our societies. It starts from the nonideal conditions of exclusion and victimization and the organizing of the activist oppressed.

Dussel's use of the term *victim* is a cause of concern for some theorists about the possibly reifying effects of the term, its eclipse of agency, its reliance on binary categories, and the possibility of constructing a romanticized portrait of the "oppressed masses." On the other hand, the disinclination to use the term *victim* may be traceable to Western overinflations of agency and the tendency to ontologize what are fundamentally social relations rather than fundamental problems with the concept itself. Particularly in the context of feminist theory, the concern about "victim feminism" that emerged in the 1990s revealed itself as a neoliberal strategy with the effect of blaming victims![22] In some cases, terms like *victim* or *victimization* are simply apt descriptions of situations with extreme inequities in operable agency. A better project than refusing its use entirely is to refine its meaning so as to avoid problematic connotations and effects.

Dussel uses the term *victim* as a way to capture a broad variety of forms of oppression and exclusion, from social to economic. Victims for him are those who are denied the possibility of reproducing their material life or of participating in their society as well as those whose way of being in the world are excluded.[23] This definition would include LGBTQ people who are able to make a living but only at the price of their social displacement from the public sphere. What unites the category of victims for Dussel is exclusion, including exclusion from material life and/or social and political participation. Thus he leaves the category open ended, recognizing that our capacity to discern victimization and exclusion is historically contextual and is likely to be altered by new social movements we cannot yet imagine. Importantly, Dussel does not portray victims as powerless but in fact quite the reverse; they are the most important and creative agents of change throughout history: "Victims, when they erupt in history, create new things. It has always been like this. It cannot be otherwise."[24] They create concepts, organizations, forms of community, and institutions, as well as new forms of cultural expression. Where formalists want to fashion procedures that will "allow" victims to speak, Dussel wants an ethics that acknowledges their leadership and the unpredictable creativity of their tactics and their demands.

Hence for Dussel, the answer to questions about who must be included and what must be debated requires a materialist and critical starting point based on an account of real-world conditions, the material necessities of life, and an understanding of the realities of domination and exclusion. In other words, procedures cannot be judged in the abstract or across contexts: the material facts of impoverishment will command the norm: "Ethics . . . is realized when it shows and normalizes the compatibility of the nonintentional formal system with the production, reproduction, and development of the human life of each ethical subject with the right to discursive participation."[25]

Dussel's varied criticisms of his interlocutors will no doubt generate debates, both substantive and methodological. He often develops his criticism of theories by situating them in their time and place, and this can yield an evaluation that looks reductive, though it can also help us to understand an inadequate theory's inordinate influence.[26] Yet Dussel recognizes that ideas can travel across contexts, changing their meanings and real-world effects, hence his attempt to subsume what is best in various theoretical traditions no matter their original provenance.

Dussel's insistent reminder that existing ethical approaches have overlooked our global crisis of poverty is compelling. Beyond the work in formalist debates, philosophers continue to produce numerous tomes on liberty, rights, freedom, bioethics, law, and so on, with little attention to the billion-and-a-half-people-living-on-less-than-a-dollar-a-day problem. Thomas Pogge's work became a watershed no doubt because he had the temerity to address this problem, and yet his solution—the global resources dividend—as promising as it is, offers redistributions of resources without fundamentally addressing the causes that generated such extreme inequality.[27] Thomas Piketty's recent book on twenty-first-century capitalism has attracted an even greater amount of attention precisely because it dares to explore the way in which capitalism has produced global impoverishment. These works stand out against a general backdrop of avoidance.

Unlike Pogge and Piketty, Dussel is doing ethics, even metaethics. His idea is that ethics needs to be significantly reframed if it is going to be forced to address life itself and its concomitant real-world, historically situated needs. Toward this end, ethics requires attending equally to three elements: validity, materialism, and feasibility. None of these elements can be fully met with an abstract formalism or proceduralism that makes questions of validity a priori and renders secondary all questions of content.

As a result of his attempt to combine materialism, validity, and feasibility, Dussel's work is a real methodological mix, with aspects that will flag some readers as modernist holdovers. He is a humanist with universalist aspirations, and although he rejects the category of naturalism, it is difficult, as I argued, not to read his insistence that ethics be grounded in the bodily capacities and needs of the human species as a naturalist turn. This is what makes it possible, he believes, to argue beyond the stalemates of incommensurable cultural identities or discursive formations. Dussel's naturalism and materialism are in the Marxist tradition of mediation: the category of need is structurally constituted, communal, and historically situated. Needs are in some cases created, he admits. And yet "the needs of the life of the human subject as such . . . cannot be created in their *ultimate* content. Eating can be done in many ways . . . but to 'eat' is necessary, and the person who does not eat . . . will die."[28] This provides the materialist universal that marks a departure from modernist versions that emphasize reason over embodiment or that value the human species' capacity to imagine and to die for ideas over its need for nourishment. Dussel's materialism leads toward a humanist universalism that renders human types of being as more alike than different from sentient life in nonhuman forms.

The Western postmodernist left today generally prefers to follow in the tradition of the "philosophers of suspicion," as they are sometimes called, from Nietzsche and Freud forward, who espouse pessimism about the implications and real motivations of a moral discourse. Dussel finds little to unite with in this tradition. Nietzsche's imperturbable elitism and Freud's fatalism are serious problems for Dussel and symptomatic of the limitations of their elite perspective. He believes the postmodernists in general remain within a Eurocentric frame that has undercut their capacity to offer politically contextualized understandings of the developing debates within philosophy. Their "surface" criticism of modern philosophy and rationality "leaves the victims absolutely opaque, shrouded, from within the horizon of a systematic rationality which ultimately goes unquestioned."[29] Despite their sophisticated ability to give systematic readings that reach below the stipulated content of a theory, the postmodernists tend to read philosophy transcendentally or outside of colonial history, following Hegel in the practice of taking only European thought as having achieved the level of abstraction required for critical thought.

Though Dussel finds much to admire in Karl Marx, Jürgen Habermas, Michel Foucault, Franz Hinkelammert, Rosa Luxemburg, and others, as he moves out of the critical and into the reconstructive part of the book, he turns increasingly to Paolo Freire, Rigoberta Menchú, the Zapatista Army of National Liberation (EZLN), and others from the Global South for a touchstone. Here is the community of victims from whom we have the most to learn. The impetus toward transformative thought and practice motivates a search for the untrue, the invalid, and the ineffective. He approvingly quotes this underused passage from Marx: "The first duty of a thinking brain that loves truth, in light of the initial explosion of the Silesian workers revolt, was not to situate itself like a *schoolteacher* in the face of such an occurrence, but instead to make an effort to study its specific character. It is clear that to do this demanded a certain amount of scientific acuity and love for humanity, while for the other procedure it was more than enough to employ a well-trodden phraseology."[30] This captures another theme of Dussel's ethics of liberation: the necessary commitment to a democratic epistemology. The central role in liberation is always played

59

60

by the excluded and the victims who have proven over and over their capacity for insight and creativity. The social movements, counterdiscourses, and reconceived institutions that communities of the activist oppressed continuously create are what drives liberation: "The *subject of the praxis of* liberation is the living, needy, natural, and thus, cultural subject, and in the last instance the victim, the community of victims, and those who are co-responsibly articulated with it."[31] There are no schoolteachers of the revolution. Instructively, Dussel takes Menchú more seriously as a thinker than any social theorist writing today. Conscientization as described by Menchú and by Freire is a process of critical enunciation and denunciation that promotes the critical and creative activity of "taking possession of reality, making it one's own."[32]

Dussel remains a Marxist in this work and in the final chapters offers analyses of both positive and negative lessons from Marxist practice in the twentieth century. He takes Luxemburg's side against Lenin and defends the insights of Gramsci, Freire, and new social movements in the Americas. Dussel is convinced that liberatory movements of the twenty-first century must eschew the vanguardism that upended twentieth-century socialism. He also rejects pacifism and defines violence as more usefully referring to illegitimate coercion, although despite the need for legitimate violence, liberation requires a symmetrical participation and communitarian intersubjectivity. Dussel criticizes both anarchists and liberal reformists, making use of Luxemburg's incisive analysis of opportunism as the unprincipled pursuit of power. But he carefully allows that in any given specific fight, anarchists and/or liberals may be on the same side as the ethics of liberation and can be supported in coalition. He avows the term *transformation* rather than *revolution* as a way to signal the long temporality of truly liberating action.[33] The goal is not the momentary cataclysm but real change in the conditions in which material life is reproduced. Anarchists, he argues, underplay the feasibility principle: that ethical directives must be tied to tactics and strategies that fulfill a feasibility threshold. And a further difference with anarchists is that for Dussel, the key concept is liberation rather than freedom: where freedom might be decontextualized as an ideal type and made use of in imperialist hierarchies of cultures, the concept of liberation will be more context bound; it can only come about upon overcoming a specific historical form of oppression. This is more in line with his constant materialist and contextualist orientation. The *Ethics of Liberation* is a culmination of Dussel's life work, not a new development. His main critics from within Latin American philosophy, including Santiago Castro-Gómez and Alejandro Vallega, are primarily concerned with Dussel's ontology: the ontologization of the category of the excluded victim and the emphasis on the material over the discursive. And yet it is difficult to understand how shifting the geography of reason, as Walter Mignolo has described the decolonial theoretical project, can be accomplished without naming social groups and tracing the effects of diverse locations. The critique of Eurocentrism requires attending to concrete contexts, particular histories, and the social identities these bring forth in spite of all their complexity. This means talking about victims not in the overly abstract tradition of Levinas and Agamben, which offers no help in explaining why particular bodies are targeted for abjection, but in the way certain social movements do about specific groups and peoples. In the idiom of today's movement, it involves the move from "All Lives Matter" to "Black Lives Matter" or "Muslim Lives Matter."

The liberatory theories that enlivened the transformative hopes of much of the world throughout the nineteenth and twentieth centuries developed from basically five countries, all from the Global North. These theories were formulated out of their local experiences and the perspectives of their largely white male authors. Social conflict was not given a racial or ethnic cast, nor was the international division of labor a central analytic. Capitalism was not explained as a development out of, or alongside, colonialism but as a replacement for European feudalism. As a result, liberatory social theories, including Marxism, developed no theory of race, no conceptualization of xenophobia, no critique of Eurocentrism, no concept of indigeneity, no analysis of the deep ties between culture and colonialism, and no analysis of the ways in which geographical hierarchies affect the making of theory itself.

Formalist approaches in our own time attempt to justify a sidelining of these topics in the doing of ethics: only ethical applications require grappling with such concrete issues "on the ground." Here Dussel makes a compelling case and offers a unique departure for a new and more truly liberatory ethics.

NOTES

This is a revised version of an essay that appeared as "The Hegel of Coyoacán," *boundary 2* 45, no. 4 (November 2018): 183–202. My deepest thanks to Eduardo Mendieta for his suggestions on this version.

1. G. W. F. Hegel, *The Philosophy of History*, trans. J. Sibree (New York: Dover, 1956), 341.
2. Enrique Dussel, *Ethics of Liberation: In the Age of Globalization and Exclusion*, trans. Eduardo Mendieta, Camilo Pérez Bustillo, Yolanda Angulo, and Nelson Maldonado-Torres, ed. Alejandro A. Vallega (Durham, N.C.: Duke University Press, 2013). This argument is elaborated in Dussel's introduction.
3. Hegel's attitude toward the colonies has finally come under some significant critical discussion by philosophers and social theorists in recent decades. Susan Buck-Morss has made one of the most important contributions in her book *Hegel, Haiti, and Universal History* (Pittsburgh: University of Pittsburgh Press, 2009). For an interesting rejoinder defending Hegel's contributions to the anticolonialist effort, see Frank Kirkland, "Hegel and the Saint-Domingue Revolution—'Perfect Together?' A Review of Susan Buck-Morss's *Hegel, Haiti, and Universal History*," *Logos: The Journal of Modern Society and Culture* 11, nos. 2–3 (Spring–Summer 2012), http://logosjournal.com/2012/spring-summer_kirkland/.
4. Dussel, *Ethics of Liberation*, 47.
5. G. W. F. Hegel, *Reason in History*, trans. Robert S. Hartman (New York: Pearson, 1995).
6. Dussel, *Ethics of Liberation*, 45.
7. Ibid., 128. See also pp. 95 and 289–90.
8. See ibid., 57–69, for his defense and use of naturalism, undoubtedly the most controversial claim in the book.
9. Ibid., 58.
10. Ibid., 346.
11. Ibid., 39. See also Enrique Dussel, *Hacia un Marx desconocido: Un comentario de los manuscritos del 61–63* (Mexico City: Siglo XXI, 1988), translated by Yolanda Angulo as *Toward an Unknown Marx* (New York: Routledge, 2014).
12. For a powerful literary rendering of this distinction, see Cesar Vallejo's *Tungsten*, trans. Robert Mezey (Syracuse: Syracuse University Press, 1989).
13. Dussel, *Ethics of Liberation*, 68.
14. Ibid., 68.
15. Ibid., 61.
16. Gregory Pappas, ed., *Pragmatism in the Americas* (New York: Fordham University Press, 2011).

17. For example, see Helen E. Longino, *The Fate of Knowledge* (Princeton: Princeton University Press, 2002); Elizabeth Anderson, "Uses of Value Judgments in Science: A General Argument, with Lessons from a Case Study of Feminist Research on Divorce," *Hypatia* 19, no. 1 (Winter 2004): 1–24.
18. Claire Colebrook, *Deleuze: A Guide for the Perplexed* (London: Continuum, 2006), 3.
19. Dussel, *Ethics of Liberation*, 115–16.
20. Ibid., 115.
21. Ibid., 116.
22. See my essay on this, "Discourses of Sexual Violence in a Global Framework," *Philosophical Topics* 37, no. 2 (Fall 2009): 123–40.
23. Dussel, *Ethics of Liberation*, xx, 290, 294.
24. Ibid., 355.
25. Ibid., 391.
26. Ibid., 77.
27. See, e.g., Thomas Pogge, "Eradicating Systemic Poverty: Brief for a Global Resources Dividend," *Journal of Human Development* 2, no. 1 (2001): 59–77.
28. Dussel, *Ethics of Liberation*, 171.
29. Ibid., 278. Foucault's work is partially exempted from this critique, since his work reveals an awareness of the exclusion of victims.
30. Ibid., 361.
31. Ibid., 385.
32. Freire quoted by Dussel, *Ethics of Liberation*, 319.
33. Ibid., 388–98.

63

CHAPTER 4

Ideality and Intersubjectivity

Dialectics and Analectics in a Philosophy of Liberation

Mario Sáenz Rovner

On the one hand, dialectical critique articulates theories of social transformation that do not shy away from an approach that is immanentist through and through. Transcendence in this approach is only the positive result of contradictions inherent to the totality; here, revolutionary subjectivity becomes aware of its other as the dynamism of change. On the other hand, analectical critique presupposes that the relationship to the other is primary, for the other lies beyond the totality in a transhistorical and transsystemic dimension; it is a distinct narrative forever present as a novelty; it is the *source* of expression that itself cannot be expressed; it is a transnarrative.

Contemporary literature expresses vividly those two paradigms, which are useful for critical theory, thus encompassing also the praxis of decolonization:

Example 1

Octavia Butler in her *Parable of the Sower* has a fascinating affirmation of incompletion or rather of Becoming as the complete meaning of the Totality through her main character, Lauren, at the heart of the novel: "Change is ongoing. Everything changes in some way—size, position, composition, frequency, velocity, thinking, whatever. Every living thing, every bit of matter, all the energy in the universe changes in some way. I don't claim that everything changes in every way, but everything changes in some way. . . . Earth-seed deals with ongoing reality, not with supernatural authority figures. God will shape us all every day of our lives. Best to understand that and return the effort: Shape God."[1]

65

Example 2

Ursula Le Guin in one of her short stories gives voice to the drive toward exteriority that is founded on the confrontation with an other who is the source of the subject's responsibility, of the self's love and desire toward an infinity never comprehended but touched by a love for which no reason can account because it's the never-ending saying that cannot be said: "He had taken the fear into himself, and accepting had transcended it. He had given up his self to the alien, an unreserved surrender, that left no place for evil. He had learned the love of the Other, and thereby had been given his whole self. But this is not the vocabulary of reason."[2]

In this chapter, I articulate philosophically the two paradigms of decolonization in two principal sections: living labor and the logic of intersubjectivity, which form the framework of the process toward liberation.

1. LIVING LABOR

In this section, I offer two distinct interpretations of Marx's concept of living labor. They will serve as the foreground for an analysis that contrasts (1) Dussel's Levinasian reading of Marx with (2) a Hegelian one. The former has the anthropological virtue of rescuing the human from totalizing irrationality but also has a problematic relation to the mystification of the human and the unintended naturalization of historically constituted social relations; the latter has the anthropological virtue of thinking of the human as immanent to the relations of their existence without a mystification of the "something" that *relates* to an inexpressible exteriority, but it does so at the risk of dismissing the posthuman novelty produced by subjectivities that rebel against their constitution. I argue, however, that the Hegelian reading is closer to Marx's view and is the more promising theoretical approach to the praxis of liberation.

(1) Dussel's reading of the *Grundrisse* is deeply influenced by a Levinasian rather than a Hegelian perspective. Dussel states that in Hegelian Marxism, the totality—that is, Being (*Sein*) or Essence (*Wesen*)—is the origin and foundation (*Grund*) of the real. Instead, in Dussel's interpretation, the origin is to be found in the exteriority of the source (*Quelle*) of value: "Living labor . . . [is] 'the *living source* of value.'" Thus while living labor is *anterior* and *exterior* to capital, the value created by living labor is the *being* of capital. Therefore, living labor in its exteriority and anteriority is the source of *being*:

> From the "exteriority" of "living labor" (which is neither "the capacity for labor" nor "labor power," a denomination that Marx does not use with certainty until 1866), from the transcendental poverty (the "pauper," as Marx writes) of the person, subjectivity, corporeality, of the worker as "not-capital" (*Nicht-kapital*), transcendental, then, with respect to the "totality" of capital, the "living labor" is "subsumed" ("subsumption" is the trans-ontological act par excellence that negates exteriority and incorporates "living labor" into capital) in the "labor process." It is from this perspective that Marx, quickly, set himself the problem of how "surplus value" (*Mehrwert*) appears and thereby discovered, for the first time in his life, the question of "surplus value."[3]

Dussel makes this point again in his 2018 manuscript *Filosofía de la liberación decolonial*: "All capital is the subsequent development of categories based on this central discovery, originary, and ontological point of departure (and even transontological) of Marx's critical theory of political economy: from what is anterior to capital (exterior to capital), living labor is subsumed (that is, 'incorporated within') as mere mediation in the Totality of capital."[4]

One of the key elements of Dussel's interpretation of Marxism is that Marx's scientific critique is based more on the critique of fetishism than on the critique of ideology. If the critique of fetishism is a central pillar of Marx's critical theory, then, Dussel argues, the subsumption of living labor in the totality of capital obscures not only living labor but also living labor's relation to value as the source of the latter: "For Marx, to fetishize is to absolutize the term of a relationship . . . thus losing its meaning. . . . Critical or scientific activity for Marx consists in explaining all categories from the category origin of all other categories: Living labor. If this relation with living labor is lost—living labor being the substance of value [that is, its 'cause' in Hegelian terminology]— value is absolutized, and it is attributed to the thing and not living labor as its objectification."[5]

This is a Levinasian interpretation of the concept of living labor: We have here a subjectivity anterior to and irreducible to all social relations to which I can point as the truth because its proximity allows me to substitute for it a relation prior to all relations,[6] including Marx's concept of relationship. Hence a key element of Dussel's thought and of his interpretation of Marx is that the *source* is the *subject* as Other and not the *relationship* as Other, a relation that disguises the ideality of intersubjectivity, or as Marx put it regarding fetishism, "A definite social relation between men . . . assumes, in their eyes, the fantastic form of a relation between things."[7]

Thus for Dussel, the fundamental question is what the origin of any economic system is. The origin is always the concrete subject, the "originary" moment of every possible economy.[8] However, Dussel's subject is not the subject of social relations and, therefore, of totalities but the Levinasian subject, an ever-present transcendence (or transascendence, as Levinas put it, borrowing from Wahl[9]) of social relations.

The logic that informs Dussel's philosophy of liberation is what he calls an "analogical pluriversality" by contrast to a "univocal universality." While the latter imposes itself on others—the imposition of self-same over the other in a logic of identity/difference—the former allows for a process of dialogue among equals on the basis of a logic of analogies of "similarity and distinctness":[10] it is grounded in fact on a metaphysics of duality that articulates "the incommensurable plenitude of reality itself" through "the cognitive finitude of the human being."[11] Hence the totality is discovered through analogy as "not-originary," as rather derivative from a drive toward Alterity and a previous metaphysical encounter with the Other. Reality is, therefore, for this logos (i.e., that of the ethical attitude of the finite being) always open, never univocal. We are thus "situated at an anthropological level (not at the level of the infinite but of the human being), in face of the revelation (Schelling's *Offenbarung*) of the 'word of the Other,' and starting from that word in search of its meaning . . . analogy acquires central relevance."[12]

The ethical drive is founded on a faith-filled decision to satisfy the urgent needs of the Other who announces those needs and who therefore lives *a la intemperie*[13] both objectively for them and subjectively for us—hence the act of faith, the logic (or *logos*) for us of an analogical faith.[14] Of course, the exposure is also our exposure because the river current that drives analogical pluriversality is an ethics of empathy and of sharing. But the logos is ours, for it is our faith, not the faith of the needy. Hence it is *our* similarity. The proximity of the other person is thus founded on a process of substitution. Our access to the other (a phenomenology of egotism based on a totalizing reason) is predicated on our openness toward the other (a transphenomenology of altruism based on faith).

Dussel says in his *16 tesis de economía política* that "the subject of *indeterminate* labor, not yet objectified in any product (and not yet subsumed in any concrete productive system), was called by Marx 'living labor' (*lebendige Arbeit*). It is the starting point of the whole productive and economic field."[15] Dussel makes an analogy between the will as the genesis of the ontology of the political field and living labor as the origin of the ontology of the productive field and therefore between *potentia* (power-in-itself) in politics and living labor in itself in the economic field. Diremption has not yet happened.

Historically, this general economic category is prenonequivalential not simply or only in a metaphysical sense but also in a system-constitutive sense: Dussel's examples are the peasant of sub-Saharan Africa in confrontation with the slave hunter (an originary face-to-face), "the human subjectivity of living labor bought integrally and substantially as a thing . . . for example, in the sugar mills of Brazil, Cuba and the American British colonies."[16]

In these examples, however, Dussel makes a subtle change from exteriority being the alterity-source of a new totality, as I previously quoted, to exteriority alterity-absorbed by a totality. He can do this because, with Levinas, subjectivity and the other that founds it ethically are anterior to social relations: they are an "interior transcendentality." They become a source of social relations but are not reducible to social relations because they are cut from a metaphysical cloth that weaves, and weaves itself into, sociality, but—as weaving, as "saying"—it is not sociality. Thus he refers to modern slavery as "the *estrangement* of living labor in the slave system, the negation of the *alterity* of the human person as it is incorporated to the *totality* of the non-equivalential economic system *par excellence*."[17]

A feature peculiar to Dussel's thought is the positing of a metaphysical origin that functions as a vitalist *apeiron* in all the fields: in the economic as we see now but also in the political and social fields. In the political field, there is *potentia* as the originating (*originario*) foundation of concrete *potestas*; in the economic field, there is precisely this reconstruction of Marx's concept of living labor as an indeterminate exteriority.

However, Dussel falls short when the *global* becomes a "universal," *metaphysical* category that has no contradiction within itself. It ends up *naturalizing* existing contradictions. For Dussel, contradiction comes to exteriority from the totality that seeks to encompass it—for example, the peasant kidnapped by the slave hunter. Alternatively, it produces the totality—for example, the living labor that is the source of all value, the heterosexual erotic relationship of his first ethics and of his latest text on political economy.[18] These two are examples, it seems to me, of a particular slant that disguises itself as a universal, a contradiction that sets itself up as an originary noncontradictory relation. Furthermore, it sets up in a problematic way a social relationship as natural. Heteronormativity is naturalized; other social relations are also normalized as if they were presocial.

Dussel is correct to look for commonality in a set of particulars. Living labor seems to be such a general category. So, of course, is God.

Dussel's concept of living labor is more akin to the concept of a transcendent God than to the concept of an immanent relationship. As I will argue later, Marx's concept of living labor refers precisely to such a relationship. Where Marx fails (namely, in his limitation to a Eurocentric conception of capitalism), Dussel succeeds (namely, through a global conception of capitalism that includes slavery and conquest as integral to the capitalist totality). Nevertheless, Marx preserves much and develops further a conceptualization of living labor as immanent to intersubjectivity and sociality.

(2) Anterior to the logic of analogy is the idealized conception of community that we find in the young Marx. In his "Comments on James Mill *Élémens d'économie politique*," Marx contrasts the true community with its caricature in the alienated society envisioned as the ideal human being (the *homo oeconomicus*) by bourgeois economic theory. Indeed, the *homo oeconomicus* of classical political economy reduces true common life to the activities of trade and exchange:

> Since *human* nature is the *true community* of men, by manifesting their *nature* men *create*, produce, the *human community*, the social entity, which is no abstract universal power opposed to the single individual, but is the essential nature of each individual, his own activity, his own life, his own spirit, his own wealth. Hence, this *true community* does not come in to being through reflection, it appears owing to the *need* and *egoism* of individuals, i.e., it is produced directly by their life activity itself. It does not depend on man whether this community exists or not; but as long as man does not recognise himself as man, and therefore has not organised the world in a human way, this *community* appears in the form of *estrangement*, because its *subject*, man, is a being estranged from himself. Men, not as an abstraction, but as real, living, particular individuals, *are* this entity. Hence, *as they are*, so is this entity itself. To say that *man* is estranged from himself, therefore, is the same thing as saying that the *society* of this estranged man is a caricature of his *real community*, of his true species-life, that his activity therefore appears to

him as a torment, his own creation as an alien power, his
wealth as poverty, the *essential bond* linking him with other
men as an unessential bond, and separation from his fellow
men.[19]

Marx follows the analysis with words that show how much this text
was a preparatory run for his *Manuscripts of 1844* and also undermines
any notion that the future concept of living labor is anything other
than the negation of the "true community." Hence the bourgeois caricature of true common life turns man's life into the "sacrifice of his life,
the realisation of his nature as making his life unreal, his production
as the production of his nullity, his power over an object as the power of
the object over him, and he himself, the lord of his creation, the servant
of his creation."[20]

Of significance here is Marx's critique of Hegel's conception of labor
as *necessarily alienated* labor. For Marx, that is the position that political
economy (i.e., bourgeois theory) has promoted concerning the nature
of labor. Hegel reduces labor to alienated labor; thus he accepts uncrit-
ically the political economy of the time, as Marx points out. Hence the
only type of intersubjective action that can be true would be outside
the sphere of labor qua material activity: "Hegel's standpoint is that of
modern political economy. He grasps *labour* as the *essence* of man. . . .
He sees only the positive, not the negative side of labour. Labour is
man's coming-to-be for himself within *alienation*, or as *alienated* man."[21]

An important point to reflect on is the critique of Hegel's conception of labor. If real, productive labor is only conceived in its alienated
form (the conception of it in political economy) that is to be transcended in morality, according to Hegel,[22] then we should examine the
connection of alienated labor to the concept of living labor that appears
in the *Grundrisse* more than a decade later. Living labor is nothing to
capital—that is, to political economy. Is its affirmation anything more
than an ethical position? There again we see a conception of political
economy similar to that of the *Manuscripts of 1844*: although political economy says that capital is nothing but "accumulated labor,"[23] or
"stored-up labor,"[24] Marx argues that it "does not consider him [the
worker] when he is not working, as a human being; but leaves such

consideration to criminal law, to doctors, to religion, to the statistical tables, to politics and to the poor-house overseer."[25]

72   It seems to me, therefore, that the concept of living labor in the *Grundrisse* as well as the *Manuscripts of 1844* is labor in its alienated form. The mistake of thinkers such as Jürgen Habermas and Michel Foucault was to reduce the concept of labor in Marx to its alienated form, whether as instrumental labor (Habermas) or as the classical episteme (Foucault). The mistake in Dussel has been to transform living labor into an ever-present transcendent exteriority. In sum, Dussel's interpretation of living labor assumes the political economy that Marx criticizes. If labor power is the form that useful labor assumes under capitalism, thus making it possible to exchange it for other expressions of value (e.g., sustenance reduced to a commodity), living labor is the "anti-form," that which asserts itself as the possibility of liberation within the capitalist totality—an "interior transcendentality," to use Dussel's germinal expression, but an interior transcendentality generated by the capitalist system itself; it transcends the system precisely because it is interior to the system as a self-negation generated by the system itself. In the language of substance conceived dialectically, it is substance as self-negation, dialectical "true infinity," as explained later.

This reconceptualization is key to the logic of Marx's critique of Ricardo's labor theory of value. For Ricardo and for all formalistic approaches, substance is conceived as a pure positivity, and thus nothing is lost when we abstract from it to develop a logical relation; value is identical to labor in Ricardo. In Marx, by contrast, labor is expressed as value when it takes the commodity form of representation under capitalism. It can do so only within the capitalist totality. Ricardo did not realize that because he assumed the self-identity of capital. Marx's labor theory of value, as Jacques Rancière notes in his discussion of the contrast between Marx and Ricardo, expresses an equality between two terms (the commodity labor power and the commodity means of sustenance for the laborer, or really, commodified labor power and commodified means of sustenance) by a "special mechanism of *representation*" that we find "in determinate formal conditions imposed by the structure in which this relation is achieved."[26]

Marx's early critique of the life denied in life of the worker is an articulation of what Marx will later analyze as "living labor" in the *Grundrisse*. "True common life" is an anthropological concept that abstracts from its historical manifestations and systemic negations by stressing the Hegelian "true" infinity expressed in the "I that is We and the We that is I"—a being with others that *precedes logically* the notion of a subjectivity that irrupts in the infinite gap that opens up when questioned by the other; the latter is Hegel's notion of "bad" or "false" infinity: the apparition to subjectivity of a presocial, preontological other; in fact, therefore, a bad infinity would also be the apparition of a presocial, preontological subjectivity, a source without sources, the sine qua non of a mystical anthropology.

For Marx, living labor is an affirmation of human life *as* negated and excluded by capital. Both are historical-ontological concepts. They are ontological because they refer us to the *being* of being human, although one of them, living labor, refers us directly to a negative relation, to an existential condition—namely, a relation to capital that negates the *being* of being human. Furthermore, they are historical categories, since they can only exist in an ensemble of dynamic social relations. The reader may want to examine the full citation that for reasons of space we cannot cite here in its totality.[27] One can gather from it that living labor arises from the "separation of property from labour" and such separation seems to be a "necessary law" of the exchange between capital and labor.

It follows, says Marx, that labor posited as noncapital is "absolute poverty . . . not as shortage, but as a complete exclusion of objective wealth." That negative positing of labor is complemented by a "positive" positing: It is "the living source of value," although by itself it is not value. Hence labor is both nothing objectively (not-capital) and everything subjectively (the source of the value of capital). It is the one because it is the other, and it is the other because it is the one.

There is no labor that is anterior and exterior to the totality in the Levinasian sense of those terms. Living labor is rather a contradiction that arises within the totality. It is an effective contradiction because it is immanent to the totality.

73

One can speak of "anteriority" in the sense that living labor is the source of value of capital, and one can speak of "exteriority" in the sense that labor is objectively excluded from capital. Nevertheless, it is not an "Other" that is the source of the totality that it nevertheless transcends; rather, it is simply an other that is the source of capital because the totality so constitutes labor and capital as well as their exchange. It transcends capital. Only transformation, not metaphysics, transcends the totality.

74

For Marx, living labor has no value precisely because it is activity only within *capitalist relations of production*. Marx makes this clear in his discussion of it in the *Grundrisse* as he distinguishes living labor from slave labor:

> As a slave, the worker has *exchange value*, a *value*; as a free worker he has *no value*; only the right to dispose over his labour, acquired by exchange with him, has value. He does not confront the capitalist as exchange value, but the capitalist confronts him as exchange value. His *valuelessness* and *devaluation* is the presupposition of capital and the precondition for *free* labor in general. . . . The worker is thereby formally posited as a person who is something for himself *apart from his* labour, and who alienates what expresses his life (*Lebensäusserung*) only as a means for his own life. So long as the worker as such has *exchange value, industrial capital* as such cannot exist, therefore developed capital in general cannot exist. Labour must confront capital as *pure use value*, which is offered as a commodity by its owner himself in exchange for capital, in exchange for its *exchange value*.[28]

This quotation, the so-called first version of *Capital*, presents the reader with one of the real contexts of living labor, shortly before the famous description of labor as noncapital that I briefly discussed earlier.[29] Living labor is nothing for capital insofar as it is the labor of a "free" laborer, free to be in himself and for himself a commodity, someone who carries within himself as his uniqueness and ownership nothing but possibility *in a capitalist world*. In the face of capital, freedom is *more* than formal indeed: it is the substantial self-expression of wage slavery. The worker is here "free" because he or she has been robbed of his or her social conditions for existence, "free" to embrace capitalism or be killed or imprisoned.[30]

Even so, the negation of capital is implicit in the possibility of the irreducibility of laborers to the inner demands of capital, for capital requires both and, contradictorily, the complete submission of the worker and the formal independence of the worker. On the side of formal independence, we encounter both the ideology that conceals wage slavery and the "true common life" of all productive activity. One of the conditions for the actualization of the latter is revolution; the other condition lies in the objectivity of the internal contradictions of capital that, alone and by itself, is a brutal machinery of social and natural de-struction; hence, it is self-contradictory. The existential question becomes, As it questions the being of being human, will it destroy not only itself but the very foundations of natural existence?

In Marx, dialectical diremption is the ontological origin of reality so that living labor is in contradiction to capital "genetically," and it is so expressed in the *Grundrisse*, where living labor is the category of the "free worker" as he or she relates to capital, not of the slave. Marx's shortcoming was not to have seen more clearly the systemic connection between slavery, imperialism, and capitalism. Dussel's ascription of the category of *living labor* to slavery[31] is not an attempt to correct that mistake, however, but simply the conceptualization of the concept of living labor as a metaphysical point of origin prior to all diremption and all contradiction.

Dussel has shown that capitalism is at its foundation an even more global phenomenon than Marx thought. Dussel thus decolonizes fundamental concepts in Marx: capitalist exploitation, surplus value, commodity, and the real subsumption of labor under capital. Marx limited himself to an analysis of those concepts within the imperial countries themselves. As I have stated, Dussel's thought becomes problematic when he privileges *some* social relations as natural: heterosexuality is clearly one of them; the mystical anthropology that grounds his conceptualization of living labor as *exterior* to the history of totalities is another one, albeit the Levinasian sense of "infinite" is replaced by an equally inexpressible Levinasian sense of subjectivity.

2. LOGICS

In this section, I offer a defense of Hegelian dialectics from the criticisms by an analectical thought that, paradoxically, attempts to subsume it.

(1) Levinas dismisses all negativity as a function of the Same.

> This reversion of the alterity of the world to self-identification must be taken seriously; the "moments" of this identification— the body, the home, labor, possession, economy—are not to figure as empirical and contingent data, laid over the formal skeleton of the same; they are the articulations of this structure. The identification of the same is not the void of a tautology nor a dialectical opposition to the other, but the concreteness of egoism. This is important for the possibility of metaphysics. If the same would establish its identity by simple *opposition to the other*, it would already be part of a totality encompassing the same and the other.[32]

Clearly then, Hegelian dialectics would not be anything other than a rationalist effort to affirm Being. It is History and therefore immanence. The other (*autrui*) resists History because it is anterior to History and resists Totality because it is beyond and irreducible to the Totality: "But to say that the other can remain absolutely other, that he enters only into the relationship of conversation, is to say that history itself, an identification of the same, cannot claim to totalize the same and the other. The absolutely other, whose alterity is overcome in the philosophy of immanence on the allegedly common plane of history, maintains his transcendence in the midst of history. The same is essentially identification with the diverse, or history, or system. It is not I who resist the system, as Kierkegaard thought; it is the other."[33]

Ultimately, infinity—whether expressed in "Greek" (Plato's Good in the *Republic*) or "Latin" (Descartes's intellectual intuition of the Infinite in the Third *Meditation*)—is for Levinas the revelation that the finite self is *in* the truth only in relation to an Other that "always" overflows the Same in an infinite "gap" because the bond between subjectivity and other (*autrui*) never constitutes itself as a totality. "False" infinity is, by contrast, the philosophical tradition that is "incapable of overflowing the Same."[34]

Hegel's thought would presumably belong to such a philosophical tradition. In principle, of course, Hegel quite explicitly defines true infinity as the ideal unity of finite and infinite within a totality. Furthermore, Hegel's racism and Eurocentrism lead him to formulate in many of his texts a conception of *universality* (understood as Absolute Substance *and* Subject) that barely disguises the *particularity* of European supremacy.[35] Imperialism contradicts the unity in difference of finitude and infinity, and the task of decolonization requires the unmasking of ideological false unities but also the affirmation of the ideality of unity in difference.

Decolonization requires, therefore, besides a struggle for recognition against the colonizing other, a struggle for recognition against the internalization of colonization expressed in the uncritical embrace of the material and discursive structures produced by exploitation and oppression. The revolutionary transformation through asymmetrical means of relationships of domination is the push from below toward the ideal symmetry of "the I that is We and the We that is I."

(2) Social structures influence the form of intersubjectivity (e.g., is it exploitative and oppressive, or is there the unity of a mutual recognition of differences?) as well as the rise of new totalities: "Men make their own history, but they do not make it just as they please; they do not make it under circumstances chosen by themselves, but under circumstances directly encountered, given and transmitted from the past."[36] Thus the affirmation of the Other carries with it the negation of the circumstances that produce and reproduce the suffering of the Other.

For Hegel, *Life* is both motion and disquiet: the latter is the sensuous condition that was esteemed by Marx; the former is the unconditioned

supersensible criticized as a hypostasized abstraction by the philosophies of existence. What is the common feature of both motion and the
disquiet? The simple essence that produces itself through self-negation.[37]

Self-negation is causality internal to life. It draws the thing toward
a projected self-realization. The "drawing" or "pulling" is part of what
the thing is in itself. To use Nietzsche's terminology regarding the will
(to power), it is a self-propelled wheel.

The motion of life is that self-propelled wheel in-itself. The disquiet of life is that wheel aware of itself as such—that is, for-itself: the
allusion to "God-is-Change" in my first illustration in this chapter is
precisely this coming to awareness. Hence being-for-itself is not a fantastic invention of "truth." Truth is both support and disclosure, so that
becoming aware is a disclosure of the real's immanent contradictions
and thus a support toward the realization of what Marx called the "true
common life."

It should be stressed that Nietzsche's will to power is not founded
on a relationship, but it is rather the source of relations, the inverse of
what Levinas called the Other that resonates in Dussel's sui generis
interpretation of the concept of living labor. Hegel's conception of
Life *is* the *relationship*: the negation of Infinite life by the finite in the
Phenomenology is a conceptualization of the negation in practice of
mutual recognition in the struggle for recognition and the dialectics
of domination. (Parenthetically, we find the same conceptual approximation in the young Marx's statement that the true common life goes
through egotism.) Nevertheless, ideality asserts itself by *overcoming*
the negation of the Infinite through the preservation of the difference
among the finite shapes:

> The fluid element is itself only the *abstraction* of essence, or
> it is *actual* only as shape; and its articulation of itself is only
> a splitting-up of what is articulated into form or a dissolu-
> tion of it. It is the whole round of this activity that constitutes
> Life: not . . . the continuity and compactness of its essence,
> nor the enduring form, the discreet moment existing for
> itself; nor the pure process of these; nor yet the simple taking
> together of these moments. Life consists rather in being the

self-developing whole which dissolves its development and in this movement simply preserves itself.[38]

Hegelian idealism is built upon the notion of contradiction at the heart of Being: Being "ex-ists" as Becoming because it is a determinate no-Being. This is not merely a claim that rests on the notion of dialectics. Rather, it rests on the concept of ground and Hegel's analysis of Kant's view that analytical judgments are grounded on the principle of contradiction.[39]

Hegel's conception of the totality (which he also calls the Infinite) is a dynamic unity of opposites that are sublated, or brought to a higher level, through their unity in dynamic difference. Opposition as such is never overcome; what is negated is also preserved. The particular is not thrown off in favor of the universal but rather brought to the status of universality, which preserves itself in the multitude of particulars that compose it. Think of the beehive, the anthill, and human highway traffic as examples of the motion of life. Think of the movement of intersubjectivity as an example of the disquiet of life.

In the struggle for recognition and the movement toward its negation and ideality—namely, "the I that is We and the We that is I"—one can observe both the motion and the disquiet of life.

Furthermore, a radically dialectical Hegelianism, a decolonized Hegel, requires the grounding of the dialectic on the major *Logic*, for it dissolves the racism integral to his *Philosophy of History* and the cultural narrowness and sexism that we find in the *Phenomenology*.[40] By contrast, Dussel's Levinasian reading assumes the impossibility of retrieving the logic from the social specificity of Hegelian racism and sexism and is thus impermeable to a concept of totality that generates its own contradictions. That is the concept of Hegelian "true infinity" I have sought to articulate here: it allows us to see the struggle for recognition in a new light, no longer as a struggle *primus inter pares* of the bourgeois ideal described by Marx in the *Grundrisse*'s section on living labor but rather in the *real* and not simply *formal* subsumption of slave labor by capital.[41] We can glimpse that decolonized conception of labor under capital in the fact that the modern slave was in fact regarded as culpable. Ona Judge after all was blamed by the first president of modern democracy as guilty of asserting her freedom by leaving the confines of her slavery. We glimpse that aspect of formal equality in the legal culpability of the enslaved in the following illustration:

> Example 3
>
> Margaret Garner's story is well known, a figure of history and also of literature and poetry. Unable to make her children free as she escaped slavery in Kentucky, she tried to kill them, killing her two-year-old daughter with a knife. Abolitionists tried unsuccessfully to free her by convincing the law of the time to charge her with murder. But federal marshals were unable to arrest her because her slave owner hid her and sold her in secret to his brother in Arkansas. Only as a murderer could she become an equal in a system of domination and hence neither equal nor free. She died a young person of twenty-four in 1858. One of the means that capitalism uses is to attempt to isolate the oppressed, to break them loose from the foundation of human reality, the community.[42]

Hegel's conception of totality as a unity of contraries is fundamental in his logic. We see it in his critique of atomism, which isolates the ego from relationships and goes as far as "naturalizing" the products of *social* relations: "In recent times, the atomistic approach has become even more important in the *political* than in the physical sphere. According to this view, the will of the *individual* as such is the principle of the state. The attractive force is the particularity of the needs and inclinations, and the universal, the state itself, is [based on] the external relationship of the contract."[43]

In his *Science of Logic*, Hegel stresses the lack of a fully developed self-consciousness in atomistic thought, which finds the power of the negative solely in the ego: "Atomistic philosophy does not know the concept of ideality; it does not take One as comprehending within itself the two moments of Being-for-Self and Being-for-It (that is, as of ideal nature), but as being simply and bluntly for-Self."[44]

On a first level of manifestation, the "I" is the *other* that *I* refuse to be or become. The "I" is thus born under conditions of struggle, of victory and defeat. At another level, we can see that the encounter with the other is an encounter that happens within a social context, even when the social context of the other comes from "exteriority," from, for example, the society conquered and colonized as well as the capitalist conditions created by capital itself, which account for the movement from the formal to the real subsumption of labor under capital.

81

The struggle for recognition in the *Phenomenology* follows that logical pattern. The Other is excluded; self-consciousness asserts itself; apparently, it is for-itself. In reality, it denies its for-itselfness by rejecting the Other. It rejects, in fact, its ideality by excluding the Other, for it is only through and with the Other that it can attain the truth of self-consciousness. Hegel's community of free selves—"The 'I' that is 'We' and 'We' that is 'I'"[45]—is the phenomenological expression of the logical relationship of the One and the Many: "Independence having reached its quintessence in the One which is for itself, is abstract and formal, destroying itself; it is the highest and most stubborn error, which takes itself for highest truth;—appearing, more concretely, as abstract freedom, pure ego, and, further, as Evil. It is freedom which goes so far astray as to place its essence in this abstraction, flattering itself that, being thus by itself, it possesses itself in its purity. Determined more closely, independence is that error which regards as negative, and maintains a negative attitude towards, that which is its own essence."[46]

Being is indeed the source of Reality, as we saw in Dussel's contrast between Hegel and his own conceptualization of living labor in the first section of this chapter; however, it is Reality as Essence that grounds Being, and essence *is* Contradiction: "Resolved Contradiction is, then, Ground, that is, Essence as unity of Positive and Negative"[47]—at its deepest level, a contradiction aware of its unity or a One that can only *be* through the preservation and affirmation of difference. That is the logic that supports the community of free selves in Hegel and "true common life" in the young Marx.

Desire of the same in the Other and of the Other in the Same is thus the essence of the intersubjective relationship—a restless process, a disquiet in life that cannot be stilled except in ideality. It is therefore the infinite, from which we are alienated intellectually through the *understanding* (*Verstand*) and passionately through the absence of *true common life*.[48]

We must move, however, beyond theories, Hegel's included, that preserve privileges for certain subjectivities, thus slicing ideality from intersubjectivity. *More* critique, beyond dialectics and analectics, is therefore welcome. Judith Butler's analysis of the constitution of subjectivity through disciplinary performances of gender and sexual roles is necessary to decolonize all forms of subjectivity and subjectification, from the performance of the finite self that gives rise to the Cartesian cogito to the acceptance of heterosexual and cisgender cultural traditions[49] as natural or originary when in fact they are saturated with "assertions of masculine privilege."[50] Only by looking toward the future and the possibilities of liberation in a posthuman condition rather than toward an "otherwise than (social) being" that elides the concealed normativities of communities can we decolonize not only the dialectic but also the analectics of a saying that refuses full thematization.

We see such refusal in the romanticization of Walter Benjamin's distinction between the irruption of divine violence in the midst of the violence of state but also in Levinas's and Dussel's projection of normative privilege into the figure of relations anterior to history and "otherwise than Being."[51]

Harry Cleaver has presented us with the foundations to the alternative I am looking for in this chapter. In his *Reading Marx Politically*, Cleaver develops an autonomous Marxism that can serve us to think about Marx's concept of living labor as a *capitalist* concept—however, as a concept that need not be thought of *therefore* from the viewpoint of capital; in the struggle, the working class defines it *for* itself. As such, it cannot be understood outside the totality of capital and of the struggle within capital: "*There are always two perspectives, capital's versus the working class's!* The analysis of every category and phenomenon must be two-sided. . . . To recognize the inevitable two-sided character of analysis is not to merely reflect the class struggle but to reproduce it."[52]

However, instead of widening the concept into a metaphysical notion, it can be broadened to encompass more than the narrow affirmation of labor in the factory. Cleaver does it to encompass not only different sectors of the salaried working class (feminist and student struggles as well as the fight against white supremacy); it can and has been broadened to encompass the ecological struggle and the neocolonial situation.

Cleaver contrasts his own position with the readings of Marx's *Capital* in Althusser, the Frankfurt School, as well as a political economy's orthodox and ideological readings, which all assume the standpoint of capital, whether by totalizing "capitalist culture" or by proposing a separation of the economy from the political in a base-superstructure model.

For Cleaver, the dialectic is a relation of contradiction in which capitalists and the working class are in a struggle with capital qua social capital and social factory: "The capitalist class creates and maintains [a] situation of compulsion by achieving total control over all the means of production."[53] It makes itself into a totality; as such, it is a totality in contradiction with itself—that is, of capital with the working class—on which it imposes through the commodity form "the zombie-like form" of labor power: "In fact, *we can define capital as a social system based on the imposition of work through the commodity form*."[54] Living labor thus "dominates itself" through the dead labor it creates. It dominates itself as capital.[55]

The commodity form is the means through which capital transforms the lives of people into labor power. Hence we distinguish between the working class's living labor and power. The working class is defined as labor power by and through capital.[56] Cleaver here uses Marx's famous Hegelian distinction (from *The Eighteenth Brumaire of Louis Bonaparte*) between class in-itself and class for-itself: The former would be the class as labor power; the latter would be the class defined politically, "when it asserts its autonomy politically, as a class through its unity in struggle against its role as labour-power."[57]

Through the separation of the producer from the means of production—a separation that wrests the individual from the community and creates instead the capitalist form of cooperation—the duality between living labor and labor power is constituted. Marx describes the separation in "The Secret of Primitive Accumulation" toward the end of the first volume of *Capital*: "The so-called primitive accumulation . . . is nothing else than the historical process of divorcing the producer from the means of production. It appears as primitive, because it forms the pre-historic stage of capital and of the mode of production corresponding with it."[58]

Nevertheless, what distinguishes the form of cooperation established by capitalism is the presupposition that the isolated free wage laborers sell their labor power to capital, thus being thrown also simultaneously into the capitalist form of cooperation. One form of community is replaced by the capitalist community through the alienation of the individual as a free seller of labor power.[59]

Cleaver's use of the distinction Marx makes between the relative and equivalent forms of value as a tool for analyzing the class struggle is, of course, based on the forceful separation of laborers from the means of production—the "primitive accumulation of capital" now continuously reconstituted through the force of law and arms—and the forms of "cooperation" imposed by capital on individuals whose dignity is reduced to isolated decisions separated from the community. Now the struggle moves to another level: Marx's Hegelian reflection analysis that shows how the relative form's value is reflected in the equivalent form is also a conceptualization of the class struggle, for capital seeks to reduce useful labor to the equivalent form of value: "We can see now that just as the relative value form finds its meaning only in the equivalent form so it is that the working class recognizes itself as working class only through its relation to capital. Indeed it is working class only within that relation. The relative form thus expresses the perspective of the working class. Destroy capital and there is no working class as such."[60]

Once brought down to its true size—the self's invention of the other by the posing of its limit through the other's face—by Cleaver's autonomism, the metaphysical desire for exteriority expresses a conception of living labor that resonates with the autonomist position proposed by Hardt and Negri in *Multitude*:

> Living labor is the fundamental human faculty: the ability to engage the world actively and create social life. Living labor can be corralled by capital and pared down to the labor power that is bought and sold and that produces commodities and capital, but living labor always exceeds that. Our innovative

and creative capacities are always greater than our productive labor—productive, that is, for capital. At this point we can recognize that this biopolitical production is on the one hand immeasurable, because it cannot be quantified in fixed units of time, and, on the other hand, always excessive with respect to the value that capital can extract from it because capital can never capture all of life.[61]

85

Negri and Hardt's term, the "corralling" of living labor by capital, suggests both immanence and failed transcendence: the immanence of living labor to life's production of life and the failed transcendence by capital of the processes of biopolitical production. Indeed, capital, as a form of biopower, cannot exhaust or destroy the biopolitical production of labor. The conceptualization of immanence also arrests the attempted transcendence of groups who claim to speak for the whole of the oppressed or represent them as a transcendent figure anterior to intersubjectivity.

Only through a struggle for the recognition of the asymmetry of the struggle can we move toward decolonization. The fighters of the Paris Commune learned that truth when a group of the oppressed refused to be silenced in the name of a historical bloc unwilling to really listen to those they wished to leave behind and far away from the trenches:

Example 4

The Paris Commune arises out of despair, abjection, and war. It also is the flowering of hope, freedom, and participatory democracy. Old traditions began to die. Workers organized to decide how to live. Women workers, traditionally superexploited, began to assume positions of power and leadership in the new community even against the misogyny of some anarcho-communists, such as Proudhon, and the conciliatory attitude of some French members of the International. The women of the Commune seemed to realize that the only way to overcome oppression as well as the colonized mind was through new structures of intersubjectivity. There was no source behind them but the Spirit of community that began to push toward a new totality. Old prejudices, patriarchal prejudices that produced the myth of motherhood and the sex-laden gentleness of women, were challenged; in the words of one of the members of the Union of Women for the Defense of Paris and Aid to the Wounded, "We have come to the supreme moment, when we must be able to die for our Nation. No more weakness! No more uncertainty! All women to arms! All women to duty! Versailles must be wiped out!" Today, we must wipe out our own Versailles. We know where it's at.

NOTES

1. Octavia Butler, *Parable of the Talents* (New York: Grand Central, 1998), 218–20.
2. Ursula Le Guin, "Vaster Than Empires and More Slow," in *The Found and the Lost: The Collected Novellas of Ursula K. Le Guin* (New York: Saga, 2017), 35.
3. Enrique Dussel, "The Four Drafts of *Capital*: Toward a New Interpretation of the Dialectical Thought of Marx," *Rethinking Marxism* 13, no. 1 (Spring 2001): 14.
4. Enrique Dussel, "Siete nuevos ensayos de filosofía de la liberación" (unpublished manuscript, 2018). My translation.
5. Ibid.
6. Emmanuel Levinas, *Otherwise Than Being or Beyond Essence* (Pittsburgh: Duquesne, 1998), 114–15.
7. Karl Marx, *Capital*, vol. 1, in Karl Marx and Friedrich Engels, *Marx and Engels Collected Works*, vol. 35 (New York: International, 1996), 83.
8. Dussel, "Siete nuevos ensayos."
9. Emmanuel Levinas, *Totality and Infinity: An Essay on Exteriority* (Boston: Martinus Nijhoff, 1979), 35.
10. Dussel, "Siete nuevos ensayos."
11. Ibid.
12. Ibid.
13. Tununa Mercado, *In a State of Memory* (Lincoln: University of Nebraska, 2001), 116.
14. Dussel, "Siete nuevos ensayos."
15. Enrique Dussel, *16 tesis de economía política: Interpretación filosófica* (Mexico City: Siglo XXI, 2014), 27.
16. Ibid., 60.
17. Ibid.
18. Ibid., 32.
19. Karl Marx, "From Excerpt-Notes of 1844," in *Writings of the Young Marx on Philosophy and Society*, ed. Lloyd D. Easton and Kurt H. Guddat (Garden City: Anchor Books, 1967), 272. Translated also as "Comments on James Mill *Élémens d'économie politique*" by J. T. Prisot (Paris, 1823), in Marx and Engels, *Collected*

Works, vol. 3 (New York: International, 1975), 217. This last citation is the translation cited.

20. Ibid., 217.

21. Karl Marx, *Economic and Philosophic Manuscripts of 1844*, in Marx and Engels, *Collected Works*, vol. 3, 333.

22. Ibid., 341.

23. Ibid., 239.

24. Adam Smith's phrase in ibid., 247.

25. Ibid., 241.

26. Jacques Rancière, "The Concept of Critique and the Critique of Political Economy: From the *1844 Manuscripts* to *Capital*," in *Reading Capital: The Complete Edition*, by Louis Althusser, Etienne Balivar, Roger Establet, Jacques Rancière, and Pierre Macherey, trans. Ben Brewster and David Fernbach (London: Verso, 2015), 106. My agreement with the author on this matter does not entail agreement with his epistemological distinction between the "ideology" of the Marx of the *1844 Manuscripts* and that of the Marx of *Capital*. That is another matter that requires an analysis of the relationship between intersubjectivity and social structure. I would argue for the irreducibility of intersubjectivity to structure, and in that regard, I am closer to the critical theory of Habermas *and* Dussel than the structuralism of Althusser.

27. See Karl Marx, *Economic Manuscripts of 1857–1858*, in Marx and Engels, *Collected Works*, vol. 28 (New York: International, 1986), 221–22.

28. Ibid., 218–19.

29. Ibid. 222.

30. Angela Davis expresses clearly the predication of freedom on oppression in a capitalist system that weaves together class domination, racism, and sexism. "We" are free because "others" are not: "Prisons tell us that we are free"; Angela Davis, *The Meaning of Freedom* (San Francisco: City Lights, 2012), 125.

31. Dussel, *16 tesis*, 60.

32. Levinas, *Totality and Infinity*, 38.

33. Ibid., 40.

34. Jacques Derrida, "Violence and Metaphysics," in *Writing and Difference*, trans. Alan Bass (Chicago: University of Chicago Press, 1978), 312n12.

35. See Enrique Dussel, *Encubrimiento del Indio, 1492: Hacia el origen del mito de la modernidad* (Mexico City: Editorial Cambio XXI, 1994), 20–25; Enrique Dussel, *Ethics of Liberation: In the Age of Globalization and Exclusion*, trans. Eduardo Mendieta, Camilo Pérez Bustillo, Yolanda Angulo, and Nelson Maldonado-Torres, ed. Alejandro A. Vallega (Durham, N.C.: Duke University Press, 2013); Mario Sáenz Rovner, "Life and Ethics: On Dussel's *Ethics of Liberation*," *Journal of Religion* 97, no. 2 (April 2017): 244–58; Adolfo Sánchez Vázquez, *Filosofía de la praxis* (Mexico City: Grijalbo, 1967), 67.

36. Karl Marx, *Eighteenth Brumaire of Louis Bonaparte*, in Marx and Engels, *Collected Works*, vol. 11 (New York: International, 1980), 103–4.

37. Kant's dual conception of Nature is pertinent here, for the motion of life is exiled from its object by the understanding itself so that we have the following: (1) Nature as constituted by the understanding produces a series of determinant judgments

that assert that Nature is a pure mechanism within the terms of content (the totality of Natural phenomena) and form (the laws that govern phenomena). (2) Whatever in Nature that is not constituted by the understanding and therefore not produced by the determinant judgment is instead a product of the reflective judgment.

38. G. W. F. Hegel, *Phenomenology of Spirit*, trans. A. V. Miller (Oxford: Clarendon, 1977), 108, para. 171.

39. Songsuk Susan Hahn refers to Hegel's critique of the paradox in Kant's use of ground in the *Prolegomena*. See Hahn, *Contradiction in Motion: Hegel's Organic Concept of Life and Value* (Ithaca: Cornell University Press, 2007), 74: "If the law [of contradiction] were valid by virtue of the concepts involved or by logical principles alone, then by Kant's tests for analyticity, asserting its denial should lead to a contradiction." Hahn refers here to the circularity in Kant's reasoning, since the law of contradiction is itself an analytic judgment. She argues that Hegel's critique of the paradox leads him to show that it rests on a synthetic judgment but that his concept of synthetic is not synthetic a priori but rather the synthesis of unity and difference or the principle of determinate negation; ibid. 77.

40. Buck-Morss raises the issue that Hegel's struggle for recognition in the *Phenomenology* was in fact mediated by Hegel's scholarly familiarity with the struggle for independence and human liberation among Haitians against the French in the colony of Saint-Domingue. If true, Hegel's analysis is not as narrow culturally as commonly thought. See Susan Buck-Morss, *Hegel, Haiti, and Universal History* (Pittsburgh: University of Pittsburgh Press, 2009), 21–75.

41. I use the Hegelian dialectic to criticize the narrowness of Hegel's struggle for recognition in the *Phenomenology* in another text. See Mario Sáenz Rovner, *The Identity of Liberation in Latin American Thought: Latin American Historicism and the Phenomenology of Leopoldo Zea* (Lanham, Md.: Lexington Books, 1999), 40–47.

42. Garner's story has been the subject of literature, philosophy, and art. Paul Gilroy's account in his *The Black Atlantic: Modernity and Double Consciousness* (Cambridge, Mass.: Harvard University Press, 1993) decolonizes Hegel. Toni Morrison's *Beloved* (New York: Vintage, 1987) is inspired by the story. There is an element to the story as well that is illuminated by Angela Davis's analysis of the legal responsibilities imposed on the slave. See Davis, *Meaning of Freedom*, 144.

43. G. W. F. Hegel, *Encyclopedia of the Philosophical Sciences in Basic Outline, Part 1: Science of Logic*, trans. and ed. Klaus Brinkmann and Daniel O. Dahlstrom (Cambridge: Cambridge University Press, 2010), 154–55, para. 98.

44. G. W. F. Hegel, *Science of Logic*, vol. 1, trans. W. H. Johnston and L. G. Struthes (London: Allen & Unwin, 1961), 183.

45. Hegel, *Phenomenology of Spirit*, 110.

46. Hegel, *Science of Logic*, vol. 1, 185.

47. Ibid., vol. 2, 62.

48. For an analysis at the level of sex of the longing for true common life, see Foucault's English introduction to the diaries of an intersex person in Michel Foucault, ed., *Herculine Barbin* (New York: Colophon, 1980): the longing for self-affirmation in the presence of the desired Other in his introduction to Herculine Barbin's diary,

an introduction that Judith Butler accused of self-contradictory and inconsistent romanticization of the subject in her *Gender Trouble* (New York: Routledge, 1990), 133.

49. Judith Butler, *Gender Trouble* (New York: Routledge, 1999), 34 and 184.

50. Simone de Beauvoir, *The Second Sex* (New York: Vintage, 1989), xxiin3.

51. Levinas, *Otherwise Than Being*, 114–15.

52. Harry Cleaver, *Reading Capital Politically* (Leeds: Antithesus / AK Press, 2000), 75.

53. Ibid., 82.

54. Ibid.

55. Ibid.

56. Ibid., 83.

57. Ibid.

58. Marx, *Capital*, vol. 1, 705–6.

59. Ibid., vol. 1, 339.

60. Cleaver, *Reading Capital Politically*, 143.

61. Michael Hardt and Antonio Negri, *Multitude: War and Democracy in the Age of Empire* (New York: Penguin, 2004), 146.

CHAPTER 5

The Upsurge of the Living

Critical Ethics and the Materiality of the Community of Life

Don T. Deere

Life and the will to live are at the foundation of both the ethics and the politics of liberation, with life understood as the vital source and measure of all human institutions, values, and norms.[1] Indeed, the central theme of Enrique Dussel's *Ethics of Liberation: In the Age of Globalization and Exclusion* is the materiality of human life as the foundation and critical touchstone for an ethics of liberation.[2] The appearance of this fundamental category expands the frame of his ethics beyond earlier works inspired by Heidegger and later Levinas. Dussel encounters the category of life in his extensive and detailed studies of Marx in the 1980s into the early 1990s, when he finds the key concept of Marx's four drafts of *Capital* to be that of living labor. Living labor is the force that animates the dead labor congealed within capital, and yet it remains irreducibly exterior to capital. Living labor is a condition of possibility for capital yet is never fully subsumed by its dialectical machinations.[3] Thus Dussel fuses his earlier Levinasian notions of totality, exteriority, and the Other with a Marxian notion of life: as a vital and irreducible animating force.[4]

In Dussel's ethics, the materiality of life will serve as a constant referent both for the critical task of liberation and as a counter to the empty formalism of the neo-Kantian ethics of Habermas, Apel, and Rawls. Dussel argues for an ethics that articulates together the material and the formal spheres—that is to say, the materiality of life together with the community of reason that sets ends for itself. Materiality thus achieves its most developed formation at the intersubjective level by the formal processes of reasoning.[5] Yet there is always the remainder of life that is not subsumed within the formalization of moral rules or the institutionalization of political laws: the life and lives that are excluded, forgotten, oppressed, and suffering under the given moral and political system. Dussel refers to the excluded or those who experience the negation of life as the victim(s). The exteriority of the lives of the victims serves as the critical point of transformation vis-à-vis the goodness claims of the prevailing moral system, when they have become fetishized and no longer produce the conditions of life that they claim for their basis of legitimacy.[6]

In this chapter, I elaborate Dussel's understanding of the normative and revolutionary force of life both at the foundation of all moral and ethical claims and also as ana-dialectical (analectic) exteriority. The analectic is not just the dialectical movement beyond totality via negation but "the affirmation of exteriority."[7] The analectic exteriority of life involves a vital upsurge that breaches the enclosure and totality of the system.[8]

First, I demonstrate how Dussel grounds his ethics on a material notion of life and how he differentiates his notion of material ethics from other similar ethics such as utilitarianism and emotivism. Next, I show how Dussel maintains that this material principle must also be coconstitutive with the principle of formal intersubjectivity. Here, I will consider how Dussel's notion of life goes beyond any liberal accounts of material normativity in that he considers the ultimate aim of life to be the will to live of the community and not simply the individualized drive for self-preservation: the formal principle of intersubjectivity shows that life itself ought to be organized by a community of the living and not simply isolated in a drive for survival, as found in the liberal tradition of Hobbes or the Nietzschean notion of will to power. Here I also consider how the *hyperpotentia* of the material (its continual upsurge from beyond, into, and against the system) mitigates against any possible fetishism of the formalism of moral rules, rights, or institutions.

1. MATERIAL ETHICS AND THE CRITIQUE OF UTILITARIANISM

Human life as a mode of reality is the ultimate reference for all morality and ethics, according to Dussel.[9] The architectonic of *Ethics of Liberation* is articulated between a set of three interrelated and mutually determining foundational principles and a mirroring set of three critical principles: the material, formal, and feasibility principles.[10] Life is not only the foundation of ethics and institutions but also the *touchstone* by which all institutions and values must be measured in critical perspective. The origin of these institutions points to the first set of foundational principles, which is to say the generative organization of life in its material, formal, and feasible moments. However, this is never a complete or perfect process. In the passage from life's pulsional force to its organization into norms and institutions, there are inevitable failures that create victims and exclusions. With the critical principles, Dussel reverses the normative perspective from the center to the outside as he refers to the life of the victims and the excluded and explicates the norms at work in the critique of the prevailing system. The failure of the prevailing system to create conditions of flourishing for the lives of the victims is put under scrutiny by the upsurge of these excluded lives.[11]

The material principle is most immediately rooted in "life" and its original upsurge in the will to live; however, it would be a mistake to think that the other principles are not determined by and rooted in their relation to the organization of living subjects. For example, the formal intersubjective level concerns the creation of rational norms and institutions, which serve to govern the community of the living. From the material to the formal, we pass from life to language and from the material body to the formality of reason. However, this is not a strict separation but a continuation, as each and every principle is mutually determined by the other principles.

In the history of European moral philosophy, the material side of Dussel's ethics has its strongest resonance in the utilitarian school of thought, while the formal side ties into a Kantian and neo-Kantian lineage exemplified by the discourse of ethics of Jürgen Habermas and Karl-Otto Apel. The aim of the ethics of liberation, however, is to overcome many of the aporias of both of these traditional schools of material and formal ethics. In the last instance, however, Dussel's ethics is better described as a material ethics that includes a formal determination and not the other way around.[12]

As a material ethics of life, Dussel is careful to demonstrate the points of overlap and profound departures with utilitarianism, the most hegemonic modern tradition of material ethics. One of the primary concerns in drawing out this distinction is to separate out Dussel's material principle from the possessive individualism that permeates utilitarianism and the liberal tradition of ethics and politics more generally. Utilitarianism is a clear and certain opponent of the ethics of liberation, yet it also shares some core principles that need to be highlighted here. Dussel will show how these core material principles can be taken in a truly liberatory direction beyond the failures of utilitarianism and its lack of critical force against practices of domination.

Utilitarianism draws from Scottish and English empiricist traditions that turn toward the body and sensibility against the preceding early modern tradition of Continental rationalism, which privileged the immaterial rational soul. Prior to the most well-known utilitarian philosophers, Jeremy Bentham and John Stuart Mill, the foundations for this moral philosophy were set by thinkers spanning from Hobbes and Locke to Hume and Adam Smith. Dussel points to a passage in Locke's 1689 *Essay Concerning Human Understanding*, which offers one of the first formulations of a hedonistic materialist moral theory: "Good and evil . . . are nothing other than pleasure or pain, or that which produces pleasure or produces pain."[13] Morality is not rooted in rational or divine commands but rather in the bodily sensation of pleasure and pain. The body and its living-affective evaluations are considered the material basis for all morality.

This materialist moral theory is scarcely developed by Locke and remains rife with contradictions as he also holds onto various vestiges of natural law theory and its natural moral commands. Bentham and Mill will, however, make this notion of pleasure the centerpiece of their utilitarian moral philosophy. The core thesis of Bentham's philosophy, for example, holds that "it is the greatest happiness of the greatest number that is the measure of right and wrong," where happiness is considered to be pleasure and the absence of pain.[14] Bentham adhered to a strict psychological hedonism, where pleasure and pain could be the sole motivators for moral action, as opposed to external rational commands that contravene desire. For this reason, there is no intrinsic value to be placed on any particular action beyond the consequences it has for the pleasure and pain of both the individual and the group. For example, lying possesses no intrinsic moral fault and can be considered good if done in such a way that it produces more happiness than suffering.

Bentham's account of utilitarianism, however, leads to several serious problems and critiques, many of which Mill will aim to resolve by nuancing Bentham's psychological hedonism. The first problem involves the baseness of pleasure as the ultimate goal of humanity. On the one hand, if the sole psychological motivation of the moral actor is the pursuit of pleasure and the avoidance of pain, is not morality reduced to a kind of animality?[15] On the other hand, if moral individuals are only driven by the pursuit of pleasures, what could motivate them to pursue the happiness of the community or the greatest number instead of their own egoistic pleasures? Mill responds to this criticism by arguing that pleasure is a more complicated and rich notion than usually thought. The human pursuit of pleasure itself follows a natural telos in which we tend to pursue the higher pleasures of the spirit, intellect, and moral sentiments over and above the base and bodily pleasures of momentary satisfaction.[16] Mill argues that a neutral judge who has experienced both the higher and lower pleasures will always rule in favor of the higher ones as qualitatively (and not merely quantitatively) better than the lower pleasures. Thus not through an external ruling that reason should rule over the body but rather through an internal process of the valuation of material pleasures themselves, Mill argues that the material human will tend to pursue the higher pleasures. The doctrine of higher and lower pleasures offers a potential solution to both critiques mentioned earlier, but it also carries new baggage of its own. Mill risks inserting a dualism between mental and bodily pleasures into the traditional account of hedonism, a dualism that would negate the material foundations of utilitarianism. Mill's perfectionist psychology, the notion that humans tend to seek satisfaction in their own self-betterment and in the fulfillment of the highest pleasures, begins to part ways with the purely hedonistic drive for pleasure.

Dussel is able to show that the problems with Mill's moral philosophy are much deeper than his debates with Bentham and hedonistic versus perfectionistic psychology. First, Dussel raises a social and historical critique. The English utilitarians are unaware of the massive unhappiness that is produced within the system they live under, and they are unable to account for the historical (and thus not natural) conditions under which that system emerges. The greatest happiness principle runs into stark contradiction with the reality of a surplus of unhappiness produced by the capitalist system in nineteenth-century England. Mill and Bentham mistake the economic laws of capitalism for laws of nature, and thus their morality of greatest happiness also naturalizes capitalist norms of individualism, private property, and inequality.

Marx's critique of political economy is one of the first to expose the greatest happiness principle for this failure and turn the supposed happiness produced by capitalist society on its head. As Marx writes, "Accumulation of wealth at one pole is, therefore, at the same time accumulation of misery, agony of toil, slavery, ignorance, brutality, mental degradation, at the opposite pole."[17] In other words, the majority of humanity suffers at the expense of the happiness of a few. The failure to account for the systemic production of the suffering of the majority, a reality that cannot be supported by the utilitarian calculus on its own terms, demonstrates the critical and material failure of utilitarianism in its attention to contemporary reality. It demonstrates, in other words, the lack of a critical element in utilitarian ethics, which would be able to disrupt the given system of moral valuation.

In addition to these problems raised by the lack of a critical social or historical principle in utilitarianism, a second problem is that there is no moral principle contained in this philosophy that stands against the suffering of the victims as such. If a minority of victims suffers in order to produce the happiness of the majority, the overall goodness tally still comes out positive according to a utilitarian calculus. For this reason, egregious moral harms such as enslavement or torture are not marked as intrinsic wrongs according to the consequentialist method of utilitarian valuation. According to Dussel's material principle, however, we must account for the suffering of each and every singular human life as well as the overall material flourishing of the community. The human life of the minority cannot be sacrificed for the sake of all the rest. It is precisely for this reason that Dussel's ethics is a *critical* one based in practices of *liberation*—it places particular ethical value on this moment of exclusion and victimization, which can never be naturalized or justified through an instrumental calculus. In sum, Dussel shows the lack of a critical vision in utilitarianism with respect to sociohistorical reality and with respect to the lives of the victims.

Dussel's material universal principle, however, offers a more robust materialist vision of ethics. Dussel states a version of the principle as follows: "One who acts morally (or ethically) ought to responsibly produce, reproduce, and augment the concrete life of each singular human, of each community to which they belong, which is inevitably a cultural and historical life, from a com-prehension of the happiness which is shared in solidarity and at the level of the drives, having as ultimate reference all humanity, and all life on the planet."[18] This principle is rooted in an understanding of life that goes far beyond liberal individualism's emphasis on pleasure, the greatest happiness, or worse, self-preservation. The moral actor is not only individually responsible for the preservation of her or his own life but also responsible to and for the other. The moral actor is responsible for the life of her or his community, but as Dussel is careful to point out against the possibility of any right-wing racist vitalism, this responsibility also extends beyond one's own community to all of humanity. The formal principle here prevents the will to live from degenerating into a will to power.

2. THE INTERSUBJECTIVE FORMATION OF THE MATERIAL

Dussel's material principle is incomplete, however, without its intertwining relation to the formal principle, where it is formalized and determined at the intersubjective level. Dussel insists that there is a dialectic between the formal and the material level: there is not one ultimate instance of determination.[19] The formal level of morality is in that sense an extension of the material level: "Human life in its rational dimension knows that life, as being in a community of living beings, is ensured through the participation of all . . . and rational argumentation is a new 'cunning' of life."[20] Reason is an extension of life, the cunning of life, where the formal level involves the mediation or subsumption of the material level. Thus the point of the formal level is to arrive at rational intersubjective principles that can be agreed upon at the level of the group that operate in the name of the material. These rational principles have their *validity* when they can be agreed upon by the consensus of the group, but their *goodness* refers back to the materiality, of which they are intended to support, organize, and give space for flourishing.

In Dussel's politics of liberation, the relation between the material and the formal is elaborated using the terms of *potentia* and *potestas*.[21] The principles of his politics of liberation, developed after the ethics, mirror the ethics in their architectonic elaboration. I will turn to the politics of liberation to understand the articulation from material life to intersubjective institutions.[22] The politics of liberation will also offer an avenue to return to a reflection and critique on the English liberal tradition at the level of political philosophy and not simply moral philosophy.

For Dussel, *potentia* refers to potential power, or the material will to live before it has been actualized or formalized into an institution.[23] *Potestas*, on the other hand, refers to institutionalized power. Thus *potentia* maps onto the material principle, while *potestas* maps onto the formal principle. Dussel also refers to *potentia* as the community of the living, based on the expression of an original will to live. In a neo-Aristotelian sense, Dussel argues that we are all herd animals who by nature tend to form communities. Thus the individual will to live is already gathered by a communal will to live. This is the original power of the people before it has been formalized and institutionalized: there is no state-of-nature myth with an isolated, competitive, defensive subject roaming about in a world of scarce resources.

The passage to politics proper, however, requires institutionalized power, *potestas*. Yet the relation between *potentia* and *potestas*, for Dussel, does not suppose the transfer of power assumed by social contract theories of modernity. While *potestas* involves the organization of rules, laws, and institutions through which a community of life is to be governed, the relationship of obedience is reversed. It is not the people who are to obey the laws and submit to the mandate of the governing. Rather, it is the governing who must remain obedient to the people and their mandate; they must command by obeying rather than command by commanding.[24]

This relation between *potentia* and *potestas* points to the dialectical relation between the material and the formal levels of politics (and ethics). The formal moment must always be justified and determined in relation to the material moment. However, there is always an inevitable scission in the process of institutionalizing power. The formal never perfectly matches or lives up to the demands of the material: there is a necessary transfer that entails a gap between the two levels, as our human will to live requires institutions to formalize its power. Yet this scission carries with it a great risk.

Over time, the formal institutionalized power may lose track of its obediential foundation in the *common will to live* and *power* of the people. This leads to what Dussel refers to as fetishized power. *Potestas* begins to rule for its own sake and mistakes the origin of its power. It believes its power to be located in its own current status: being in power means to them that they possess the power. When this happens, *potestas* is prone to lose its legitimacy. However, it requires the rebellion of the people, the reassertion of the original upsurge of the community of the living, in order to delegitimize this fetishized power. The rebellion of the people against fetishized power is referred to as *hyperpotentia*. *Hyperpotentia* involves a struggle against the material suffering of the victims (critical material principle) and the organization of a critical intersubjective consensus to expose this suffering imposed by the prevailing system (critical formal principle).

3. THE WILL TO LIVE VERSUS SELF-PRESERVATION

Contrary to the critical liberatory force of *hyperpotentia*, the tradition of liberal political philosophy initiated by Thomas Hobbes requires relinquishment of the material vital forces of the body and its passions for the establishment of political institutions. The subject must transfer all of his or her rights and power (*potentia*) *to* the formal ruling sovereign (*potestas*). This is done in the name of security and preservation of the individual, providing salvation to the individual from the state of nature that only the sovereign, the mortal god, can offer.[25] The rebellion of the people, *hyperpotentia*, is thus strictly forbidden in Hobbes once these subjects have transferred their *potentia* over to the institutional *potestas* of the sovereign. Furthermore, the possibility of a critical consensus that turns against the abused and fetishized power of the sovereign is out of the question.

The only intersubjective consensus that occurs in Hobbes's materialist philosophy is this first one, moving out of the state of nature that involves a complete and irretrievable transfer of the subject's *potentia* over to the *potestas* of the sovereign. There is no dialectic between the material and the formal, only the formal that completes and closes off the material. The passage from the state of nature to the sovereign is the passage from passions to reason, without return: "Outside the commonwealth is the empire of the passions . . . ; within the commonwealth is the empire of reason."[26]

Though Hobbes seeks to establish an empire of reason and absolute obedience to the sovereign, the fundamental premise from which his materialist philosophy begins is nothing more than a body in motion. The fundamental desire of that body is to continue in motion without imposition. For Hobbes, this is the material mechanism of life.[27] In a protoutilitarian manner, the body seeks to obtain those things that increase its pleasure and its power, and it seeks to avoid pain and anything that diminishes its power. However, Hobbes sees the pursuit of bodily pain and pleasure taking place within a state of scarcity wherein the increase of one's pleasure and power means the decrease of another's. Unlike the greatest happiness principle or Adam Smith's invisible hand, the pursuit of individual pleasure does not yield an overall increase of pleasure for the group.

For this reason, the mechanisms of the body are not yet fully normative in Hobbes given that they cannot enforce general norms applicable for all: prior to the establishment of political laws, for Hobbes, there is no justice and no sense of good and evil beyond that which pleases and displeases each individual. The passions and strivings of each individual body and his or her sense of "good" naturally conflict, and this conflict is what takes us into a state of war and the need to fundamentally alter the human community through law and the sovereign.

Yet through this maelstrom of passions and bodies in conflict, rules of reason still emerge based on a universal principle that seeks to preserve life.[28] The natural right of each individual to everything is superseded by a higher striving that sees the need to preserve one's life and sees the impossibility of doing so within the state of war. As Hobbes writes, "A Law of Nature, *Lex Naturalis*, is a Precept or generall Rule, found out by Reason, by which a man is forbidden to do, that, which is destructive of his life, or taketh away the means of preserving the same."[29] Natural law is then the reason that emerges out of life and allows for the formulation of general rules for the preservation of life, which can escape the particularism of each individual passion. Natural law forces the individual to lay down his or her right to everything (which is, in its most extreme, even a right to the life of the other) and to instead "*seek peace and follow it*"[30] not for the sake of the *communal life* but for the sake of *individual self-preservation*. For Hobbes, life qua self-preservation is the one sacred thing that must be preserved at all costs by the individual, and it is only accidental that this happens to coincide with a need to lay down our right to harm the other. It is important to point out here that the one right that the subject can never relinquish through a contract is the right to self-preservation and resistance when his or her own life is at risk.[31]

Following out this reading of Hobbes, we might ask how Dussel's material principle of life does not conceal or simply contain a more primary drive for self-preservation, will to power, or a will to life that expresses itself as the domination of others.[32] Perhaps Dussel gets dangerously close to a similar hedonistic calculus when he draws from neuroscientific research to found the material principle. Citing thinkers such as Antonio Damasio, Dussel writes, "In principle (that is to say, as fundamental objective state), what leads to the reproduction of life produces pleasure; pain as a system of warning announces death, ultimately."[33] Without further qualification, the natural affective evaluation of the human subject may lead to a Hobbesian universe of scarcity where the success of others means the pain for the self and the pleasure of the self are tied to an increase in power over others.

Yet if we recall Dussel's earlier critique of utilitarianism, we can return to it here to respond to the threat of Hobbes. Utilitarianism naturalizes its own historical social conditions and considers a certain kind of historically contingent subjectivity to be natural and ahistorical. Similarly, Hobbes, living in early imperialist England and writing out of conditions of civil war, considers materiality to be naturalized as the struggle of individuals over scarce resources. For Dussel, to the contrary, the material principle is not individuated into a competitive subject in a system of scarcity. That is to say, insofar as we are materially determined to compete for scarce resources and see the social field populated by competitors rather than potential subjects of solidarity, we are living in an unjust material system that demands transformation through solidarity: a material system that requires a critical vantage developed through the recognition of suffering of the victims and the critical consensus of the victims.

Critical ethics and liberation movements see the failures of the prevailing system to produce, reproduce, and uphold the conditions in which living human communities can materially flourish. By critical ethics, I refer to the second part of Dussel's architectonic of ethics. Critical ethics does not offer foundational normative principles, which is what the first part of Dussel's architectonic offers. Instead, this aspect of the ethics requires that practice and critical awareness unmask the failures of the prevailing system: critical ethics (like critical politics and the rebellion of the people) begins with a moment of negation. The suffering of the victims and the material negation of life demand a critical ethics of life with a critical material principle. This leads further on to the need to recognize the sources of this suffering and to articulate a critical consensus in response to this fetishized system with its failure to uphold its claim to goodness. The critical consensus or antihegemonic consensus of the victims is the material affirmation of these living communities that have been excluded from or oppressed by the prevailing system.

Both Hobbes's liberal political philosophy and the liberal moral philosophy of utilitarianism in general falter due to a lack of formal intersubjective validity. For Hobbes, the only intersubjective moment of reason is formulated in a state of fear and terror and leads to an irreversible abandonment of the future possibility of intersubjective organization: absolute submission to the sovereign is required. Similarly, utilitarianism is not able to move beyond the individual as the ultimate moral unit and as such is unable to allow for a critical consensus of the community.

The reciprocity and mutual determination between the formal and the material levels of Dussel's ethics help us understand how material life is never simply a problem of individuality or liberal competition but always embedded within a community of reason. Political and moral liberalism, on the other hand, fails to live up to its promise due to its formalism of rights. In this, contemporary liberalism is also reminiscent of the strict sovereign of Hobbes, who permits no *hyperpotentia*—that is to say, it pays no attention to the material suffering of those who cannot make use of formal rights for their material flourishing.[34] The material moment always returns us to the shortcomings of the prevailing system, and critical ethics allows for the exposure of these formalisms. This is often evidenced in the United States, where the formalism of rights is often paraded against the struggles and suffering of those who are least well off. These rights are supposed to grant access to all forms of material flourishing and therefore negate the need to even speak of material suffering or locate its causes in the nature of the prevailing system.

4. CONCLUSION

In this chapter, I elaborated on Dussel's notion of critical material ethics and the dialectical relation between the material and formal principles. In critiquing the material ethics of utilitarianism and the liberal political philosophy of Thomas Hobbes, I have intended to show that the materiality of Dussel's material principle is not based simply on the individualized and hedonistic evaluation of pains and pleasures or the naturalization of the competitive subject of capitalism or scarcity. Rather, the dialectic between the formal and material points to an always already intersubjective constitution of the community of life. Ethics and moral philosophy fall short when they only account for the well-being of the isolated individual and when they take the isolated individual as the only possible unit of measure for all moral action. This is a sociohistorical and economic bias rooted in the possessive individualism of capitalism, which fails to give ethical or normative weight to systemic forms of critique or the power of the critical community.

103

Due to the dynamic and vital upsurge of the community of the living, formalist moralities and fetishized claims of goodness falter under the delegitimizing force of *hyperpotentia*. The upsurge of this force is not a guarantee but rather the critical reservoir from which the praxis of liberation springs, a force that must be activated and energized through the will of the people. While morality may use "goodness" claims to justify the domination of the prevailing system, ethics in Dussel's sense is more concerned with the negative moment of mitigating, reducing, and removing suffering. Neither is ethics concerned with the simple instrumental calculation and inflation of the greatest happiness of the greatest number. Ethics, in the strict sense, refers to the exteriority of the system, the excluded life, the other, the life that remains free from the reductive determinations of the system, which is not to say that it is founded not simply on the positive claim to produce and reproduce the flourishing of human life in general but rather on the analectic material moment that turns to the lives of the victims and their suffering as the original critical moment. It is not the comfortable majority, the model liberal citizen, or the industrious individual but rather the victims and the excluded that are the main protagonists of an ethics worthy of the call of liberation.

NOTES

1. I would like to thank the *APA Newsletter on Hispanic/Latino Issues in Philosophy* for permission to reprint sections of this chapter that previously appeared in a review essay. Cf. Don T. Deere, "Review of *Ethics of Liberation: In the Age of Globalization and Exclusion*," *APA Newsletter on Hispanic/Latino Issues in Philosophy* 13, no. 2 (2014): 17–21. I would also like to thank Frederick B. Mills for his valuable dialogue and comments on an earlier draft of this chapter.

2. Enrique Dussel, *Ethics of Liberation: In the Age of Globalization and Exclusion*, trans. Eduardo Mendieta, Camilo Pérez Bustillo, Yolanda Angulo, and Nelson Maldonado-Torres, ed. Alejandro A. Vallega (Durham, N.C.: Duke University Press, 2013); hereafter cited as *EL*.

3. Cf. Enrique Dussel, *Towards an Unknown Marx: A Commentary on the "Manuscripts of 1861–63*," trans. Yolanda Angulo, ed. Fred Moseley (New York: Routledge, 2001), 239–45; and *EL*, 228–34.

4. He furthermore discovers the categories of totality and exteriority as key elements in Marx's corpus alongside the questions of life and labor.

5. It should also be remarked, however, that life itself in its prereflective and preindividuated materiality is itself already communal in the proximity that precedes the individuated subject who stands against external objects.

6. In this sense, *ethics* is always critical for Dussel, while *morality* is foundational and refers to the normative rules of the prevailing system.

7. Enrique Dussel, *Philosophy of Liberation*, trans. Aquilina Martinez and Christine Morkovsky (Maryknoll, N.Y.: Orbis Books, 1985), sec. 5.3, 160.

8. There is a complicated relation to be teased out between the exteriority of life as anadialectical and its position within the system as negated. For now, it may be considered that there is always a vital remainder beyond the negation imposed by the system. For a discussion of this issue, cf. George Ciccariello-Maher, "Latin American Dialectics and the Other," in *Decolonizing Dialectics* (Durham, N.C.: Duke University Press, 2017), 103–21.

9. On life as a mode of reality, Dussel is influenced by Xavier Zubiri's account. Cf. Xavier Zubiri, *Dynamic Structure of Reality*, trans. Nelson R. Orringer (Champaign: University of Illinois Press, 2003).

10. More recently, in *14 tesis*, he expands and subdivides the critical principles into one strictly critical negative set and one positive set of building anew. Cf. Enrique Dussel, *14 tesis de ética: Hacia la esencia del pensamiento critico* (Madrid: Editorial Trotta, 2016).

11. In this chapter, I limit the analysis to the material and formal moments of the foundational and critical set of principles and leave aside for the moment the question of the feasibility principles.

12. In this sense, Dussel finds his project in a profound kinship with the Aristotelian understanding of the relation between form and matter: "The contemporary relevance of Aristotle consists precisely in this unity or articulation of the *material* and the *formal*, although it has, as is evident, premodern limitations"; *EL*, 108. Aristotle thinks of the unity of reason and the passions in his articulation of the theory of virtue. For example, when he describes the process of practical moral decision (*prohairesis*), he explains that temperance (*sophrosune*) preserves our practical wisdom (*phronesis*).

13. John Locke, *An Essay Concerning Human Understanding*, ed. P. H. Nidditch (Oxford: Clarendon, 1975), bk. 1, chap. 28, sec. 5; cited in *EL*, 71.

14. Jeremy Bentham, preface to *A Fragment on Government and an Introduction to the Principles of Morals and Legislation* (Oxford: Blackwell, 1948), 3; cited in *EL*, 72.

15. As Aristotle writes, the life organized around the pursuit of pleasure is a life for grazing animals. Cf. Aristotle, *Nicomachean Ethics*, trans. Terence Irwin (Indianapolis, Ind.: Hackett, 1999), bk. 1, chap. 5.

16. John Stuart Mill, *Utilitarianism* (Indianapolis, Ind.: Hackett, 2001), 6–15.

17. Karl Marx, *Das Kapital*, vol. 6 of *Karl Marx-Friedrich Engels-Gesamtausgabe* (Berlin: Dietz, 1987), sec. 2, 588; cited in *EL*, 70.

18. Dussel, *14 tesis*, sec. 5.7, 69.

19. Dussel writes, "Against those moral theories (or ethics) that are founded on one solitary principle, we will justify the multiplicity of principles that found diverse moments constitutive of practical action"; ibid., sec. 6.01, 71.

20. *EL*, 108.

21. Enrique Dussel, *Twenty Theses on Politics*, trans. George Ciccariello-Maher (Durham, N.C.: Duke University Press, 2008), 13–21.

22. Drawing from the politics makes sense insofar as Dussel does not see a strict divide between ethics and politics in the sense often presupposed by modernity. Further, the dialectic between the material, the formal, and then the excluded or oppressed material (its *hyperpotentia*) is particularly striking in the politics.

23. The Latin distinction between *potentia* and *potestas* is most prominently developed in Spinoza's work, and it has also been central more recently in the work of Michael Hardt and Toni Negri.

24. Dussel draws this principle of obediential rule from the Zapatista National Liberation Army (EZLN) and their communities that have been in rebellion and asserted their own autonomous governance structures for over twenty years in Chiapas. This is their central governing principle, which one will see posted at the entrance to Zapatista territory: "You are in Zapatista territory. Here the people [*el pueblo*] rule and the government obeys."

25. "This is the Generation of that great Leviathan, or rather (to speake more reverently) of that *Mortall God*"; Thomas Hobbes, *Leviathan*, ed. Richard Tuck (Cambridge: Cambridge University Press, 1996), 120. See also "By *Kingdome* (which is an estate ordained by men for their perpetuall security against enemies, and want) it seemeth that this Salvation should be on Earth"; ibid., 316.

26. Thomas Hobbes, *On the Citizen* (Cambridge: Cambridge University Press, 1998), 116.

27. "Life is but a motion of limbs"; Hobbes, *Leviathan*, 9. Hobbes's view of life is purely mechanistic as opposed to Dussel's own vitalism.

28. Like Dussel, Hobbes is a monist and sees the generation of reason out of the materiality of the body.

29. Hobbes, *Leviathan*, 91.

30. Ibid., 92.

31. "And therefore there be some Rights, which no man can be understood by any words, or other signes, to have abandoned, or transferred. As first a man cannot lay down the right of resisting them, that assault him by force, to take away his life; because he cannot be understood to ayme thereby, at any Good to himself"; ibid., 93.

32. For a more detailed account of how Dussel works through his own critique of Hobbes, cf. *Política de la liberación*, vol. 2, *La arquitectónica* (Madrid: Editorial

Trotta, 2009). See also *Twenty Theses*, where the main critiques of Hobbes tie him to the Eurocentric tradition of the will to power and domination as opposed to the will to life.

33. *EL*, 64.

34. Dussel, *14 tesis*, sec. 6.1, 71.

CHAPTER 6

Ethics of Liberation and Discourse Ethics

On Grounding the Material Principle of Life

Jorge Zúñiga M.

1. INTRODUCTION: THE DUSSEL-APEL DIALOGUE, AN ATTEMPT TO CLOSE THE GAP BETWEEN NORTH AND SOUTH

The dialogue between Enrique Dussel and Karl-Otto Apel in the 1990s should be understood as an attempt to close the gap between two philosophical traditions, the European and the Latin American one. I understand this effort as an attempt, since it is a fact that Latin American philosophy is still excluded and ignored by some of the most important philosophical discussions on ethics, politics, and the history of philosophy.

Nevertheless, it should be mentioned as well that in some topics and some points of view, the Latin American philosophy is nowadays more debated than before.[1] The specific case of Dussel and the philosophy of liberation in general is that both present and represent a school of thinking that is more than comments on specific topics of Latin American philosophy. This has been the main contribution of the philosophy of liberation. This is the reason, in my view, it stands out as the most well-known Latin American philosophy outside of this region.[2]

This scope of Latin American philosophy—and specifically of the philosophy of liberation in the sphere of the global north-south dialogue—is seen in the debate with Apel as well. Apel recognized the influence that the philosophy of liberation provoked for him. It challenged him to advance an ethics of responsibility to complement part A of discourse ethics (the part that deals with the grounding). Apel states in his debate with Habermas, "That there could be a reflection deficit in the whole European–North American discussion about democracy has been suggested to me in the last ten years through the discussion with Latin American theology and the philosophy of liberation, which never tires of denouncing the ethnocentrism of Northern philosophical discourse."[3]

This was, in a certain way, the gain of Apel's discourse ethics during the dialogue with Dussel and other Latin American thinkers such as Franz Hinkelammert and Raúl Fornet-Betancourt, among others. However, Apel's deficit in this dialogue, despite his concern with bridging the gap between north and south, is that he was unable to subsume categories and concepts related to the material dimension of the ethical, presented by the mentioned philosophers from Latin America, into the framework of his transcendental pragmatic and discourse ethics.

To explain this, I suspect there were three main reasons for this deficit within discourse ethics. On the one hand, one could maintain, the transcendental pragmatic was, in Apel's view, sufficiently grounded and did not need to be transformed or revised through the contributions of the philosophy of liberation; on the other, Apel saw potential contributions only in regard to the social field, to empirical politics (what Apel called part B of discourse ethics—namely, the part dealing with application and implementation), and thus not as a philosophy that could contribute to the metalevel of discourse (part A of discourse ethics—again, the part dealing with normative grounding). A third reason may be that Apel saw the philosophy of liberation as one that was not able to contribute to the question of the conditions of the possibility of valid knowledge and the normative conditions of discourses as they are elucidated by the philosophy of language.

The situation was different for Dussel. He was capable of subsuming the contributions of transcendental pragmatics and discourse ethics within the architectonic of his ethics of liberation by making it more complex and elaborate than before. As a result of his encounter with Apel, Dussel reformulated his practical philosophy from the perspective of a deontic ethics, including the contributions of the philosophy of language. As a consequence, Dussel grounded six practical principles in his renewed practical philosophy: three positive principles and three critical ones. Among these principles, two discursive (of intersubjective validity) principles are included (positive and negative). It should be noted that in Dussel's case, there was the possibility of subsuming contributions that differ from his philosophy in order to make it stronger for contributing to practical solutions, since he has understood his philosophy as a praxis-oriented one. Thus Dussel has gained much more than Apel in this dialogue.

In this context, in this chapter, the topic that I will discuss is inspired by the dialogue between these two great philosophies. Actually, I focus on the specific topic of the grounding (*Begründung*) of the material principle of life. This topic represents, in my view, two important aspects of the dispute between Dussel and Apel—namely, (1) the confrontation of two primacies: of language and discourse and of life, and (2) the founding of the material principle of life, which was Apel's challenge to Dussel. To these two points Dussel gave answers. The answer to the first question was Dussel's proposal in relation to the grounding and formulation of six practical principles.

The answer to the second question—namely, of the grounding of the material principle of life—was presented by Dussel in his formulation of the positive material principle of life as well as in his formulation of the critical negative principle of life. I focus in section 2 on the grounding of the positive material principle of life by Dussel. In section 3, I enter into the problem of the grounding of the material principle with my own perspective and proposal.

2. THE GROUNDING OF THE MATERIAL PRINCIPLE OF LIFE IN DUSSEL'S SECOND ETHICS OF LIBERATION

Dussel grounded life as the material moment of ethics both in its positive side into the given practical order and in its negative aspect into the construction process of new practical orders that come from the negativity of the present practical system—namely, from the perspective of its victims and excluded. I refer later directly to this material moment of his architectonic for the purpose of the present chapter, but it is worth mentioning in short that this material moment is articulated in the framework of the architectonic of this ethics of liberation with the formal moment—that is, the moment of intersubjective validity—and the feasibility moment. This coarticulation is presented in both the positive and the critical (i.e., the negative principles) parts of the architectonic.

In the second architectonic, inspired in part by Xavier Zubiri,[4] Dussel states that "life is a mode of reality of the human being," and it refers to the concrete life of the human being. Dussel points this out as follows: "Human life is a 'mode of reality'; it is the concrete life of each human being from which reality is faced, constituting it from an ontological horizon (human life is the preontological point of departure of ontology) where the real is actualized as practical truth. . . . Human life is never the 'other' of reason; rather it is the absolute intrinsic material condition of rationality. . . . I will defend then that human life is the source of all rationality, and that material rationality has human life as criterion and ultimate 'reference' of truth and absolute condition of its possibility."[5] Dussel refers here to the fact that the subject interprets objective reality from his or her condition as a living being. That life is a mode of reality means that the subject exists as a living being. That is to say that from that fact, the real (that which is discovered in the long run and can later become objective reality) is faced by the subject. In this process, the subject discovers the means that make his or her existence possible in reality. This is what Dussel means by the term "practical truth": the subject interprets means, discourses, and practices from the possibilities that they open up for producing, reproducing, and developing his or her life—in other words, from the possibilities that any mediation opens for the subject with regard to his or her material life.

On the other hand, he states that life "is the source of all rationality." This is to say that a means that is used for an end could be determined as "rational" only if it makes the production, reproduction, and development of human life possible. In other words, the rational character of something has to do with the possibility of developing the subject's life. Thus Dussel's point contrasts with the rational theories of action that place at the center of their concept the utility and preferences of the subject, like the theories of rational choice in microeconomics. Naturally, the human being has to live first in order to decide what to do or not to do, what to buy or not to buy, even to have the chance to choose.[6]

Rational, or choice, theories of action presuppose a subject without needs. Therefore, like Hinkelammert, Dussel's proposal is to have a concept of material rationality that has at its center human life as a criterion of practices and actions. We find this in Dussel's words in the following way:

> Human beings access the reality that they confront every day from the ambit of their own lives. Human life is neither a goal nor a mere mundane-ontological horizon; human life is *the mode of reality* of the ethical subject (that is, not that of a stone, of a mere animal or the Cartesian angelic "soul"), which gives content to all of its actions, which determines the rational order and also the level of its needs, drives and desires that constitute the framework within which ends are fixed. The "ends" (with reference to Weberian formal instrumental reason) are "put in place" by the exigencies of human life. This is to say, insofar as the human being is a living entity, it constitutes reality *as objective* (for practical or theoretical reason) in the exact measure in which it is determined as the mediation of *human* life.[7]

In Dussel's sense, life is the condition of the possibility of human existence and is related to three moments: its production, its reproduction, and its development. Human acts have as a reference point one of these three moments, and ultimately, each act has, as its practical reference, these three moments as a whole. Thus life is a material criterion of ethical acts that are carried out always within a community. He articulates the material criterion as follows: "The one who acts humanly has as content in the act, always and necessarily, some mediation for the self-responsible production, reproduction and development of the life of each human subject in a community of life, as the material fulfillment of the needs his or her cultural corporeality (the first of all being the desire of the other human subject), having as ultimate referent all of humanity."[8] Life, as a mode of reality, is the horizon from which the subject interprets his or her given reality and in which he or she exists. This given reality is naturally institutional and socialized and is thus normative. Many examples regarding human practices could be provided, and through them it could be shown that they are more or less related, at least, to one of the three mentioned life moments or to all three at the same time. Against this background, Dussel formulates a universal material principle that finds its way into the architectonic of his ethics. That is to say, since life makes the practices and actions possible, there is a requirement for a universal practical principle that makes ethical acts possible. Then Dussel proposes its formulation in the following terms:

> The one who acts ethically *ought* (as an obligation) to produce, reproduce and develop self-responsibly the concrete life of each human subject, in a *community of life*, and inevitably out of a cultural and historical "good life" (from the subject's way of conceiving happiness, with a certain reference to values and to a fundamental way of comprehending being as an ought-to-be, and for that reason also making a *rightness* claim) that is shared instinctually and solidaristically, having as ultimate reference all of humanity. In other words, this is a normative statement that makes a *practical truth claim* and, further, a *universality claim*.[9]

This principle, which is formulated in terms of "ought to,"[10] is articulated furthermore with the two positive principles—namely, of intersubjective validity and of feasibility. The practical application of these principles makes possible the act that would have a claim to goodness. The goodness claim belongs, according to Dussel, to institutions and practical systems as well, since they are built from practices and actions. Therefore, these positive principles, for Dussel, are "the conditions of ethical possibility of the norm, actions, subsystem, institution, or ethical system, and the frames that frame such 'possibilities.'"[11]

Thus an institutional decision or a decision within a practical system (the practical order) takes into account the goodness claim whose practical realization is possible by means of the fulfillment of the three ethical positive principles (material, formal, and feasibility).[12] This is to say, not only at the level of the individual acts but also at the level of the community in its institutions, there are decisions with goodness claims, as long as they affect the human being. The transition from an individual act to institutional decisions is the relevant passage in the sense of the recognition of an institutionalized community within which the subject already exists.

113

Thus far I have focused my exposition with an emphasis on Dussel's positive grounding of life, which is not, paradoxically, the main point to which he wants to come within the frame of the architectonic of his ethics, for his goal is, since his first ethics of liberation,[13] the grounding of critical ethics that is oriented by the victims of the given system. Nevertheless, I followed this theme, for the grounding of the material principle, as it is presented by Dussel, seems to me to be insufficient in order to provide, in particular, a grounding that renders indisputable and objective the universal validity of life as a criterion for practices, actions, and social mediations such as institutions.

In the dialogue with Apel, the material criterion of life and its principle were disputable, for Apel showed Dussel that, on the one hand, the material principle was not sufficiently grounded, since from the perspective of the ethics of liberation and even any critical thinking, argumentative discourses are always already presupposed in order to critique the noncircumventability (*Nichthintergehbarkeit*) of language and argumentation. To this extent, arguments raise validity claims of truth, rightness, and sense. To deny this implies, according to Apel, a performative self-contradiction. This is the core of the challenge that Apel poses for Dussel, since Apel's philosophical proposal consists of a grounding in which the transcendental presuppositions of argumentation, such as those of universal validity claim, truth claim, or meaning claim, cannot be denied in argumentative discourse without at the same time committing performative self-contradiction. This is what Apel calls the *ultimate foundation* (*Letztbegründung*).[14]

Against this, Dussel realized that the material principle of life needed such a grounding, and he made a really big effort for it. However, as he himself recognized, such grounding was still lacking in terms of demonstration. He points out,

> I will offer a detailed formulation of the *discourse of the grounding* of this material principle of ethics below. A *positive* and material grounding, such as I have merely sketched, is needed. But a *negative*, or *ad absurdum*, grounding is also and equally needed, to demonstrate the impossibility of its opposite. In this case, the argument will not take on the skeptic who puts in question reason in general; it will argue against the cynic who pretends to justify an *ethical* order grounded in the acceptance of death, killing, or collective suicide, as when a Friedrich von Hayek justifies the elimination of those who are defeated by "competition" in the market. . . . *The impossibility* of arguing ethically without performative self-contradiction in favor of an order where the norm, action, microstructure, institution, or ethical system proposes the development of an ethical order based on death, killing, or collective suicide (Heidegger's "being-unto-death" or Freud's "thanatos principle"?) will have to be demonstrated. . . . The claim of this type of grounding would be to show that no ethical norm, human act, microstructure, just institution, or system of ethical life may contradict the enunciated principle.[15]

Dussel points out, moreover, that such a universal principle "may be improved in its formulation, but is not falsifiable—even taking into account the uncertainty of finite reason, because if it were falsifiable we would lose the ethical grounding of falsifiability, of reason itself: we would fall into an originating and abysmal performative contradiction."[16]

As one can see in these referred parts of the second ethics of liberation,[17] Dussel continues the dialogue with Apel, since he refers to the performative self-contradiction, but he does this in the context of a practice, norm, or institution whose arguments for universal validity are based on an ideology of death. However, one should notice that the performative self-contradiction has to do, in the first place, with language and with the presuppositions of argumentation such as the truth claim, truthfulness claim, or the claim to sense. To this extent, it is imprecise to link performative self-contradiction with life or death, for this kind of contradiction is, in fact, a pragmatic test for the validity (*in actualita*) of universal presuppositions of communication (Habermas) and argumentation (Apel).[18] However, here is seen at the same time the limit of Apel's important concept of performative self-contradiction, for an ideology or a system of arguments commits no contradiction as long as they argue,[19] excluding all other kinds of contradictions.

115

Dussel saw this and the limit of the performative self-contradiction and was clearly aware that he should work on such a concept or on a similar kind of arguing that demonstrates the impossibility of "arguing ethically without performative self-contradiction."[20] In addition, Dussel was clear that this kind of grounding was needed, even previously to a founding of deontic principles in the way he formulated in his second ethics of liberation. He himself recognized that a grounding ad absurdum allows one to argue against the cynic, who justifies a death principle—for example, the current neoliberal economists and politicians,[21] as Dussel points out in relation to von Hayek.

But what is the principle Dussel wanted to ground? What is the discourse of grounding of the material principle in the terms mentioned by Dussel? These important topics went unanswered by Dussel.[22] Instead, he decided to undertake the task of the subsumption of the deontic ethical principles into politics[23] and the economy,[24] and the important task of grounding the material principle of life in an objective manner[25] was missing.[26] It deals with making explicit the noncircumventability of life as well.

3. THE NONCIRCUMVENTABILITY OF LIFE: TWO WAYS OF SHOWING THE NECESSITY OF LIFE FOR PRACTICAL REALITIES

This missing task of grounding is, however, important, since this, on the one hand, allows us to show clearly the death principle defended by the totalizing system (the fetishized order) and its representatives and, on the other, helps provide an additional grounding for the critical principles defended and formulated by Dussel's ethics of liberation.

Against this sketched background, I attempt in this section to provide another argumentative strategy to ground the principle of life of the subject and nature in order to show unambiguously the universal validity of the material principle of life. Thus I present two strategies for it: on the one hand (3.1), I present a proposition in the form of a principle of impossibility that aims to show the noncircumventability of the subject's life and nature in a more precise way than Dussel does in his second ethics of liberation,[27] and on the other (3.2), I show another way to demonstrate the noncircumventability of life from a transcendental argument.[28]

3.1. The Principle of Impossibility of the Living Subject and Nature: Life as a Condition of Possibility

In my view, Dussel has articulated sufficient arguments throughout his works that support the thesis that the life of the human being and nature are factual conditions that make any kind of practical reality possible. This can be seen when Dussel affirms that the human being is a living entity that constitutes reality as objective within the boundaries of life and death. We do not want, naturally, to reduce his contributions to this argument, but in my view, it synthesizes an important point—namely, the noncircumventability of the living subject and nature.[29]

Dussel presents the life of the human being and of nature as a factual presupposition for the acts and practices within a community—in other words, as the condition of possibility for any kind of practical reality, as I have tried to show. Nevertheless, in my view, through the term *noncircumventability*, which is taken first from Karl-Otto Apel's transcendental pragmatics, we can express the fact that we cannot go back from the situation that the subject must live in order to develop any kind of practical reality, or in other words, it is ineluctable that the subject must live in order to carry out any act or practice. Both the subject (or human being, in Dussel's words) and also nature are already living, and in order to develop, create, and transform practical realities, they must continue to live. And these two facts are ineluctable. Or how could we go beyond this factual situation?

Now from this noncircumventability, we could think of a principle that could contain it. This means a principle that could make it explicit. This step is possible and legitimate if we accept that it is objective and universal. This principle is, however, not a moral principle but a principle that outlines just the starting point of the practices and the construction and transformation of a practical reality. This principle is, moreover, any statement that pretends to *describe* all practical relations as a whole, for they express the limits from which we interpret, know, and act in practical reality. Its grounding pivot, so to say, is exactly its noncircumventability.

Another problematic aspect is how we formulate the principle to make it visible. As I mentioned, Dussel's principle is formulated in the context of a discussion on morals and ethics by way of an "ought to" (deontic ethics). Naturally, I share the point that from the sketched background, we can derive an ethical principle, but I also maintain that this belongs to a second moment. In contrast, I am seeking a principle that contains and expresses the objectivity of the already mentioned noncircumventability. That is to say, I want to go to a more basic level and seek the formulation of a principle that is both practical and epistemological and whose formulation is unambiguous.

We find, therefore, in the principles of impossibilities, the model for formulating such a principle, since we can prove through its form that it is factually unavoidable. In a recent paper,[30] I have given an explanation of this kind of principle in detail. Here I give a brief summary.

On the one hand, these principles, which are displayed by Hinkelammert through a critical review of Popper's thought, show the limits of practical action, and on the other, they act as a presupposition for the empirical and social sciences, as long as they continue being related to practices. Here, Hinkelammert reformulates Popper's affirmation in which Popper refers to "logical impossibilities," even though they are, in fact, as Hinkelammert points out, empirical impossibilities.[31] This means that what Popper states as logically impossible is not as such but is empirically impossible.

117

From this distinction, Hinkelammert maintains that from empirical impossibilities, principles of impossibilities related to the natural[32] and social world[33] can be inferred. Thus the way of inferring these kinds of principles comes not directly from a reflection on the moral but from a description related to empirical reality. They express, through statements, impossibilities that are not yet explicit, which build their core. They are, moreover, discovered (formulated) through the reflection on experience. The statements are the principles of impossibility; through them the limits of empirical reality are recognized (such as, for example, the impossibility of constructing a perpetuum mobile). They are synthetic statements, synthetic judgments. These principles that highlight the starting point for practices and actions, and practical reality as a whole, allow the establishment of theories of practical relations as well.

Hinkelammert himself formulates in *Utopie und Ethik* (Utopia and ethics), one of his late works, a kind of holistic principle of impossibility related to social relations. He states, "A society whose productive relations appear as incapable of reproducing the concrete life of human beings and that of nature destroys itself and is not sustainable in the long run. In order to survive, it must make its productive relations compatible with these conditions of surviving for the reproduction of the concrete life and therefore to transform them."[34] Against this background, I want to display another formulation of a principle of impossibility that aims to be more unequivocal (unambiguous) or even more precise than that of Dussel and that of Hinkelammert. I display in fact two statements that are compatible with each other. I formulate them as follows:

1. No human act or any practice is factually possible without the living subject and nature.
2. No human reality can be realizable without the living subject and nature.

Here we are faced with two principles of impossibility in which both are mutually implied. The one is an extension of the other. Both are based on the acceptance that human reality (intersubjective practical reality) is created, developed, and transformed through practices, actions, and thoughts of the human being.

This is what we refer to as practical reality, since it implies a face-to-face relation. Thus practical reality means that reality is possible and depends on our thoughts and our praxis. This practical reality is distinguished from the natural one, which has its own logic and exists regardless of our thoughts and our *praxis*.[35] From this view, the relation between these two kinds of reality cannot be seen as conflicting; rather, it has to be seen as a symbiotic relationship. To this extent, the practical subject naturally is in charge of seeking ways of relating to it.

On the other hand, the sense of the human being, in the context of the principles formulated earlier, means whoever belongs—through a socialization process—to a community, with its rules, customs, and institutions, is capable of assuming moral responsibilities as well as capable of transcending his or her given reality.

To go beyond these two mentioned principles finally implies an approximation to the opposite side—namely, the dissolution of human reality. In other words, to try to go beyond something that practically and factually is impossible seems to be the beginning of the practical no-reason and with that the beginning of irrationality, to speak alongside Hinkelammert and Dussel. These principles enable us to regulate the practices, customs, and institutions for the development of practical realities. And here, practical philosophy and the social sciences (practical sciences) have much to say. Hence the principles previously elaborated—what I call the principle of impossibility of the living subject and nature[36]—are both practical and epistemological.

3.2. No Envisioned Practical Reality Without the Living Subject and Nature: The Transcendental Necessity of Life

In this section, I elaborate a second way of demonstrating the noncircumventability of life, as I previously mentioned. I want to frame this second strategy in terms of praxis and its relation with the transcendental ideas that guide it. These transcendental ideas can be both a utopia or a regulative idea of *praxis* and goals and ends that the subject follows. These ideas can be regulative ideas or transcendental models that, however, cannot be taken as achievable goals rather than ends toward which practice can tend but that nonetheless can never be completely accomplished. Examples of these kinds of holistic transcendental ideas are the neoliberal idea of the free market, the anarchist idea of the elimination or abolition of the state, or the holistic idea of the Popperian open society.[37]

But future actions or practices presuppose the transcendental as well. The fact of hoping to arrive tomorrow at an appointment on time is transcendental as well in the sense that that fact is beyond the present time and conditions. To this extent, to achieve goals and ends presupposes transcendental thinking. Thus when we talk about transcendental thinking, we can refer either to the achievement of a goal or to the historical realization of a transcendental model through practice, actions, and thought. In both cases, it should be noticed the strategic-instrumental rationality is in play in this scheme as well. In order to materialize something that was envisioned, the means for its accomplishment needs to be delimited. This is the means-end rationality that Weber and the social and political theory in general have worked out. So far, there is nothing new to suggest.

But when we consider the scheme of means-end rationality from the perspective of those who can suffer the realization of the transcendental ideas or the negative consequences of the achievement of ends and goals, then the realization of those ideas begins to create victims. These are the ideas that have become fetishized. These are ideas that are placed in the center of the human action: the goal or end is no longer the reproduction, development, or increasing of life, to speak with Dussel, but the reproduction of the idea itself. This is, for example, the case of the neoliberal thought whose realization of the idea of the free market and privatization is producing global victims. Thus the realization of the neoliberal transcendental idea is bringing the global population to a situation in which the quality of life and the quality of democracies are drastically decreasing—they respond no longer to the subject but to capital.

I have concentrated on the realization of current neoliberalism, since this is our global situation and the horizon from which critical thinking should contribute with its critical insights. However, the realization of idealizations or transcendental ideas that instrumentalize the life of subject and nature in order to reproduce the idea itself corresponds to totalizing systems that take themselves, rather than human life in community, as the points of reference.

Something that is shared by these fetishized idealizations is that they present a concept of subject and nature in which they appear as infinite, with unlimited capabilities, and not as finite entities and without material needs. Thus the subject is submitted to endless work or even sacrificed in the current neoliberalism.

In this context, I want to present the second in order to show the necessity of the subject's life and nature. I think of this second form in a direct relation to the realization of transcendental ideas and social models (social utopias, for example). This has to do, evidently, with *praxis* as well. To this extent, I want to propose the following rule: *we cannot envision a possible practical reality without the living subject and nature.*

Thus we can envision a social reality without capital but not one without the living subject and nature. We can envision a social reality without a perfect planning but not one without the living subject and nature.

4. LAST WORDS: DECOLONIZING ETHICS AND DISCOURSE ETHICS

The foundation of the material principle of life has a direct relation to the decolonization of ethics, especially in the context of Dussel's ethics, since the material criterion, considered this way, has fallen into oblivion in dominant modern thinking and philosophy in which, since the ancient Greeks, reason is the last instance. Discourse ethics as a modern contemporary philosophy related reason to language and discourse. For this reason, this moral philosophy maintained that reflection and praxis could not circumvent language.

Against discourse ethics, Dussel affirms and defends that there are agreements, reciprocal understandings, and consensus (the practical goals of discourse ethics) that can systematically deny the subject's life as well as the sustainability of the earth's ecosystem—that is, of nature. With regard to Hinkelammert's critique of Apel and of discourse ethics, we can maintain that a consensus is valid only if the subject, the human being, can live in it. In other words, a consensus is capable of acceptability to the extent that it allows life for the subject and nature. The unacceptability of consensus is discovered by the incapability to produce, reproduce, and develop the subject's life and nature, which is the case of the global institutional consensus. This means the discursivity of *praxis* needs a material complement (criterion), and this is life as such. These are complementary criteria of action, and this was well understood by Dussel and not by Apel, because for Apel, reason was the last instance, and reason is language.

On the contrary, an important part of decolonizing ethics (critical ethics) for Dussel means avoiding the last instance as a criterion of action and to ground different complementary criteria and principles related to action. However, there was a philosophical task that was left aside by Dussel: the grounding of the material principle of life. I intended to complete this task (in a summarized way) in the present chapter, only so we can ground in a better way the critical sciences and philosophies, including naturally the philosophy of liberation and decolonial theory.

So long as we try to show in a universal way criteria, principles, and noncircumventabilities that seek to go beyond the modern way of thinking and acting, we cannot stop arguing and grounding. This naturally is something we can learn from Apel.

Finally, were I to link discourse ethics and ethics of liberation in a sentence, I would state the following: since we live, we can make explicit by means of language the noncircumventability of life, and speech-acts are always intersubjective—that is, communal acts.

NOTES

1. The most evident example are the works that have been published in the often-quoted *Stanford Encyclopedia of Philosophy*. Cf., e.g., *The Stanford Encyclopedia of Philosophy*, ed. Edward N. Zalta, Spring 2018 ed., s.v. "Latin American Philosophy," by Jorge Gracia and Manuel Vargas, August 14, 2013, https://plato.stanford.edu/archives/spr2018/entries/latin-american-philosophy/; *The Stanford Encyclopedia of Philosophy*, ed. Edward N. Zalta, Winter 2016 ed., s.v. "Philosophy

of Liberation," by Eduardo Mendieta, January 28, 2016, https://plato.stanford.edu /archives/win2016/entries/liberation/; *The Stanford Encyclopedia of Philosophy*, ed. Edward N. Zalta, Spring 2016 ed., s.v. "Philosophy in Mexico," by Guillermo Hurtado, January 20, 2016, https://plato.stanford.edu/archives/spr2016/entries /philosophy-mexico/; among many others. Cf. Frederick Mills, *Enrique Dussel's Ethics of Liberation: An Introduction* (New York: Palgrave Macmillan, 2018). One should mention as well the enormous work made by the *CLR James Journal*, edited by Paget Henry.

2. Jorge Gracia and Manuel Vargas maintain the following: "Although analytic philosophers (whether in Latin America or abroad) have generally ignored the philosophy of liberation (or else dismissed it as unrigorous or unphilosophical), this philosophical perspective has arguably had more impact outside of Latin America than any other Latin American philosophical development. In particular, Dussel has been in dialogue with a variety of philosophers in Europe (including Apel, Ricoeur, and Habermas), and with Continental-influenced philosophers in the United States and elsewhere (e.g., Rorty, Taylor, Alcoff, and Mendieta)." Gracia and Vargas, "Latin American Philosophy."

3. "Daß hier ein Reflexionsdefizit der gesamten europäisch-nordamerikanischen Demokratie-Diskussion vorliegen könnte, hat sich mir in den lezten Jahren nahegelegt durch die Auseinandersetzung mit der lateinamerikanischen Theologie und Philosophie der Befreiung, die nicht müde wird, den 'Ethnozentrismus' (auch) des philosophischen Diskurses des Nordens anzupragern"; Karl-Otto Apel, *Auseinandersetzungen: In Erprobung des transzendental-pragmatischen Ansatzes* (Frankfurt am Main: Suhrkamp, 1998), 749; my translation. In a later work, Apel comes to the point of a challenge for discourse ethics, not the problem of the skeptic but the problem of the *cynic*. Cf. Karl-Otto Apel, *The Response of Discourse Ethics* (Louvain: Peeters, 2001), 81–83.

4. Xavier Zubiri, *Estructura dinámica de la realidad* (Madrid: Alianza, 1989), chap. 8.

5. Enrique Dussel, *Ethics of Liberation: In the Age of Globalization and Exclusion*, trans. Eduardo Mendieta, Camilo Pérez Bustillo, Yolanda Angulo, and Nelson Maldonado-Torres, ed. Alejandro A. Vallega (Durham, N.C.: Duke University Press, 2013), 434.

6. I follow here Hinkelammert's critique of these kinds of social theories. Cf. Franz Hinkelammert, *El mapa del emperador* (Costa Rica: DEI, 1996), chap. 1.

7. Dussel, *Ethics of Liberation*, 92.

8. Ibid., 95.

9. Ibid., 104; emphasis in the original.

10. Here one is able to see the methodical philosophical change of Dussel's ethics. While its first version was analectic-phenomenological, its second version, from the discussion with neo-Kantian ethics, was regrounded in terms of a deontic ethics.

11. Dussel, *Ethics of Liberation*, 365. I have led the present exposition at the level of the fulfillment of the three positive principles. However, what Dussel wants to ground, at least in his second ethics of liberation, is the fulfillment of the critical-ethical act whose conductive principles are the material one (from the victim's perspective), the critical-discursive one (antihegemonic validity of the community of victims), and the liberation principle. Dussel exemplifies the fulfillment of the critical act

through Rosa Luxemburg's thinking: "One cannot undertake 'any action'—or use any means or choose any ends, and so on—one can only decide, provide a discursive foundation regarding only 'those' actions that are 'possible' (founded or applicable) within the narrow frame delimited by such principles. In an amazingly accurate way—at the level of strategic organization—Luxemburg points out that 'principles' delimit and contain criteria 'both regarding (a) at the ends [Ziele] to reach, (b) as well as the means of struggle, and finally, (c) the forms of struggle.' These three levels of strategic instrumental reason define the horizon of mediation"; ibid., 365–66.

12. Ibid., 184–203.

13. Cf. Enrique Dussel, *Para una ética de la liberación Latinoamericana*, vols. 1–3 (Buenos Aires: Siglo XXI, 1973).

14. Cf. Karl-Otto Apel and Enrique Dussel, *Ética del discurso y ética de la liberación* (Madrid: Editorial Trotta, 2004), chap. 3.

15. Dussel, *Ethics of Liberation*, 105; emphasis in the original.

16. Ibid., 105–6.

17. As one can see, I distinguish between Dussel's first ethics of liberation (*Para una ética de la liberación Latinoamericana*) and his second ethics of liberation (*Ethics of Liberation: In the Age of Globalization and Exclusion*). The current chapter is based on this second one.

18. This is one of the starkest points of Apel's transcendental pragmatic. With the concept of the performative self-contradiction, he shows another kind of making explicit of universal presuppositions of practices that are, to Apel, discursive and situated in social contexts. In my view, the concepts of last foundation and performative self-contradiction have been misunderstood insofar as their explanations have not been placed in the context of a contemporary discussion in logic. In other words, the performative self-contradiction and the ultimate foundation have to do with a postmetaphysical logic.

19. I do not want to reduce and summarize Apel's transcendental pragmatics to the concept of the performative self-contradiction, even though it is really important for its architectonic, since complementary to it, Apel worked out discourse ethics as an ethics of coresponsibility for solving practical problems as well as for assuming coresponsibility for unexpected consequences. Cf. Apel, *Response of Discourse Ethics*, chap. 7.

20. It is important to mention that Hinkelammert saw this limitation of discourse ethics as well. Cf. Franz Hinkelammert, *Cultura de la esperanza y sociedad sin exclusión* (San José: DEI, 1995), 225–72.

21. It is important to take into account that the horizon within which Dussel places his critique of the given order is the ideologies and utopias of death.

22. Dussel received many critiques referring to his proposal of the grounding of the material principle. Some are regarding a naturalistic fallacy. Others are regarding the suicide in the sense that from Dussel's grounding, the fact that someone *should not* commit suicide is not justified, among others. Cf. Enrique Dussel, "Sobre algunas críticas a la Ética de la liberación. Respuesta a Julio Cabrera," *Dianoia* 49, no. 52 (2004): 125–45; Enrique Dussel, *Materiales para una política de la liberación* (Mexico City: Plaza y Valdes / UANL, 2007), chap. 12; Enrique Dussel, "¿Fundamentación de la ética? La vida humana: De Porfirio Miranda a ignacio

Ellacuria," *Andamios* 4, no. 7 (2007): 157–205. In these works, Dussel answered in terms of "ought to"—that is, in terms of the duty of doing something or not. Thus, for example, with regard to suicide, he answered showing that someone who commits suicide is irresponsible—like, for example, a father who abandons his children and his wife in the act of suicide. In this scenario, says Dussel, the father should not commit suicide.

The perspective of the grounding I intend offers an alternative answer to this problematic. Life is presupposed even in the suicide act insofar as the subject who intends to commit suicide presupposes life for carrying out that act. In short, life is presupposed even in the act of suicide.

125

23. Cf. Enrique Dussel, *Política de la liberación: La arquitectónica* (Madrid: Editorial Trotta, 2009); and Dussel, *Ethics of Liberation*.

24. Enrique Dussel, *16 tesis de economía política: Interpretación filosófica* (Mexico City: Siglo XXI, 2014).

25. It should also be mentioned that Hinkelammert had already formulated the principle of feasibility in the sense in which Dussel retakes it for the grounding of his third principle in the second ethics of liberation. Hinkelammert's principle states that what is logically possible is empirically impossible: "Las imposibilidades lógicas forman una 'frontera ciega' del conocimiento y la acción. En las ciencias empíricas, en cambio, lo imposible es lógicamente coherente (en este sentido: lógicamente posible) pero, de hecho, imposible. Declarando su imposibilidad, aparece el ámbito de lo posible que no puede ser expresado de ninguna otra manera. Trascendiendo lo posible se llega a lo imposible, y la toma de conciencia de este carácter imposible de lo imposible, marca el espacio de lo posible"; Franz Hinkelammert, *Crítica de la razón utópica* (Bilbao: Desclée, 2002), 59. If one compares Apel's grounding of the discursive principle and Hinkelammert's founding of the principle of feasibility, it can be seen that they were able to display a grounding whose validity (universal acceptance) is immanent to the practical reality. Such a grounding was needed in the case of the material principle of life.

26. I retook this task in a recent work where I specifically show the way how the material principle of life should be grounded and a formulation of it as well. Cf. Jorge Zúñiga, "The Principle of Impossibility of the Living Subject and Nature," *CLR James Journal* 23, nos. 1–2 (2017): 43–59.

27. I sketched this first in an extensive way in ibid.

28. I presented this second strategy for the first time in my doctoral dissertation at Frankfurt University—cf. Jorge Zúñiga, "Hypothese für eine Theorie der praktischen Wahrheit und der praktischen Gültigkeit" (Ph.D. diss., Goethe-University Frankfurt, 2016)—and continued the argument in recent works.

29. Something I showed in "The Principle of Impossibility of the Living Subject and Nature" is that Dussel's argumentation is parallel with Hinkelammert's. In many of their works, one could see an argument for showing the noncircumventability of the living subject and nature.

30. Zúñiga, "Principle of Impossibility."

31. Hinkelammert, in *Crítica de la razón utópica*, refers to the following fragment by Popper: "The term 'society' embraces, of course, all social relations, including all personal ones; those of a mother to her child as much as those of a child welfare officer to either of the two. It is for many reasons quite impossible to

control all, or 'nearly' all, these relationships; if only because with every new control of social relations we create a host of new social relations to be controlled. In short, the impossibility is a logical impossibility. (The attempt leads to an infinite regress; the position is similar in the case of an attempt to *study* the whole of society—which would have to include this study)"; Karl Popper, *The Poverty of Historicism* (London: Routledge & Kegan Paul, 1994), 79–80.

32. An example of impossibility related to natural sciences is that pointed out by Einstein: "Thus the science of thermodynamics seeks by analytical means to deduce necessary conditions, which separate events have to satisfy, from the universally experienced fact that perpetual motion is impossible"; Albert Einstein, *Ideas and Opinions: Based on "Mein Weltbild,"* ed. C. Seelig, trans. S. Bargmann (New York: Crown, 1960), 228.

33. In *Crítica de la razón utópica*, Hinkelammert discusses the Popperian idea of an omniscient entity; cf. Hinkelammert, *Crítica de la razón utópica*, chap. 1.

34. "Eine Gesellschaft, deren Produktionsverhältnisse sich als unfähig erweisen, das konkrete Leben der Menschen und der Natur zu reproduzieren, zerstört sich selbst und ist nicht auf lange Sicht lebensfähig. Um weiterleben zu können, muß sie ihre Produktionsverhältnisse an diese Überlebensbedingungen einer Reproduktion des konkreten Lebens anpassen und daher verändern"; Franz Hinkelammert, *Utopie und Ethik* (Costa Rica: 2001), 8, https://www.pensamientocritico.info/libros/libros-de-franz-hinkelammert/aleman.html; my translation.

35. Here, I follow both the Peircean and Apelian distinction between social and natural reality. Cf. Karl-Otto Apel, *Paradigmen der Erste Philosophie* (Berlin: Suhrkamp, 2011), 350.

36. Cf. Zúñiga, "Principle of Impossibility."

37. In the aforementioned *Crítica de la razón utópica*, Hinkelammert analyzes these kind of transcendental models from a critical position. He continues the reflection on this in *Utopie und Ethik* and in Franz Hinkelammert, *Crítica de la razón mítica* (Mexico City: Driada, 2008).

CHAPTER 7

On the Apophatic Urgency of Now

A Future for the Philosophy of Liberation

Oscar Guardiola-Rivera

1. MOVING FORWARD, SEEING BACKWARD: A QUESTION FOR THE PHILOSOPHY OF LIBERATION

In the course of a lecture delivered at Universidad de Murcia, Enrique Dussel explained the key criterion of his lifetime work by means of a visualization: the image of the Last Judgment in the ancient Egyptian weighing of the heart ritual, also known as the trial of the scales. The image can still be seen in an artwork known as the Hunefer papyrus on the upper floor of the British Museum of London. The Hunefer papyrus may be the oldest document to provide us with a visualization of justice. Justice appears as the act of walking upright and forward into the light. The image of the trial of the scales also works as a form of memory that condenses all other bodily senses, but it does so in a way that is previous to the overemphasis on linguistic mediation and plot and the overinterpretation of data that the look carries, as in a dance.[1]

I will argue in this chapter that as such, as a visualization that comes before words (and in that respect, a "prophetic" vision), Dussel's invocation of the trial of the scales not only points toward a decolonization of the image and the gaze from the bounds of language and interpretation;

128

it reenacts the memory of the process of its own coming-to-be as a totality in the very moment of its invocation, as an experience of salvage and rescue in and of the present that condenses all bodily and spiritual senses. But Dussel's visualization also sets in motion a shift toward an act of memory- and dreamwork or awakening into history. The whole of history—or "global" history, as he would say—awakening here and now, from the slumber and the dreams of our (colonial) parents. And in that sense, an act of awakening after the de-struction of the history of ethics (the ethics of our colonial parents) brings us closer to salvaging what lies in the hearts of those who in the present refuse the logic of the present, come what may. We shall speak, in that precise sense, of an aesthetic shift within the decolonial turn and in Dussel's philosophy of liberation, which completes the sequence initiated in the 1970s with the publication of *Para una de-strucción de la historia de la ética*; thus we shall speak of a double twist aiming to free ourselves from the double bind that keeps us inside the prison of dreams and the spectacle of the present.

Dussel observed during the Murcia lecture that his lifelong work on an ethics of liberation revolves around a single criterion: living, material, sense-intelligent corporality, or "corporalidad sentipensante y viva."[2] Further, he referred to the way such a criterion would have evolved from a close reading of Hermann Cohen's investigation of prophetic vision, Ernst Cassirer's reworking of Kantian imagination, and Walter Benjamin's treatment of allegory in *The Origin of German Tragic Drama*—specifically, the latter's conclusion concerning the tendential loss of eschatological certainty in a redemptive end of history leading to the presentation of political struggle in a material setting, here and now, in the shape of a visual (but also kinesthetic, tactile, and auditory) universe incorporating cosmic and bodily dimensions, an enactive metonymy arranged in accordance to the rhythms of nature and the body (a "materialist" messianism, according to Dussel).[3] Furthermore, Dussel emphasizes the significance of the body and its material rhythms in relation to such allegorical images as Ma'at, Anubis, Thoth, and Osiris in the trial of the scales scene, reenacted in different ways from Egyptian and Semitic (archaic) formations to the interplay between Christian eschatology and profane sovereign violence.

As he pointed out in the lecture, during the trial of the scales, jackal-headed Anubis would question mortals as to whether they fed the hungry, gave water to the thirsty, a roof to the homeless, or safe passage to the exiled, the forcibly displaced, and the foreigner. Thus in accordance to this archaic image of justice, the criterion of a good life is neither success in business nor the accumulation of riches ("Lo, none is allowed to take his goods with him," states the Inyotef Song) but whether we have been true to our heart's desires and, in accordance with its commands, cared for the living body of the hungry and the foreigner.

In this scenario, the heart is a site of receptivity and the presentation of life-giving sunrays. It receives the image or true likeness of the sun, thereby becoming the engine of sense and sensibility, the immanence of the solar disc. It's the place of collaboration between the contrasting model of creation (nature and cosmos) and creative natural bodies. We think of the brain or the eyes (but also of "the intelligence of a machine" such as the cinematograph) and their dance-like relation with the surrounding environment in a similar manner.

Reborn each and every day without fail, the sun and its illuminating presence constitute the model out of which the world and everything that is of it and in it has come to be, which makes it in beauty and fairness. The heart is an engine of desires and the seat of likely images received through the sun's radiation. These cosmic images that affect the body give us a sense of orientation as we transit through life. Such a sense of existence is explicit in the *Great Hymn to the Aten*, a composition found in thirteen vertical columns of hieroglyphs in el-Amarna, the site of Akhenaten and Nefertiti's utopian vision for a city that would be "the horizon" of the sun disk: a city whose people would "live on truth" (*ankh em maat*), intensifying life and happiness rather than death, giving importance to the here and now instead of the gloomy morrow, and living bodily sense-intelligence.

This kind of anthropographic reasoning is widespread among archaic formations and may correspond to an activity of symbolization that can be universalized. Here the good connects to the beautiful cosmically. The creation of symbolic forms through the connection of the body or parts thereof with other natural bodies, chief among them cosmic bodies, is the key to the making of cosmologies that perform a social memory function as well as one of orientation in space-time. Consider this excerpt from the *Hymn to the Aten*: "For you are risen from the eastern horizon and have filled every land with your beauty; For you are fair, great, dazzling, and high on every land." Here the light of the sun is linked with the motion of the human body filling space and walking upright and forward, just as in the moment of our ethical and material transition from darkness and dream to awakening and light, as the following passage specifies: "The land is in darkness, in the manner of death. People, they lie in bedchambers. . . . But the land grows bright when you are risen from the horizon. . . . The two lands are in a festival of light—Awake and standing on legs, for you have lifted them up." There's a sense of gathering in equality and justice as well as moving toward their realization (walking upright into the light, "standing on legs") associated with the image of sunrays shining over the manifold of being, not in spite of but because of their difference: "All things which are on earth, which go on legs, which rise up and fly. . . . The foreign countries of Kharu [Syria] and Kush [Nubia], and the land of Egypt / You set every man in his place . . . each one having his food and the reckoning of his lifetime."[4]

Ditto, the connection between the good and the beautiful is here a matter of sense and sensibility, of receptivity, motion, and orientation, a matter of exaltation and happiness rather than austere moderation, as the poem makes clear through its use of upward- and outward-oriented imagery emphasizing wakening light and life over darkness, slumber, and death. In other words, the poem, which is to be sung by people in a gathering, performs a dramatic intensification of enjoyment and happiness. It's an engine for the creation of a space-time of joy and happiness to be incarnated here and now in a city whose people would live on truth. The affect created through such gathering, invocation, and performance of the poem's images is like the joy we feel before the vision of the rising sun (the paradigmatic model), which is comparable to the sense of our transit (becoming, appearance, presentation) from darkness into light.

Strictly speaking, this metaphorical transit or oscillation is allegorical, at least in the precise sense given to that term by the critic and sentry of dreams Walter Benjamin. In accordance with Benjamin's understanding of allegory, the performative force of such an image (presentation, demonstration) raises the importance of a natural body dramatically in the midst of darkness and catastrophe. In such a void, an image becomes present as both tendency and orientation (or "spirit")—that is, a vital attitude that draws its impulse from the visualization and intensification of the interrupted projects of the past latent still but silent in the present. Such visualization not only condenses all the senses of the living body but intelligently focuses and drives forward (as a tale or a cosmology) the living experience of a situated and self-conscious sense in the funk of existence, which is common (with others) and initiates a sequence (instead of a plot) that pertains not only to the significance of things but also to the forward-driven orientation and importance of all existence.

As can be seen, the question raised by Dussel through its invocation of an archaic image in the Murcia lecture is as old as philosophy itself: What is the relation between the aesthetic and the ethical? Plato's encomium of love, *Symposium*, may indicate for some the starting point for a philosophical inquiry on the relationship between the good and the beautiful. More interestingly, in his prose hymn of the cosmos, *Timaeus*, and in the *Republic*, Plato proposes to engage the pre-Socratic's treatment of *eoikos* (likeness) as alluding to the notion of telling lies like truth and to the study of the power of images. According to Plato, the modellic account of the cosmos offered by these images in the world is a likely likeness—that is, not only beautiful and truthful but also an orientation for action. Arguably, it's precisely in this sense that Enrique Dussel speaks of the ethical as a cosmic "fact," one that emerges in time, is of it, and makes it. The phrase "sculpting time," used by painters and filmmakers to indicate the power of images, can be used also in this sense: to clarify the relation between the aesthetic act and an ethical action that transforms the current shape of things.[5]

Dussel prefers to point beyond Greece to the cosmology and philosophy of ancient Egypt. Let's provide further documentary evidence of his suggestion that a material criterion for ethics can be found in the archaic cosmology of Egypt and its imagery. In the Inyotef Song, a different emphasis on cosmic dawn and happiness, exaltation and excitement, replaces the more traditional concern with the Osirian west and its connotations of finality and death. Its message "Make holiday, Do not weary of it!" echoes the 1300 B.C.E. Harper's Songs ("Follow your heart as long as you live! . . . Follow your heart and your happiness. Do your things on earth as your heart commands!"). This veritable aesthetic of self and others—follow your desire, eat, drink, and be merry—is a sign of the time during and following the revolutionary pharaoh Akhenaten and his wife Nefertiti, of the ideological upheaval that came in the wake of their intensification of the significance and importance of the presence of the sun disk. Arguably, it caused philosophy to flourish and new ideas that celebrated joy, excitement, and exaltation rather than austere moderation or bodily happiness here and now instead of grim concern for the afterlife, extolling life on earth and "belittling the region [and religion] of the dead."[6]

This message, halfway between aesthetics and the ethical-political, resonates with Dussel's interpretation of the well-known weighing-of-the-heart ceremony. In the Murcia lecture, Dussel himself acknowledged he had taken up this sense of the living body and the material criterion of his lifelong philosophy of liberation from the contrasting structure of the Last Judgment and ancient Egyptian cosmology, its Semitic and Christian iterations, and their theorization in the horizon of classical German philosophy.

2. THE ARTWORK OF THE FUTURE: REENACTING THE QUESTION FOR THE PHILOSOPHY OF LIBERATION

During and after the Murcia lecture and as elaborated further in the 2016 *14 tesis de ética*, in the prologue to the 2017 *Las metáforas teológicas de Marx* (in which Benjamin is invoked once more), as well as, furthermore, in the 2018 "Siete hipótesis para una estética de la liberación," the emphasis falls on the self-positioning of peoples and natural bodies throwing themselves on the side of contrast with the present system of beliefs and signs—that is, as unbelievers or even atheists in relation to current civic theology and its pantheon, presided over by money as its god fetish. Such a materialist position is not contradictory to popular religious ethics, Dussel says, just as there's no contradiction between the latter and atheism provided one posits the question "Atheist in relation to which god?" and responds accordingly, with a likely vision. Hence Dussel's renewed emphasis on Hermann Cohen and his successors: Ernst Cassirer, Franz Rosenzweig, Emmanuel Levinas, and especially Walter Benjamin as well as Ernst Bloch. Dussel sees them (Levinas, Benjamin, and Bloch, the latter two given progressively more importance) as aesthetical-critical readers of the philosophy of history. Whereas for Cohen, the correct way to diagnose the contrasting asymmetries of the state and the situation described by classical German philosophy is to position ourselves as witnesses of poverty and oppression (i.e., in the place of the hungry, poor, foreign body) so as to denounce the state and the situation (which is what prophets do), for Benjamin and the others, such denunciation would be insufficient if it were not accompanied by a likely visualization and action.

133

Which act? What vision? Let's speak of a performative act that will have dramatically intensified the possibilities inherent to the interrupted projects of the past still latent in history but nearly invisible, which are but not yet, so as to reawake them from their slumber in history and us with them. Let's speak of a vision, not just a vision of the future (utopia), but one orienting us in the present, by way of contrasts, to go closer to what is being salvaged from the present in the hearts of those who refuse to heed the present's logic. First comes the positioning of the witness, which is a matter of the intelligent sensibility and sense of the body, not just any body but that natural body that, because it occupies the place of contrast, can denounce it as the symptom of an asymmetry constitutive of the system and of its sense (significance and orientation) as a whole. Such a body or bodies gather and engage in protest appealing to a justice (or a sense of fullness) that is absent and, thus, accompanied by a hope that in the future this justice may be established. Such hope, however, is not the first reason for the protest or the work (of art) being made. We protest (or paint, photograph, etc.) to save the present moment, to make better sense of it. This making sense of and (hopeful) vision in respect of the present as it accelerates toward the future is the second move. But not only is it not the first; it's also insufficient. Thus the third move is to awaken the possibilities coming from the past and inherent to the present, to save them and save the present moment, whatever the future holds. This thing, this not-yet or *possibility*, becomes a sign of the cosmos attached to a natural body in the universe or in a system of signs. Its importance is dramatically intensified as it is opted for or "redeemed" in a likely theory or likeness of the cosmos in the world (an "account of the universe," which has its history as Dussel says), incarnated in the body of the hungry and the oppressed.[7]

In order to avoid an overgeneralized conception of victimhood (We are all victims! We are all privileged as such!), it is important to recall Dussel's tripartite aesthetical-ethical move and add to it a fourth one: that a protest is not principally a collective sacrifice made in the name of some alternative past (Make X Great Again!) or future (It will be better in the next life! It shall be better in the time to come!). Rather, to quote art critic John Berger, another follower of Benjamin, "[to protest] is an inconsequential redemption of the present. The problem is how to live time and again with the adjective inconsequential."[8]

If so, as a further elaboration, a reenactment of our question for the philosophy of liberation could be rephrased as follows: How do we live with the in-consequence and in-completeness, the silent lucidity, of our ethical and political actions? First, notice that the adjective is temporal. Second, the tradition I have just referred to as "silent lucidity" (the *via negativa* of apophatic theology and mystics like Juana Inés de la Cruz but also the reflective silence of ceremonial, theatrical, and cinema gatherings) may have something to teach us about visualization and, in particular, hopeful visualization. Given that the adjective *inconsequential* is temporal, perhaps an adequate response to the question "How do we live in the inconsequence and incompleteness of our ethical actions?" is spatial, provided we move between space and time in a nonreductive manner as it happens—for instance, in a theatrical montage and other forms of visualization. I believe this is what the *via negativa* explored by Dussel's strategy of de-struction and later his discussion of the power of images and visualization (metaphor) but also montage, drawing, and sculpting time (as in Third Cinema, or the Zapatista creolized/*crisol* aesthetic exemplified in *Zapantera Negra*) can help us with.[9]

It's known that the term *de-struction* emerged early on within the philosophy of liberation circle in Argentina, specifically in the wake of Osvaldo Ardiles's appropriation of Heidegger's and Levinas's investigation of the framing of being and in dialogue with the Frankfurt School's critical reading of Marx. Less known is the fact that in the course of such a dialogue, the emphasis falls on an ontological locus, thereby paving the way to an aesthetics of liberation from the outset: this is the (post-Hegelian) insight that the frame and the act of framing must be included in our accounts of being. On the one hand, such a change of standpoint reveals the negative aspect of being, the "not" in the sense of not-yet-in-process or incomplete being. On the other hand, it is as if beneath the ontological text lies another one: it belongs to the order of proximity, gathering, the advent or presentation of the other taking place beyond the order of knowledge and the effects of power. These are the two sides of the project of liberation, oscillating between the silence of negativity and the event of encounter, emerging from Ardiles's 1973 *Bases para una des-trucción de la filosofía en la América indo-ibérica* all the way up to his 1980 *Vigilia y utopía*.

In this context, the term *de-struction* alludes, on the one hand, to existential philosophy "not as a 'philosophy of crisis' but as a 'crisis of philosophy,' a cleansing that opened the doors to contemporary thought, helping us let go, perhaps definitively, of the omnipotence of self-consciousness . . . toward a new reading of Hegel and post-Hegelian social thinking, always from the perspective of the priority of being over thinking."[10] On the other hand, notice how the title *Vigilia y utopía* combines the apophasis of *vigilia*, the silence of words vis-à-vis the always fragmentary essence within all existing objects (incompleteness, the opening of an interval in space-time, the visualization of such an interval that is prior to words), with the need to study the "social being" of utopia. It not only makes explicit Ardiles's and Dussel's challenge to consider face-to-face social relations in order to pave the way "towards the cultural-political specificity of the oppressed in 'Latin America's exteriority'" but also makes a case for the connection between the aesthetic and the ethical early on in the history of philosophies and sociologies of liberation. This is precisely the point where post-Hegelian social thought (for instance, Bloch's or Benjamin's work) meets the challenge that we research what has been referred to as "the utopian human" under the aegis of the encounter (as in Levinas's study of the byways of utopia)—that is, to study the order of the social (of interval and proximity) in terms of the collaboration between oneself and the other as model (as in the case of the appearance of an image in the act of painting) or of the other as such in her incomparable uniqueness.[11]

In Dussel's case, this investigation (via Levinas and Xavier Zubiri but also and most crucially because of his engagement with the issue of belief and disbelief in popular culture and religiosity, together with Ardiles and Juan C. Scannone in Argentina as well as social theorist Orlando Fals Borda in the Caribbean)[12] ends up calling the fundamental character of ontology into question. In accordance with this line of questioning, the source of prophetic vision or utopia lies elsewhere: not in the co-relation between knowing and things out there but rather in the advent or presentation of the ethical relation, the manifestation of the human. In this respect, the emergence of the human from being no longer has the form of conquest, self-affirmation, the highest place in the hierarchy of creation, or the authority of place and origin. Instead, its form is that of outward-oriented motion, or walking (upright) into the light of the other, outward to the other. This motion is also a form of *des-encubrimiento* or dis-(un)covery. Let's add here that if the discovery and conquest of a place cover over or conceal the other, exteriority, and history's incompleteness, through the representation of space-time as an empty vacuum or an enclosed and calculable plane (linear perspective), to uncover what has been covered over is to make present space-time as an exteriority or a void that is full of yearnings, imaginings, and possibilities, as in a visualization—in other words, the discovery of the no-place, the interval, which is the beyond of (and which haunts) every place. The unfolding of such a negativity into possibility and a different beginning (the interval, uchronia, utopia) is of the same kind as the inconsequential nature of our actions, their incompleteness, and the fragmentary essence within all objects. It is because we must learn to live time with the inconsequential time and again that we learn to see ourselves as being in time, of time, but also responsible for the making of different time, understood here as social alterity.

Being escapes framing in this sense: not in the sense of being as such but simply in the sense of incomplete being, of inconsequential being. Moving toward completion (to fullness and justice) means moving toward a social alterity or a different beginning. This is the work of (making) the future: to imagine or visualize such alterity, which is not impossible (in the sense that a square circle is impossible) but merely compossible or not in the concrete context. If so, an adequate response to the question of the temporality of the inconsequential is spatial: to move toward the no-place that haunts every place—in other words, to move beyond the present context and closer and closer to the thing that is being redeemed from the present. This thing is what I call the artwork of the future, which is iconic at least in the sense of the persistence of no-place, of utopia and denunciation throughout the centuries. To avoid political-theological language, let's better speak of iconicity without belief, that which becomes paradigmatic in the hearts of those who refuse the logic of the present. A painter can sometimes do this. A storyteller can sometimes do this. A playwright can sometimes do this. A *palabrero* or shaman can sometimes do this. A *community of values* can sometimes do this. Their refusal becomes "the feral cry, the rage, the humour, the illumination of the women, men and children in a story." These are all ways of making a moment indelible, in the sense in which images when seen and stories when heard and dramatic rituals when they gather us in collaboration can stop the unilinear flow of time "and render the adjective inconsequential meaningless." Such is the artwork of the future.[13]

3. AN AESTHETIC / SOCIAL SCIENCE OF LIBERATION (WITH A PLEA FOR BLACK REALISM)

To be precise, I am seeking to develop an interpretation of Dussel's most recent work—in which an aesthetic turn becomes more evident—as it completes the sequence initiated by the project of de-struction and to suggest a future for the philosophy of liberation with the idea that a thing becomes a sign, a model, a paradigmatic icon, or a likely likeness when it is experienced as having a place in a system (a system of signs, including no-place) or a *universe*, to make Dussel's words ours.[14] This location is its value or importance. Such a thing could be placed in a linear sequence or a repetitive pattern of occurrences, objects, or signs (a syntagm, a historic route, or a linear plot), but at each of its locations or repetitions, this thing (i.e., a cosmic thing like the sun or the living body) is experienced as an object opted for, in the same sense that we opt what to look at and to look for as well as to look forward to, or (evolutionarily speaking) selected from a set of alternatives or possibilities that coexist in just that place in that syntagm or that moment in a historic route, which haunts such a place. The set of excluded possibilities that I have referred to as no-place (utopia, uchronies) constitutes the source of value and importance of all that exists, in existential terms and in terms of visualization as well as in linguistic ones; such is the paradigm.

We may thus reinterpret Dussel's material criterion for an ethics of liberation, the living sense-intelligent body, in connection with the kind of cosmological imagery evoked in the wake of his Murcia lecture as an acknowledgment that, grounded in a variety of contrasts (such as I-thou, above-below, east-west, or north-south), the human body—its parts and functions—will appear or come to be present as iconic signs, as likely likenesses or images (e.g., the heart as the site of desire and the sun's illumination, according to the analogy "as above, so below"). We may also propose to extract a method for a science of the sense of liberation out of Dussel's anadialectical or contrasting perspective on the body as a living, hungry, thirsty, forcibly displaced, ruptured, and rupturing entity, both a sign system and that which sign systems signify.

Philosophers have known for some time that a sign exists as such only in reference to a paradigm or a set of significant but exclusive possibilities. As Dussel puts it, an existent thing in and of the cosmos and its relations become significant only when they can be seen within a contrasting set of other significant things or likenesses of the same ontological totality, or world in the universe, and are successfully accounted for as such—that is, as likenesses in a likely relation, thing to thing, state to state, event to event, any one of which could have been opted for rather than the one actually occurring or in use, all of them existing with equal value or importance and/or coexisting as (latent) possibilities. Ditto, this set of dialectically contrasting possibilities is paradigmatic.[15]

The first task of our science of liberation would be to construct the paradigm: a set of contrasting possibilities according to the vision and from the perspective of the living, sense-intelligent, hungry, thirsty, ruptural, and rupturing body. But let's take stock of the fact that natural bodies and parts not only rarely appear in the company of words; bodies also appear as images before doing so in the company of words. This is a crucial point that Dussel does not make explicit but that I believe follows from his emphasis on natural, living bodies, specifically human sense-intelligent bodies listening to what their eyes tell them about history's rhythms. For natural human bodies, seeing comes before words. The body sees before speaking. A child looks and recognizes before he or she can speak. If so, the second stage of our science of liberation from the perspective of the body is to analogically describe and produce the signifieds, what can be seen, sensed, or perceived even if they seemed invisible before—like the bodies and inventions of the enslaved, the colonized and the disappeared, or the peoples pushed "out of history": to make visible the invisible by means of the works of bodies, artworks, and their relations.

There is also another sense in which seeing comes before words. It is seeing that indicates our place in the surrounding world; we may explain that world with words and useful patterns, but neither words nor the conventional patterns that stabilize certain word agreements can undo the fact that we are surrounded by the cosmos in the world. For instance, the useful *knowledge* that the earth is turning away from the sun and that this accounts for the fact that each morning we *see* the rising sun never quite fits the sight itself. In this sense, there's an exhaustion of words opening toward the uselessness of contemplating a sunrise and its inconsequential nature. And yet we must learn to live time and again with this inconsequence, not only to make it significant, but more precisely to turn it around and transform it into sense and orientation. That's what our collective visualizations do; what painters can do; what storytellers, playwrights, and filmmakers can do: memory work, giving testimony to the persistence of utopia and the search for happiness, and dream work, not merely to help us escape into the dreamscape of other utopian worlds but to make the trip back to the incompleteness of the present situation, to illuminate it, helping us make better sense of it, and then to move upright toward the light of fullness and justice or to acquire a social sense of (ethical and political) orientation. The exhaustion I speak of on the basis of Dussel's aesthetic turn can be understood thus as the silence of useful knowledge and words (connected to a civic theology of utilitarian needs that binds gods and nature to their function—giving us their favor or purifying us) vis-à-vis the manifest presentation and sight of what's coming-to-be. Such is the beginning of critique: starting from the apophatic gesture of a *via negativa* to the visualization of what haunts this place and the present, to save in it and from its predatory logic what lies closer to our hearts, come what may. Exhaustion (of the useful), openness, or incompletion, which may be a fact of the cosmos itself, constitutes the commencement of critique and the opening of the doors of a different perception and beginning.

Black surrealists like Pierre Yoyotte and Wilfredo Lam, the Léros, and René Ménil expressed this much better than I could when they spoke of social convention, plot, and repetition in the following manner: "The Useful—social convention—constitutes the backbone of the bourgeois 'reality' that we want to break."[16] They point out that we must position ourselves in the contrast or ambivalence, "which permits the elimination of the contradiction decreed by logic," the logic of the present, what is and is lacking here and now. To be precise, their criticism of reductive realism and its contradictions (the logic of the present) is aimed at the present's decadent morals that prescribe that before an object of affective value, we must respond with either pure love or pure hate. Such logic always places or "frames" the real and possibility under stringent conditions. The result is a much-reduced sense of the possible. Paradoxically, this state of the situation is taken for the totality of being, all that is and can be, and such an understanding is termed *realism*. It is precisely in this respect that mainstream "realist" philosophies continue to ignore the notion of possibility in its fuller sense and constrain living experience to mere predatory survival. Such realism is, therefore, a sad and reductive one.

It's accompanied by the affect that Ernst Bloch called "eternal pessimism," an indeterminate form of negativity. Such is the affect we express when we are persuaded that our actions would make no difference, that current oppression is tantamount to social death from here onward, and that every attempt to make the world a better, different place will end in tears, as when philosophers speak of "the end of history" or when pundits argue that all attempts to realize utopian visions will inevitably end up becoming totalitarian, as if they knew the end of the story beforehand.[17]

According to the Black surrealists, such indeterminate negativity and the pessimism that accompanies it are in fact the symptoms of a more profound malaise. They refer to its cause as "the misery of desire," arguing that "in order to do justice to capitalism, it is urgent to insist on the economic poverty produced by it, as well as its other consequence—a psychological misery that must be differentiated from the first in its essence, as well as in its processes." Capitalism has received and maintained the poverty that Christian feudalism knowingly sustained and transmitted. "That is the antagonism between the suppressed human emotions of ego-materialistic desires," useful wants or *needs* such as the wish to accumulate all the women in the group and satisfy one's sexual drive regardless of what women want (in violation of the law of incest/reciprocity, as anthropologists and their Amerindian interlocutors would say) or the need for supremacy, on the one hand, and "idealized collective emotions such as the group 'attachments'—family or fatherland, and abstract passions" such as established religion and essentialized culture, on the other. Further, developing their argument along the lines of social psychology, they observe the following:

> Wherever a minority seizes the upper hand in the satisfaction of its own desires, psychological constraints are imposed to moderate the desires of the majority of individuals.
>
> And not only the majority because under the watchful eye of the powerful but oppressed majority, the advantages gained by the oppressors such as the nobility, the clergy or the bourgeoisie, can only be preserved in relative secrecy; this requires

142

a modicum of self-restraint. Sometimes consciously, and more often simply objectively, a hypocrisy both painful and degrading imposes itself on the surplus-value profiteers, and the repression of *desires* by psychological constraints creates an equally shared emotional misery in capitalist society.

In the higher classes, however, wealth offers desire such abundant opportunities that it often overrides constraints. . . . But below a certain level, one not easy to define, at the level of those whose "small properties" distinguish them from the pure proletarians, the *misery of desire* is usually greater than economic poverty. . . .

What results is the original and paradoxical contradiction of capitalism—a form that, on the one hand, develops sublime sentiments and on the other, represses and irritates them, thus preparing a *psychological misery* as intense as the *misery of desire*.

Therefore, if the proletarian minority wants a revolution to solve the economic misery to which emotional misery is linked, the majority of the . . . middle classes, burdened as they are with a moral guilt—reinforced against desire *and* mocked by money—are absolutely ripe for a *counterrevolution of emotions and ideals that is directed against both money and desire, a revolution in which a few material demands will come about hypocritically hidden by repressed emotions.*[18]

The quote may be long, but it is necessary given its significance in today's context. In fact, the insight of the Black surrealists may be more relevant now than it already was back in the 1930s. For we are going through such a counterrevolution, with alt-right and neofascist populists using effectively the local and historical aggravations of psychological misery. We would do well to add to Dussel's emphasis on the living sense-intelligent body (the poor) the Black surrealists' insight that compared to material satisfactions, "the emotional or mystical ones (or those of the horde) have the advantage of a long history. Their infantile victories over primary desires endow them (as in war) with the appearance of paradise." This is how, they teach us, through such a displacement, which reduces the space of institutions and rhetoric (including the power of trope and images) to their persuasive function, and the mediation of sentimental and emotional satisfactions, the oppressors co-opt the middle classes and in doing so manage to contain all the affective aspirations of the 143 majorities and their successive generations. "This was the invention of Hitlerism and Mussolinian fascism" as well as Spanish Francoism, taken up and reinvented for the twenty-first century by those propping up the Trumps, Dutertes, Johnsons, and Bolsonaros of our world. "It was just a matter of masks to forget the money battles after the kisses, and to hide—as if it was dirty—the necessity of love and pleasure. Emotions survive on masks not realities," explains Pierre Yoyotte in his manifesto *Antifascist Significance of Surrealism.*

This is, I believe, the political import of an aesthetic turn within the decolonial turn and the philosophy of liberation. Following the example of the Black surrealists, let's claim an expansive notion of the real that includes what I have called the no-place haunting every place. Following that, let's position ourselves and our science on the side of a surplus of realism. The connection between Black surrealism and Dussel's philosophy of liberation is what the aesthetic turn allows, via the work of Caribbean sociologists like Orlando Fals Borda, whose impact in the very project of a philosophy of liberation has been acknowledged by Dussel himself.[19]

From such a renewed perspective, the contradiction pointed out by Yoyotte and the others appears indeed as symptomatic. As they said, it's "a function of the Useful," of conventional stability and standards. Crucially, conventional stability and standardization exhaust their remit when it comes to the most intense experiences of our lives, when we fall in joyful love, and do not exist in it or in the dream, as Yoyotte observed.[20] When in love, the sight of the beloved has a fullness that no words can embrace or match. This sense of exhaustion, silence, and incompletion, or the apophasis of words and conventional patterns as well as the institutions underpinned by them, is an aesthetic fact—perhaps even an ontological fact—of huge ethical and political significance. For the Black surrealists of the early twentieth century, it indicated their orientation to take flight from "assassinated conventions" and to undertake "the destruction of ideals," as Yoyotte put it in

1934, before Ardiles and Dussel spoke of de-struction. Dussel's initial ethical orientation—termed in 1970 a "destruction of the history of ethics," which in 2003 he situated in the vicinity of Fals Borda's critical sense-intelligent social science (*una sociologia sentipensante para América Latina*) before adding the link to Benjamin and Bloch in the wake of the aesthetic turn announced in the Murcia lecture—is not far at all from that of Yoyotte and the other Black pioneers.

Rather than advancing some "po-mo" cliché (postmodern, postcolonial, etc.) against grand narratives, my point is that the interlocution between the totalizing cosmologies motivating current creolized struggles in the Americas and the turn toward the question of the artwork of the future in the philosophy of liberation, after the de-struction of the history of ethics and the Benjaminian (and Fanonian) *dèrive* of the liberationist approach, has the potential to rekindle one of the most undertheorized elements in the Marxist legacy of the critique of political economy to weaponize it against the neofascists—namely, the picture that expresses the tendency toward political fragmentation resulting from the divisions *within* (not just between) classes and, therefore, the need for like efforts guided by a likely image (a social myth or dialectical image) to overcome such atomization.

NOTES

1. Enrique Dussel, "Walter Benjamin y la Política de la Liberación" (lecture, Universidad de Murcia, Spain, February 27, 2017), accessed December 20, 2018, http://www.youtube.com/watch?v=JuGyjGosmR4; hereafter cited as Murcia lecture. See also Silvia Rivera Cusicanqui, *Sociología de la imagen: Miradas ch'ixi desde la historia andina* (Buenos Aires: Tinta Limón ediciones, 2015), 22–25, for my use of such terms as *visualization* and *memory work* and the distinction between plot and sequence hinted at in this paragraph.

2. Murcia lecture.

3. Ibid.; see Cusicanqui, *Sociología de la imagen*, 23–25. I am also citing Benjamin's *Trauerspiel* on allegory, contrasting sequencing, and anthropographic visualization as "motion according to rhythm and breathing"; Walter Benjamin, *Ursprung des deutschen Trauerspiels* (Frankfurt am Main: Surhkamp Verlag, 1963), 24.

4. See Nicholas Reeves, *Akhenaten: Egypt's False Prophet* (London: Thames and Hudson, 2005), 137–38, for my quotes of the *Great Hymn to the Aten*.

5. Enrique Dussel, *14 tesis de ética: Hacia la esencia del pensamiento crítico* (Madrid: Editorial Trotta, 2016), 15–25, especially 15n1; see also Jenny Brian, *Likeness and Likelihood in the Presocratics and Plato* (Cambridge: Cambridge University Press, 2012), 161–95.

6. Dag Herbørnsrud, "The Radical Philosophy of Egypt: Forget God and Family, Write!," *Blog of the American Philosophical Association*, December 17, 2018, https://blog.apaonline.org/2018/12/17/the-radical-philosophy-of-egypt-forget-god-and -family-write/, for the Harper's Song and my interpretation of the period, which is in contrast with Reeves's; see also Reeves, *Akhenaten*, 135, for a different interpretation and my quotes from the Inyotef Song.

7. Dussel, *14 tesis*, 15n1; Murcia lecture. The three levels of open positioning (as opposed to foreclosed self-affirmation), interpretation, and critique become the three vectors of aesthesis (*áisthesis*) or the subsumption of the physical-cosmic properties of the real in the world in the aesthetic field: (1) openness to the real, (2) constitution of the real as significantly beautiful, and (3) the real thing as incarnating both (1) and (2) in the world or universe. Thereafter, they are presented as three levels of aesthetic openness, production-interpretation, and critique, indicating an orientation from absence to fullness constitutive of the work of art and of the ethical act. See Enrique Dussel, "Siete hipótesis para una estética de la liberación," in *Siete ensayos de la filosofía de la liberación: Hacia una fundamentación del giro decolonial* (Madrid: Editorial Trotta, 2020).

8. See John Berger, *Bento's Sketchbook* (London: Verso, 2011), 79–80, for quotes and some of the ideas in these paragraphs.

9. On this, see Marc James Léger and David Thomas, with Emory Douglas, eds., *Zapantera Negra: An Encounter Between Black Panthers and Zapatistas* (Brooklyn: Common Notions, 2017); and Anne Garland-Mahler, *From the Tricontinental to the Global South: Race, Radicalism, and Transnational Solidarity* (Durham, N.C.: Duke University Press, 2018), especially 36–105, for Third Cinema, the metonymy of color, and the aesthetic roots of today's protest movements. See also Dussel, "Siete hipótesis."

10. Editorial Bonum, "Dos palabras," in *Hacia una filosofía de la liberación latino-americana*, by Osvaldo Ardiles et al. (Buenos Aires: Bonum, 1973), 5. According to the authors, "Philosophy, traditionally understood as a 'theory of liberty,' now hopes to become a 'knowledge of liberation'; to do so it must throw itself, passionately and without reservation, on the side of the denunciation of all objective oppressive totalities, including the concept of 'liberty' itself. It must also try to salvage and rescue the concrete human in his or her incomparable uniqueness and differentiation, that which makes him or her radically 'other.' . . . The risks are high . . . the task difficult insofar as we desire to place ourselves in a position of self-critical lucidity . . . and yet, *every difficult task is as such beautiful* and because of that worthwhile. It's worth taking an absolute risk, as old Plato said"; ibid., 5–6.

11. Osvaldo Ardiles, "Bases para una des-trucción de la filosofía en la América Indo-Ibérica," in *Hacia una filosofía*, 7–26; and Osvaldo Ardiles, *Vigilia y utopía: Problemas de la filosofía contemporánea* (Mexico City: Universidad de Guadalajara, 1980). Also Osvaldo Ardiles, "Instructivo," in *Montaje temático de la obra de Bertolt Brecht*, ed. O. Ardiles and W. Vogt (Guadalajara: Universidad de Guadalajara, 1990). For quotes, see Orlando Lima Rocha, "Osvaldo Ardiles y

las Filosofías de la Liberación: Elementos para una ubicación de su pensamiento," in *Revista Pelícano*, vol. 1 (Córdoba: Agosto, 2015), 59–72, at 65, accessed August 5, 2019, http://revistas.bibdigital.uccor.edu.ar/index.php/pelicano/issue/view/305; and Adriana Arpini, "La filosofía de la liberación," in *Revista de Filosofía Latinoamericana: Argentina entre el optimismo y el desencanto*, ed. Clara Alicia Jalif de Bertranou (Mendoza: Instituto de Filosofía Argentina y Americana, Facultad de Filosofía y Letras, Universidad de Cuyo, 2007), 192–230. See also Ernst Bloch, *The Principle of Hope*, vol. 1 (Cambridge, Mass.: MIT Press, 1995), 370–75; and Emmanuel Levinas, preface to *Utopie et socialisme*, by Martin Buber (Paris: Aubier-Montaigne, 1977), 10.

12. See Enrique Dussel, "Philosophy in Latin America in the Twentieth Century: Problems and Currents," in *Latin American Philosophy: Currents, Issues, Debates*, ed. Eduardo Mendieta (Bloomington: Indiana University Press, 2003), 11–56, at 32, for acknowledgment of his debt to Ardiles and Fals Borda as part of a "Latinamericanist ontological current [which] developed this philosophy with a political consciousness, from an analysis of continental reality as it was practiced by nascent Latin American critical social science . . . and arising from militant engagement." He references Orlando Fals Borda, *Sociología de la liberación* (Bogotá: Siglo XXI, 1968). See also Orlando Fals Borda, *Una sociología sentipensante para América Latina* (Bogotá: Siglo XXI and CLACSO, 2015), 9–19 (for the notion of sense-intelligence or *sentipensante*), 81 (for the "stereophonic" register of social science), and 439 (for the concept of "rhythm" in relation to the dynamics of history).

13. Berger, *Bento's Sketchbook*, 80.

14. Dussel, "Siete hipótesis," 104, 125n341.

15. Ibid.

16. Etienne Léro, Thélus Léro, René Ménil, Jules Marcel Monnerot, Michel Pilotin, Maurice Sabas-Quitman, Auguste Thésée, and Pierre Yoyotte, "Légitime Défense Manifesto" (1932), in *Black, Brown & Beige: Surrealist Writings from Africa and the Diaspora*, ed. Franklin Rosemont and Robin D. G. Kelley (Austin: University of Texas Press, 2009), 36–38, at 37.

17. Ernst Bloch, *Despedida de la utopía?* (Madrid: A. Machado Libros, 2017), 23–25, distinguishing between the "eternal look *ad pessimum*, the no of the expert," and "a look *ad pessimum* such as that of the detective, which Marx knew well, attentive to the causes and interested in remedying them." Whereas the earlier corresponds to what Hegel would term a "reified negation" and the highest degree of defeatism, the latter corresponds to a "determinate negation," which puts the finger on the thing that's lacking here and now, which lies closest to the heart of those who recognize the "incompleteness of insufficient being" and denounce it as "insufficient and terrorizing." It uncovers the lie of defeatism and "turns it into outrage and rebellion."

18. See Pierre Yoyotte, "Antifascist Significance of Surrealism," in *Black, Brown & Beige*, 42–44, for this long quote and the shorter ones in the previous paragraph.

19. Enrique Dussel, *Philosophy of Liberation*, trans. Aquilina Martinez and Christine Morkovsky (Maryknoll, N.Y.: Orbis Books, 1985), 32.

20. Léro et al., "Légitime Défense Manifesto," 37.

CHAPTER 8

An Introduction to Liberatory Decolonial Aesthetic Thought

A South-South Path, from Indigenous and Popular Thought in América and from the Sense of *Xu* in Chinese Painting

Alejandro A. Vallega

It appears possible to philosophize in the periphery . . . only if the discourse of the philosophy of the center is not imitated, only if another discourse is discovered. To be different, this discourse must have another point of departure, must think other themes, must come to distinctive conclusions by a different method.

—ENRIQUE DUSSEL, *PHILOSOPHY OF LIBERATION*[1]

Así es la vida, tal
como es la vida, allá, detrás
del infinito; así, espontáneamente,
delante de la sien legislativa.
So it's life, such
as life is, over there, behind
the infinite; spontaneously
in front of the head's legislative temples

—CESAR VALLEJO, "ESCARNECIDO ACLIMATADO AL BIEN"[2]

The title of the conference at which this chapter was first read (Decolonizing Ethics) is as ambitious as it is difficult. It not only seeks a place in which liberation and decoloniality touch but gives to this relation a place, the ethical. The ethical that must be decolonized, liberated. The place of gathering then would seem to be the urgency for decolonial liberation: urgency that arises as a force, a drive, a pulsation. How do we understand this force, this drive? I believe that it is in engaging this pulsation that a decolonial philosophy of liberation may find fruitful—indeed, distinct—pluriversal fecund paths. In the following chapter, I depart from and think with Enrique Dussel's philosophy of liberation, as I first show the aesthetic basis of philosophy of liberation and then develop this insight into an aesthetics of liberation. Aesthetics here is delimited and understood not as the study of the beautiful and works of art but as the preconceptual and prelinguistic dimensions of the temporalizing-spacing movement called traditionally "life" but now rethought in terms of the affective, memorial, and bodying levels of livingdying in a gerundive sense. As will become evident, my reflections also move progressively away from westernizing thought, from Dussel, to Kusch, to ancient or classical Chinese thought.[3]

1. AT THE LIMIT OF THE AESTHETIC DIMENSIONS OF LIBERATORY DECOLONIAL THOUGHT

For Enrique Dussel, concrete life is the universal material principle that calls for and grounds all politics and ethics of liberation.[4] In the *Ethics of Liberation*, this principle is itself grounded on sensibility. As Dussel explains in the *Ethics*, the universal material principle of all ethics arises as "a principle of 'corporeality' as a 'sensibility' that contains the pulsative cultural-valorizing (hermeneutic-symbolic) order of all norms, actions, microphysical structures, institutions or systems of ethical being."[5] Here one finds a fundamental aesthetic dimension inseparable from the first material principle or pulsating life that directs the ethics and politics of liberation. I want to push here and complicate the "hermeneutic-symbolic" by bringing it to touch on the preconceptual, as I suggest that corporeality as sensibility must refer not only to the gesture, image, and word but to the aesthetic dimension of understanding: as I see it, the ground of concept, logics, institutions, and ideologies—that is, the very happening of the composing of consciousness—bears and occurs with prerational elements, such as affectivity, emotion, memorial rather than historical memory (trauma, loss, involuntary memory), concreteness (*concrescere*), and the temporalizing-spacing movement in bodying, which in various configurations we call "bodily." As Dussel indicates, this aesthetic sensibility traverses the various levels of life and the production, reproduction, and development of life. Furthermore, since the material and formal principles, as well as the principle of feasibility, occur under this sensibility, the very possibility of a politics as well as an ethics of liberation will depend on keeping attuned to that sensibility, on remaining with such grounding originary preconceptual sensibilities/experience.

Life here leads to a preconceptual level. The sensibility in question appears already in *Philosophy of Liberation* (1975–77). In this work, the grounding experience for liberatory thought is indeed a sensibility. In chapter 2, "From Phenomenology to Liberation," one finds that at the heart of liberatory movement appears pulsating life, revealed as a fundamental relation of/in alterity.[6] For the capitalist vision and for the coloniality of power, existence is a matter of production of value and meaning, grounded on subjective rationalism, the *ego conquiro* and then the ego cogito, over against a world to be conquered and dominated by willful force and utilitarian calculative reasoning. This system grasps the world as a matter of thinghood: the world, nature is a collection of things out there. Thus existence happens as a tension between a subjective interior consciousness and the extended world outside of it. At the same time, the ego cogito recognizes itself as the rational entity among entities. Thus existence, Being, comes to be composed of entities, rational and nonrational, and the space-time between them. The world is a world of things, and the logic and concepts that sustain such intelligibility and perception are structured accordingly. To be human in such a schema is to be a double being, mind and body, subject to the laws of nature as well as free in one's internal rational consciousness. In terms of the coloniality of power and knowledge, we are speaking of the reification of living into a specific concept of "life":

at its center, rational subjectivism, the separation of body and mind, the exclusion of the aisthetic from reasoning, and the leveling of the phenomena as the other of instrumental calculative rationalism, as reason's genitive negativity, "nature." It is this disposition that will develop and populate modernity with the violent, irrational, racial, and capitalist power differential so well identified by Aníbal Quijano. Dussel calls this traditional way of being—this modality of being-in-the-world that underlies the totalizing concept of Being—"proxemia."[7]

In contrast to this way of interpreting and encountering existing as mere physical and conceptual phenomena, Dussel introduces the experience of proximity: "It is a matter, then, of beginning with somebody who is encountered beyond the world of ontology or Being, anterior to the world and its horizon. From proximity-beyond physical closeness, anterior to the truth of Being—we come to the light of day when we appear, when our mother gives us birth. To give birth (maternal act) is to appear (filial act)."[8] Here the world of Being proves insufficient with respect to the modality of being-in-the-world of the human. Humans, unlike things, appear through a relationship of radical proximity, a face-to-face that reveals one's place and sense of existing out of that very being-with-others always already in distinct senses. Dussel's explication reaches back to the moment we are in the womb. It is that proximity in alterity—that most proximate being with another and yet being distinct in that relation—that is the foundation for the ethical. In the natal experience, there is always already two and yet one.[9] This of course becomes more evident when one considers transthought, the fact that to be human is to be humanx. Our consciousness then appears in utmost proximity and exteriority in/with a distinct other at the same time: this I call radical exteriority, since the principle for communication is in the difference that is always already operative in the claim to identity. In other words, identities and dialogues are given in difference and not sameness, not through universality but in pluriversal distinctness. Commonality is always predicated upon difference, found in the encounter of distinct ways-of-being (gerundive). As I understand this insight, communication is interpellation and not a dialectic of identity in which difference will serve as a negativity of (genitive) a totality or autonomous heterogeneous identity. Indeed, Dussel writes,

"To approach in justice is always a risk because it is to shorten the distance towards a distinct freedom [*una libertad distinta*]."[10] Justice, as all our relationships and senses of existence (from the arche or beginning through to the eschatological moment or the end), happens out of a fundamental human proximity in distinctness—that is, as we approach the other as other and as we sustain our relationships in the consciousness of the other's distinctness, hence the danger of rejection that grounds justice. Mother, lover, brother, friend, animal, earth, but also work of art, culture—these are found in light of relations of proximity sustained by profound radical exteriority. Only out of such a sensibility and in attunement to it may we begin to recognize life in its pulsation, and it is thus that one may recognize the dignity and potency of life as such.

One implication is that the ground of philosophy of liberation is not rationality or conceptual knowledge alone but the very movement of thought; its quickening occurs out of preconceptual sensibility. More specifically, I want to underscore that this radical exteriority is found at the affective, concrete, and memorial dimensions of the movement of existing. I do not use the word *bodily* because *body* too often already imports a sense of thinghood that undermines the issue of the dynamic way of being-with through which one finds identities as mental and bodily. In my view, body, like gender and race, is a term that operates as a border, a site of resistance and configuration, an ecological attunement through which one negotiates existing by engaging lineages, transforming, and imagining identities in the process.

But if life is such movement, then speaking of life is not sufficient: living in its gerundive sense will be much more fitting, since in the active gerundive life is heard its transformative resisting and spacing temporalizing dynamics. However, this is not to deny identity but to gain a position from/with/through which to engage living-life, in contrast to life as primarily phenomena, events of fact, a matter of subjective rational consciousness and its "other" (genitive) "nature," of written history and institutional determinations.

In my discussion of Dussel's sense of proximity, I have drawn a sense of life as gerundive movement that is aesthetic, transformative, always already distinct, and not necessarily determined by things, their presence and logic, or the ways of representational thinking determined by the need to measure, manipulate, and produce being(s). Furthermore, I have also underscored that the very insight into liberatory decolonial thought is preconceptual, at the limit if not outside rational utilitarian ways of comprehending the movement of existing in living.

At the same time, with this insight, I want to bring the discussion to some profound difficulties; the need for liberation and a decolonial turn remains no longer at the conceptual, logical, historic-dialectical, or institutional levels. The oppressed, excluded, exiled, and colonized experience their situation and its perpetuation also at preconceptual levels. My point here is that what appears in Dussel's works as the material condition gives way into the aesthetic condition, not in the sense of works of art, but in the sense of the affective, concrete, emotional, and memorial ways of coloniality. This much one already finds in Frantz Fanon's work on psychiatry, as well as in his famous chapter on the condition of the negro in *Black Skin, White Masks*, where he brings us into "heptic" bodily dimensions of colonized-being.[11] Moreover, the issue here is as much interior as exterior, thus breaking the Cartesian model of existence, since it refers us to the entire psyche, to levels of temporalizing-spacing, desiring, projecting, configuring archetypes, to the somatic-horizontal-understanding, the bodying of living. As I have discussed extensively in *Latin American Philosophy: From Identity to Radical Exteriority*, this aesthetic dimension presents an aporetic moment for any liberatory decolonial thinking, since concepts, goals, projections, historical memory, institutions, new ideas and ideologies, all of these arise in light of the aesthetic, and this means that for as long as there is not a decolonizing of these dimensions of psyche, liberation and decoloniality cannot occur sufficiently.[12] In fact, I would venture that it is perhaps because of this dimension of coloniality and power that revolutions often repeat the errors of their oppressors. One should also at least keep in mind that while the eventual reification of the periphery as a new center appears as a necessary outcome in Dussel's dialectical sense of philosophy of liberation, the potential of the periphery's decolonizing affirmations can be seen as other than fated to become the center if one thinks with the arising of the periphery in their concrete transforming movement of livingdying—in other words, in particular as conceived beyond Western thought (a case in point, Andean Indigenous thought, its cyclical temporalizing movement, the sense of "estar" when understood along with *Pachakuti*, as does Rodolfo Kusch in *Popular and Indigenous Thought in América*).[13]

153

As we have just heard, it is not enough to rehearse the analysis of the coloniality of power and knowledge, to identify and critique its structures, to turn the harrow to one's archeological past to critique and deconstruct. The issue is a turn in the sensibility that situates one's thought and from which concepts are wrought, a turn with and from one's concrete living in departure / beyond the senses of "life" in light of which critique and reason are formulated and take new forms of expression, always reverting to domination. In the very mouth, in the harrow or frame of the teeth of the way of being so well invoked by the term *homo homini lupi*, one's situation is not theoretical. Rather, as Professor Dussel reminds us in *Philosophy of Liberation*, unlike the cat who may play with the mouse, for the mouse, living is a matter of "life and death." I think that this formulation only has a chance if it is taken from "life" in its racist instrumentalist rationalist capitalist and neocapitalist globalizing drive. I want to turn, to leap here and then to liv-ing, concretely, seminally said, to livingdying (gerundive).[14]

But how do we engage in this leaping toward livingdying? How would one come to think through and with the dynamic articulate experiencings in/with/through which living moves? In what follows, I move toward liberatory decolonial thinking by way of first interpolating Rodolfo Kusch's engagement with popular and Indigenous thinking and then through a second interpolation with the introduction of the Chinese character *xu*. But first I address the question of living in the gerundive and "life" in liberatory decolonial thought.

2. GERUNDIVE LIVING

If philosophy is liberatory and decolonial, the thought that articulates the distinct situation critically and affirmatively leaps to take risks and to come to pass in its arising. The thought of liberation cannot find its fitting path in being grasped as something to be given through an account of it offered by a subject in the sense these terms operate in/with/through westernized modernity. Moreover, living is movement, and hence one seeks a thinking that is a transport, a traveling exilic flight. Therefore, no final conclusion will follow from living except that of a temporalizing-spacing movement, neither inside nor outside but an in-between, a *transito, transitus, transire*, literally "going across," in the sense of transformative passages. This articulate movement of life, concrete, irreverent, hungry, hard-as-rock-malleable-as-pulp, at times far on the horizon, at times the horizon of a past that welcomes and threatens—such temporalizing-spacing awakens us into and toward a determinate physicality, again, a bodying as a portal to concrete originary transformation. This movement must resist its first habit, to become a matter of gravity, "bodily"—that is, resist being inscribed "naturally" into the modern economy of body over mind, welcomed through inclusive exclusion into the house of the totality of Being.

Perhaps philosophy that is liberatory disciplines one to living *sin mas*, from/in/through the situation with which one finds selves, meanings, directions—that is, in living that is only living if without redemption or alibi, in/with/through the unjustifiable pulsation of living: corruptible, subtle, ephemeral, memorial, arising in coming to pass, hence livingdying germinal life.[15] I find such living echoes in Dussel's ethics of liberation through his quotation from Fabien Eboussi Boulaga's *Crisis of the Muntu*:

> Time passes and returns, the force that expands and begins again manifests the eternity of Power in its incessant emanation and expansion from its origin. . . . Periodicity is the substantial time of things. . . . Everything is alternation and rhythm. . . . Rhythm is vital. . . . It is rhythm which produces ecstasy, that flowing out of one's self that is identified with the vital force. . . . It would not be exaggerated to affirm that rhythm is the *architectural framework of the self*, which for the human being of the civilization for which this philosophy is expounded, is the most fundamental experience, which

eludes all of the trappings of malign genius [as Descartes would put it], which remains free of all doubt, and which is *Je danse, donc je vie* [I dance, therefore I am alive].[16]

155

But how does one think with such liberatory movement, in departures, at the limits and beyond the single auspice of onto-theological and later onto-technological and rationalist "identity," "subjectivity," and their "freedom"? Can one engage in a decolonial way such that the epistemic structures that sustain modernity, the subject, thinghood-nature, its expansive logical teleology of production . . . will move, shake, resonate onto distinct rhythms?

3. "VER PARA SENTIR": THE AESTHETIC OR AFFECTIVE DYNAMIC DIMENSION OF LIBERATORY DECOLONIAL THOUGHT

In Quechua, the term for "life" is *kawsai*, which means energy that may be engaged or drawn. *Kawsai* also refers to the temporalizing-spacing in-between life and death. *Kawsai* then refers us to the movement of living that is livingdying-birthing, the germinal movement. As such, living appears also in a word in Quéchua and Aymara impossible to fully translate or grasp: *pacha*, which means space, place, depth, time, the state of affairs, the cosmos, and, with the term *Pacha-mama*, the living cosmos. These terms, although clearly distinct, are relational and must be understood simultaneously. *Pacha* in turn refers to three inter-active elements: *ana-pacha*, *kai-pacha*, and *uku-pacha*, which mean sky, mountains and valleys, and the depths of the earth, respectively. Existence, livingdying, is the circular movement between sky, mountains, and deep earth. But the issue is how this is thought in some of the Andean Indigenous traditions. I will turn briefly here to Rodolfo Kusch's *Indigenous and Popular Thinking in Latin America*.

As Kusch explains, for us, existence, the world, is populated by objects. Indeed, the very term *ob-jectum* bespeaks a world made up of things thrown in front of us, "a reality before the subject."[17] This reso-nates with Dussel's distinction we saw earlier between the proxemic, which refers to the objectum, and the proximity, or the "human to human," as Dussel puts it. As we will see now, in contrast to Dussel, in the case of Kusch, we move away from the subject.

For Kusch, two terms from the Aymara introduce things in their manner of disclosure in Andean thinking. *Cunasa* refers to things as "anything." And the term *yaa* refers to things with a distinct attribute, not only in terms of physical attributes, but more importantly for us in terms of things being either favorable or unfavorable, auspicious or inauspicious in terms of the cosmological movement of the *Pacha*. The language shows us that this thinking is not focused on things as objects but on their dynamic movement. The words aim to articulate happenings, how something happens, "the way of doing," and not a final result or effect. The example Kusch gives is the verb *to carry* in Aymara, which is conjugated depending on the way the carrying is done: whether the one carrying is person or animal, whether that which is being carried is heavy, light, or long.

The point is that in Aymara, movements, the processes of becoming, are registered before things. What is said then is not meant as an abstract idea of a thing "out there," but it indicates the modality of a thing's happening. And such understanding refers us to a distinct sensibility: one does not understand with/through an analytical or rational logical process but with one's emotional feelings, which are not rationally determined. One could say that each experience's happening has a certain tonality that is felt. Now the issue is not to replace things or rationality but to begin to realize that understanding may be much broader than as narrowly construed and, with its broadening, to begin to understand and experience the coming to pass in becoming through distinct necessary aesthetic sensibilities.

Kusch elegantly says that in this way of understanding, one "sees to feel."[18] It is not that one does not see things, the world, but that seeing in terms of an objective world "out there" is only an indication of another dimension of understanding. Grounded on emotion, affect, and their concrete undergoing or happenings, understanding refers to aesthetic sensibilities: "Emotion is what drives one in the face of reality."[19] This means that reality is not experienced as the stage of stable things out there. The kind of assumed stability granted to things and their seeming unchanging static qualities gives way to insight into the movement of becoming in passing away. Things in the world appear through a modal understanding in which one understands reality through affect and as the unveiling of auspicious or inauspicious aspects or moments of becoming. This is why Kusch writes that "the indigenous person registers reality as the affect it exercises on him before registering it as simple perceptual connotation."[20] Understanding happens with an emotional affectivity that focuses on the intense movement of becoming that is beyond the world of things, on a movement or happening that is ultimately cosmological and yet concrete. Indeed, Kusch finds that in contrast to other terms, the Aymara word *utcatha* is a term for being-in-the-world more fitting to Indigenous "feeling or sensibility" ("mas propio del sentir indigena").[21] The *ut* in *utcatha* relates to "dwelling at home" (*estar en casa*) and in the form *utcaña*, to the seat or chair and also to "the mother or womb where woman conceives."[22] *Utcatha* indicates a manner of living linked "to concepts of shelter and germination."[23] A similar and certainly enriching discussion of these concepts occurs in Maria Lugones's "Towards a Decolonial Feminism," where Lugones takes up Filomena Miranda's distinct sense of "living well" (*suma qamaña*) by being *chachawarmi*.[24] Lugones sets out by discussing Miranda's explanation about the meaning of the words *qamaña* and *utjaña*, terms usually translated as "living." *Utjaña* refers to the *uta*—that is, to dwell in the community and the communal land. For Filomena Miranda, living in the sense of *qamaña* is impossible without living in the sense of dwelling within the community on the communal lands (*utjaña*). Here the seat or womb bears a fuller sense, since for Miranda, *utjaña* requires that she take a leading role in the community, sometimes as father (*chacha*), sometimes as mother (*warmi*). But as is the case with ancient Andean thought, the role is not a matter of an either/or, but *chachawarmi* is one term, a unity—that is, in the sense of a distinctness held in germinal unity. One finds here a sensibility that understands with the happening of existing livingdying that is always linked to the cosmological.

In his analysis, Kusch is not saying that Indigenous people feel rather than know (a westernized binomial presupposition); he, as does Lugones, is showing that Indigenous thought happens in a broader range of understanding and knowledge found through aesthetic sensibilities and the discipline of such profound affective aesthetic understanding, ways of aesthetic understanding we hardly use in westernized thought.[25]

4. *XU*: MOVING AT THE EDGE OF SILENCE AND EMPTINESS

In the same paragraph we were just discussing, Kusch concludes that "the indigenous take reality . . . as a screen without things but with intense movement."[26] The movement of livingdying-birthing is not related to a static ontic ontology; there is not a material teleology of potential things and potential egological reasoning or grasping of reality.[27] Indeed, the movement of livingdying is a dance in emptiness. This does not mean meaninglessness but merely that perceptual and conceptual experiences arise in movements, not other than the movement as movement, concrete rhythmic livingdying played out in/with emptiness and silence.[28]

Emptiness, the empty screen, is not a thing and also is not the absence of a thing. The dialectic of appearing and not appearing is not followed here. Moreover, thought is not a representation of an *x* something and therefore is not the abstract operation in absence of a representation. Rather, emptiness does not follow the potentiality-actuality schema in terms of things that are, not as the privation of presence in terms of things; emptiness is the silence of the movement in which the world happening appears and resonates. But the point here is that although not understood in terms of entities, existing is experienced, interpreted, and undergone, and this experiencing or understanding is different from the understanding available to utilitarian subjective rationalism and its abstract logic. This is because one engages existing-living without an ontology and teleology (ideal or factual) the likes of westernized thought. As a result, one finds a living-existing revealed as a holding-freeing movement, a cosmological germinal dance of livingdying-birthing. In order to develop this sense of emptiness further, I will turn now to Chinese traditional painting, a millenary tradition that springs with calligraphy, a writing-painting that remains at the heart of Chinese thought to date. In doing so, I am seeking a sensibility in thought not determined by rationalist subjectivism and its natural ontology or objectification of living. The point is to turn to a way of thinking that permits the release from such ontology in order to be able to engage that emptiness and silence one finds not only in Chinese painting, poetry, and thought but also analogously with Andean Indigenous thought's sense of dynamic germinal living as discussed by Rodolfo Kusch.

Guo Xi's remarkably complex classic *Early Spring* (1072) offers the occasion for engaging some of the complex aspects of Chinese classical painting.[29] Traditionally the aim of Chinese painting and poetry is the poetic feeling or charm experienced from and with the energy of existing, a sense hardly translatable into the term/concept of *nature*. This movement finds articulation through the tension between two aesthetic elements: "void or emptiness" (*xu*) and "solidity" (*shi*).[30] Atmosphere, feeling, and the poet/painter's vision are fully engaged and conveyed only if and when one enters the temporalizing/spacing of the tension between void or emptiness (*xu*) and the solid (*shi*). As Cao Jun, one of the major exponents of this tradition in contemporary Chinese painting, indicates in his collected writings, "The criterion for assessing whether a painting is good or not lies in the arrangement of *Xu* void or emptiness and *Shi* the solid, which requires an artist to value the '*Xu*,' in his painting."[31] In other words, one must turn toward emptiness, silence.

Existence's momentum and experience may be engaged by remaining with this tension, and this means that the painter must be able to engage in an articulate manner that which is not objectively present/absent. Thus as in *Early Spring*, in traditional Chinese painting (which is called *shan shui*; literally "mountain water"), often mountains, rivers, and land appear shrouded in a mist or covered by clouds. In this way, a kind of density and opacity sets the feeling of the painting toward nonobjective understanding in the engagement of emptiness. In other instances, in mountain and water paintings, the background is left blank (as is the case in the high mountain sky in Guo Xi's painting). These two aspects refer to the poetic and atmospheric force of the paintings, but more importantly, they are an essential part of engaging the energy and movement of existing in its distinct density and sense. The aim of the painter is not to give an image of things, as if photographed or a matter of scientific fact. Rather, the issue is to capture the atmosphere of the moment, of the distinct happening, the sense and energy of living, by being exposed to the dynamic movement of existing/living. This is why the empty spaces in Chinese painting are not passive or neutral as in most of Western painting but active to the point of providing the vibrancy of the picture.[32]

Interestingly, Chinese painting is not done en plein air, as was the case with Western impressionism's vivid concern with nature and its atmosphere. Chinese traditional painting is done in the studio. And this means that the painter would work not from historical fact or the impression of things but from memorial experience—that is, by looking into the feeling and bodying memorial dimensions—in a kind of reminiscing or recollecting. This recalling would require immense concentration, since no image could capture what the painter seeks: the feeling of the living experience, its energy. Indeed, *xu* works in distinct degrees through the handling of each line, brushwork, and color-splashing. This is a discipline well beyond technical skill that requires listening and seeing to feel, an attunement of heart-body-mind in being-with the movement of existing/living. While *shi* can be depicted in a conscientious way, *xu* is the outcome of aesthetic sensibility that does not rely purely on things, and therefore it is ultimately indescribable. This is why Cao Jun writes that *xu* "is a kind of artistic state, other than a kind of ability."[33]

The blank spaces and opacities have a further significance. In the play of *shi* (the solid) and *xu* (void or emptiness), paintings find their ultimate vividness and strength, and this occurs when the viewer engages emptiness and through this living and existing. Thus the master painter knows to leave space for the image to be gathered as it is viewed. Such gathering of sense and image requires the affective-aesthetic involvement of each singular viewer, an involvement that is nonrepresentational and yet understood, undergone through aesthetic understanding. I might add that in this under-standing, the subject goes under to recover out of emptiness to stand with that which is seen and in finding a perspective (this is a process along the lines of what I previously called "bodying"). This occurs at the physical as well as the psychic level: the painting or poem can only be understood, undergone through the movement of heart-mind, an understanding that does not separate body-heart-mind (a profound distinction from Western art). Through this experience, not only are image, sense, and viewer config- ured, but the viewer comes into and out of the becoming momentum of existing and through this into living.

Xu is not nothing; it is the opening onto the non-ontic-ontological movement of living, and it is not understood through the epistemic system of post-Cartesian Western subjectivism and natural ontology. Whereas in Western painting the blank spaces are neutral and passive, in Chinese painting, emptiness (*xu*) is active and originary through the tension with the inverse solidity of the world (*shi*). The aesthetic dimen- sion of thought with *xu* operates not over against reason but in and with the movement or happening in/with which coming to presence, identity, representation, and the logic of subjective rational knowledge is configured. Emptiness affords one the engagement with the sense of the movement and density of existing without the a priori gravity of thinghood and rationalist utilitarian subjectivism of westernized knowledge. Out of silence and emptiness, the dance of world-ing may be engaged in, through, and with them. At the same time, as sinolo- gist and philosopher François Jullien points out, emptiness in painting, poetry, and thought is not heroic or tragic but "bland," in the sense of setting one's sensibilities beyond the pragmatic search for the essence or the control of things. Emptiness does not mean, nor does it have value, nor is it a first and only rational principle.

To speak of "feeling" and "emptiness," of "atmosphere" and "mood," may immediately sound abstract if not like a form of outdated romanticism to the Western ear, particularly given our emphasis on historical and scientific facts and on the separation of the aesthetic from reason and our dedication to the production and classification of things and virtual pecuniary value. But a close look at Chinese painting reveals that not only is emptiness felt in the works, but atten- tiveness to *xu* does not take us away from con-crete life. Instead, as the word *con-crete* indicates in its Latin source *con-crescere*, or to grow with, through the aesthetic engagement with *xu*, one is exposed with/ through the very elemental and originary rhythm and movement that underlie and occur with every moment of existing/living. In listening out of the silence of emptiness, one understands living through the elemental energies westernized thinking calls, among other names, "life," "nature," "existence," and ultimately "Being."

One finds this same aesthetic gerundive feeling throughout contemporary Chinese art. This is clear if one takes, for example, some of the works in the exhibit "Ink Art: Past as Present in Contemporary China" at the Metropolitan Museum of Art in New York between December 2013 and April 2014.[34] In *A Book from the Sky* (1987–91) by Xu Bing, there are four volumes filled with four thousand invented characters. Xu Bing is a master printer, and the work he does, the books and four thousand made-up characters, put into question the specificity of language, meaning, and production and the perpetuation of institutions through the way of understanding the world specific to books—that is, history. It is from emptiness that these books speak, and emptiness remains inseparable from things at their limits in the great alphabet of a silent and empty nonlanguage language. In Gu Wenda's *Mythos of Lost Dynasties Series—I Evaluate Characters Written by Three Men and Three Women* (1985), the judgment and evaluation of the characters happen in light of the empty background of the paper, which places the operation and claim of power in relation to emptiness, and ultimately the operation of power must be dissolved into the emptiness of the background. In *Family Tree* (2001), Zhang Huan engages emptiness in his body or bodying, as the characters cover him to the point of his disappearing into opacity, beyond language and signification (one may think of Anzaldúa's bodying). Finally, *xu* echoes and resonates in its profundity and blandness in the minimalist canvases of Qiu Shihua. His "Untitled" (1996) is well known as an example of "serene blandness" paintings. Her subtle paintings are not representational or abstractions. As do the other works, this painting remains with the tension between *shi* and *xu*. Before moving to the conclusion, I should add here one more painter, Wu Shanzhuan. In his work *Character Image of Black Character Font*, one sees the influence of calligraphy, as the character becomes through the contrast and tension between *xu* and *shi*, between presence and erasure, ambiguity and emptiness: in this work, the graphic mark—and with it, writing—remains held in midair between emptiness (the background, in Western terms) and the solidity of the world (the calligraphy-like strokes), held as one is also held between that temporalizing-spacing, taken up by the intensity that reveals living in the tension of becoming. In all five cases, emptiness does not figure a mere withdrawal from things and society and its reality; rather, it operates as a non-space-time, as elemental in the spatializing-temporalizing movement that transforms the immediate, utilitarian concerns with and the perception of things, identities, ideologies, and objective valuation of existence. Much like the "clave" in Latin music, which disappears, as it is often not played during the tune and yet organizes the rhythm, *xu* (emptiness) remains with living, opening it to its livingdying seminality, to the repetition and rhythmic understanding of becoming (to say it in terms of ritual and Kusch's analysis of Indigenous altiplano consciousness).

163

Ultimately, through this brief discussion, I have wanted to open a decolonial option—that is, not only is there nothing behind the appearing of the world, but engaging living through such a nonontological or nontranscendental idea makes possible engaging life as a concrete gerundive originary or germinal movement in departure, at the limit, and beyond westernized thinking and the coloniality of power and knowledge.

5. CLOSING REMARKS: TOWARD A LIBERATORY DECOLONIAL AESTHETICS

Given the density of the discussion, in closing, I should take a couple lines to rehearse my central hypothesis: as we saw in the penultimate section of the discussion on Kusch's work, "life" may be better engaged in terms of dynamic or gerundive or seminal livingdying (rather than the binary opposition between life and death). In the last section, in taking up *xu*, one finds a certain alterity operative in all determinations of identity and ultimately in the very dynamic of living. Here emptiness figures a certain openness beyond the totalizing westernized reification of living into egological subjectivity and natural ontology, into presence and representation, and into the infinite production of meaning in such terms—elements central to the power differential of the coloniality of power and knowledge. The openness occurs as these basic epistemic expectations or structures are displaced, decentered. This openness/displacement is found in senses of emptiness in Indigenous Andean thought and Chinese thought—that is, in modalities of seminal livingdying that have traditionally been excluded from philosophical knowledge through their association with magic, mythical thinking, the idea of the soul, and other obscuring ideas projected from the central position of the rationalist utilitarian ego cogito. Our encounter with the distinct possibilities of engaging livingdying in the seminal sense occurs through modalities of aesthetic understanding, or to use Dussel's fitting term in his "Siete hipótesis para una estética de la liberación," through "intelligent-sensitivity" or "sensitive-intelligence," such as the modalities of being in/with the movement of world/cosmos Kusch identifies as "estar" rather than the reifying *ser* in Spanish and with the concrete seminal *utcatha* in Indigenous thought. Aesthetic modalities also appear in distinct ways in the tension between "emptiness" (*xu*) and "solidity" (*shi*) in Chinese thought, a tension central not only to Buddhism but in the philosophy of the Dao (the path or way) as well as Confucianism. Ultimately, our discussion leads to an aesthetic thinking in/with livingdying in concrete rhythmic fluidity, in pluriversal ways, in a south-south dialogue that stands affirmatively and not only critically beyond westernized understanding.[35]

NOTES

1. Enrique Dussel, *Philosophy of Liberation*, trans. Aquilina Martinez and Christine Morkovsky (Maryknoll, N.Y.: Orbis Books, 1985), 172–73; hereafter cited as *PL*.

2. César Vallejo, "Escarnecido aclimatado al bien" [Mocked acclimated to goodness], in *The Complete Posthumous Poetry*, trans. Clayton Eshleman and José Rubia Barcia (Berkeley: University of California Press, 1980), 134–35.

3. In section 4 of this chapter, I revise parts of my work on Chinese painting as developed in Alejandro A. Vallega, "Poetic Sensibility on the Work of Cao Jun," in *Cao Jun, Hymns of Nature*, ed. John Sallis (Boston: McMullen Museum of Art, Boston College, and University of Chicago Press, 2018), 9–14.

4. Enrique Dussel, *Ethics of Liberation: In the Age of Globalization and Exclusion*, trans. Eduardo Mendieta, Camilo Pérez Bustillo, Yolanda Angulo, and Nelson

Maldonado-Torres, ed. Alejandro A. Vallega (Durham, N.C.: Duke University Press, 2013); hereafter cited as *EL*.

5. *EL*, 104.

6. *PL*, chap. 2, "From Phenomenology to Liberation," 16–66.

7. *PL*, 16–17.

8. *PL*, 17.

9. *PL*, 16–17.

10. *PL*, 17.

11. Frantz Fanon, *Black Skin, White Masks*, trans. Richard Philcox (New York: Grove, 2008).

12. Alejandro Vallega, *Latin American Philosophy: From Identity to Radical Exteriority* (Bloomington: Indiana University Press, 2014).

13. Rodolfo Kusch, *Indigenous and Popular Thinking in América*, trans. María Lugones and Joshua M. Price (Durham, N.C.: Duke University Press, 2010); hereafter cited as *IPT*. This is the path I seek when I talk about emptiness in this chapter.

14. See Charles Scott, "Livingdying," *Mosaic: An Interdisciplinary Critical Journal*, special issue, *A Matter of Lifedeath* 48, no. 2 (2015): 211–17. See also Charles E. Scott and Nancy Tuana, *Beyond Philosophy: Nietzsche, Foucault, Anzaldúa* (Bloomington: Indiana University Press, 2020), chap. 8.

15. Liberatory decolonial thought through one's bodying, as I attempt it here, is not defined by or of the timely line of order and progress, of organizing concepts, given laws, judgments, institutions, nor does it seek the freedom of transcendental duties. Liberatory decolonial thought forgets its alternatives and chance once it enters the purview of the "I" as *ego conquiro*—that is, the "I see, I grasp, and thus I doubt" (a skepticism won by excluding the other through doubt), and I control: a thinking that asserts "its own" and in doing so gives to itself an I to exist. By contrast, perhaps one would best find one's place along the lines of a sense of doubt. As Augustine would render existence before Descartes, "I contradict myself; I exist." Not the certitude of doubting that inflicts a consciousness upon a living movement but the originary transformative movement of a concrete "contra-dictum," the undoing of the subject in the saying and acting, and with it the undoing of its other, nature-body-thinghood. This does not mean falling into nihilism or abandoning concrete existence: here, to exist is *vivere*, or to live. Living. And yet, unlike Augustine, liberatory decolonial philosophy does not offer salvation by Christ; no promise is required of time's temporalizing movement.

16. *EL*, 50, quoting Fabien Eboussi Boulaga, *La crise du Muntu: Authenticité africaine et philosophie* (Paris: Présence Africaine, 1977), 55.

17. *IPT*, 11.

18. Ibid.

19. Ibid.

20. Ibid.

21. Ibid., 5.

22. Ibid.

23. Ibid.

24. Maria Lugones, "Toward a Decolonial Feminism," *Hypatia* 25, no. 4 (2010): 750.

25. As Kusch states in the next section, the whole cultural tradition of the Indigenous peoples he engages "indicates that the ability of indigenous people may reside in

the use of mental functions that our Western style of life does not customarily use"; *IPT*, 17.

26. *IPT*, 5.

27. Here open immense difficulties, as one cannot think of the dynamic in the sense of subjective willful production of meanings, things, and values as opposed to the static or nonproductive. This westernizing dichotomy does not fit the thought under discussion. This is because neither rational subjectivism nor the will or desire of an ego has a determining role in the concept of motion. In this sense, the philosophy of liberation offers a path beyond philosophy as held by modern westernized thought.

28. This is analogous to what Rodolfo Kusch engages in when discussing the face of the gods on stone in *América profunda* (1962), Obras completas 2 (Córdoba: Editorial Fundación Ross, 2000), 1–254.

29. Image available at https://commons.wikimedia.org/wiki/File:Guo_Xi_-_Early _Spring_(large).jpg.

30. Yanfang Tang, "Translating Across Cultures: Yi Jing and Understanding Chinese Poetry," *Intercultural Communication Studies* 23, no. 1 (2014): 192.

31. Cao Jun, "Value Vagueness in Painting" (unpublished manuscript, November 8, 2013). The manuscript is with the author.

32. The latter is a dynamic emptiness one finds, curiously enough, in Daguerre's first photograph of a human as well as in Francis Bacon's electric interiors in his paintings.

33. Cao Jun, "Value Vagueness in Painting."

34. All images from the exhibit are free to access at the Metropolitan Museum of Art's website, New York City, https://www.metmuseum.org/exhibitions/objects ?exhibitionId=2cca0d85-6307-4ac7-9674-c4e4f675c08e&pkgids=237.

35. These are ways of understanding not often explored by our studies and critiques toward a decolonial turn. In part, I suspect given our proximity to the urgency of things and their logic and to the fear of losing existence in letting one's thought not impose itself, as if one would cease living in no longer accomplishing the representational identification of subjective calculative consciousness, the ego cogito's self-*valuation*. Perhaps it is the case that we do not engage emptiness because such a turn would deny us the limit that gives us a sense of being through the conscious instantiation of egological ontology: sap and sum of our "practical rationalist world," a world that grows in depth and intensity in living through aesthetic decolonial liberatory thought.

CHAPTER 9

The Ethics and Politics of Progress

Dussel and the Frankfurt School

Amy Allen

Enrique Dussel's *Ethics of Liberation* is a monumental book, ambitious both in its philosophical aims—which include the articulation of the ethics that guides the philosophy of liberation and the call for the liberation of philosophy from its Hellenocentric and Eurocentric histories and paradigms—and in the sheer number and variety of its philosophical sources. Given the daunting breadth of those sources and the vast scope of the work, my proposal to isolate just one strand of the rich tapestry of this project—Dussel's relationship to Frankfurt School critical theory—may seem overly selective. However, focusing on this aspect of Dussel's project will prove fruitful, I think, for two reasons: first, and most importantly, because it will enable me to articulate the complex and ambivalent conception of progress that runs through Dussel's ethics, forming an important part of its normative framework, and second, because it reveals some as yet unexplored connections or points of concordance between Dussel's work and the Frankfurt School, connections that I hope might be mutually enriching.[1]

Dussel characterizes his relationship to the Frankfurt School by emphasizing the break and discontinuity between what he calls the first and second Frankfurt Schools. As he explains, in 1968, "the 'first'

Frankfurt school, critical, from the Heideggerian, Weberian, Marxist, and Freudian horizons, . . . gave way to the 'second' generation of the Frankfurt school—pragmatic, but no longer critical. The philosophy of the second Frankfurt school is a fin-de-siècle one, social-democratic, of a Europe of late capitalism, and builds a bridge to Anglo-Saxon thought (with North American pragmatism and the *linguistic turn*)."[2] Although Dussel emphasizes that his ethics of liberation has much to learn from the second Frankfurt School, and although he does incorporate certain features of Habermasian and Apelian discourse ethics into his overall ethical framework, his judgment that this project is pragmatic but no longer critical is quietly damning. Dussel's reception of the first Frankfurt School is, by contrast, more positive. In part 2 of the *Ethics of Liberation*, where Dussel articulates his critical ethics, he notes the affinities between this tradition of thought and Latin American liberation philosophy, even going so far as to call the first Frankfurt School "a direct predecessor of the philosophy of liberation, which developed in the heart of the crisis of late Modernity within capitalism's central core."[3] However, as we shall see, Dussel is also critical of a "lack of *positivity*" and an "insufficiently clear *exteriority*" in the work of this tradition.[4]

This question of Dussel's complex reception of the Frankfurt School is of more than mere scholarly or hermeneutical interest, as it is related to his own complicated and ambivalent conception of progress—a concept that is, I think, central to both the critical and the reconstructive aspects of his critical theory. Like the first Frankfurt School and unlike Habermas, Dussel is highly critical of progressive philosophies of history that present European modernity as the outcome of a process of civilizational development. To Benjamin's and Adorno's critiques of the concept of progress, he of course adds a comprehensive, detailed, and devastating critique of the Eurocentric, colonial, and imperial logics and implications of such a conception of history. As such, Dussel is deeply aware of and acutely attentive to what we might call the *politics* of progress: the entanglement of this concept with a complex history of exclusion, domination, and exploitation of the subjects of colonial domination. However, perhaps surprisingly, Dussel does not for this reason abandon all talk of progress or development. Rather, he refigures these notions, defending not only the vital importance of hope for the philosophy of liberation but also the possibility of what he calls qualitative (as opposed to quantitative) progress or development in the future. The realization of this hope has as a necessary (but not sufficient) condition the achievement of the kind of formal, intersubjective validity that is central to Habermasian discourse ethics. As such, Dussel is equally attentive to what we might call the *ethics of progress*.

169

The primary task of this chapter is simply to try to work out the relationship between these two aspects of Dussel's conception of progress—first the politics and then the ethics—as they are articulated in his dialogue with the Frankfurt School. At various points in this reconstruction, I will point out some striking resemblances between Adorno's conception of progress and Dussel's. These resemblances suggest, on the one hand, some ways that the relationship between the politics and the ethics of progress might be made more explicit in Dussel and, on the other hand, possibilities for radicalizing Adorno's critique of progress by infusing it with a decolonial perspective on the notion of humanity. My aim in mapping these concordances is neither to suggest that Dussel's work stands in need of validation or legitimation by being connected to the work of Adorno nor vice versa. Rather, my aim is simply to make a modest contribution to the fruitful north-south dialogue between Dussel and the Frankfurt School that his own work has already begun.

1. THE POLITICS OF PROGRESS

What I am calling the politics of progress—the entanglement of ideas of progress, development, and modernity with the exclusion, domination, and exploitation of the victims of colonialism and imperialism—is already announced in the subtitle of the *Ethics of Liberation: In the Age of Globalization and Exclusion*. As Dussel explains, the subtitle of the book "seeks to capture the double movement that the global periphery is caught between: on the one hand, the supposed modernization occasioned by the formal globalization of finance capital ('fictitious' capital as Marx characterized it); but, on the other hand, the increasing material, discursive, and formal exclusion of the victims of this pur-ported civilizing process."[5] This complex double movement is explored more fully in the book's introduction, which contrasts two paradigms of modernity. First, there is the Eurocentric paradigm, according to which "the phenomenon of Modernity is *exclusively* European," devel-oping out of the Middle Ages and then spreading to the rest of the world.[6] According to this paradigm, Europe possessed "exceptional *internal* characteristics that allowed it to supersede, through its ratio-nality, all other cultures."[7] This paradigm is contradicted by the second, the planetary paradigm of modernity, according to which "European Modernity is not an *independent*, autopoietic, self-referential system, but, instead, is 'part' of a world system: its *center*."[8] Moreover, according to the planetary paradigm, Europe's centrality to the world-system is decidedly *not* a function of its internal superiority. Rather, it is the effect of European conquest and colonization of Amerindia, which itself rests on a contingent historical fact: because Portugal had exclusive rights to the Cape of Good Hope, Spain's only route to India or Central Asia was across the Atlantic Ocean. "Because of this," Dussel notes, "Spain 'bumps' into, 'finds without looking,' Amerindia, and with it the entire European 'medieval paradigm' enters into crisis."[9] Thus it is far from the case that the developmental or civilizational superiority of European modernity led it to assume a central role in the world-system; rather, its centrality to the world-system was made possible by colonialism, which gave Europe a "comparative advantage" over India, China, and the Ottoman Empire. It is this centrality, in turn, that gave rise to the belief in the civilizational superiority of Euromodernity. As Dussel puts it, "Modernity is the fruit of this happening, and not its cause."[10]

As is well known, Dussel insists both that modernity begins with this event—that is, with the "discovery" of the Americas in 1492—and that acknowledging this beginning is central to leaving the Eurocentric conception of modernity behind. On Dussel's view, there are in fact two modernities: the first, the Hispanic-Renaissance modernity that begins in 1492, and the second, the later modernity of Anglo-Germanic Europe. Whereas the central philosophical question of the first moder-nity was what right—if any—Europe had to dominate its colonies, by the time of the second modernity, these questions had been settled in Europe's favor, and as such they tended to go unthematized from that point forward. As a result, Eurocentrism goes unquestioned in the second modernity.[11] To the extent that debates about modernity presuppose that the second, Anglo-Germanic modernity, is coextensive with modernity as such, they tend to remain within the Eurocentric horizon of that conception.

This is true for Habermas's influential—but controversial—discussion of the philosophical discourse of modernity, which according to Dussel remains within the framework of the second modernity and caught within a developmentalist conception. Developmentalism views modernity "as an *exclusively European* phenomenon, which *expanded from the seventeenth century on* through all the 'backward' cultures. . . . Modernity in this view is a phenomenon that must be concluded."[12] Dussel's position, by contrast, emerges from the periphery rather than the center of the world-system and aims at "the overcoming of the world system itself, such as it has developed for the last five hundred years."[13] Although Dussel is happy to "recuperate what is redeemable in Modernity," his primary aim is neither the completion nor the conclusion of the project of modernity but rather the negation of the exclusion, domination, and exploitation of the victims of the current world-system—all of which are themselves central components of modernity.

These reflections on modernity form part of what Dussel calls the "World History of Ethical Systems," which makes up his introduction to the *Ethics of Liberation*. Although Dussel does not discuss the first Frankfurt School in this part of the book, his critique of the developmentalist conception of modernity finds a clear echo in his later discussion of their work. As he explains, the *Ethics of Liberation* "subsumes the critical stances of the 'great critics' (Feuerbach, Schopenhauer, Nietzsche, Horkheimer, Adorno, Marcuse, and particularly Marx, Freud, and Levinas), and the Latin American experience, to the extent that they criticize the aspects of Modernity and modern reason that foster tendencies toward domination."[14] In section 4.2, Dussel explores the resources that can be found in the work of the early Frankfurt School for the philosophy of liberation. This discussion is organized around the account of the methodology of critical theory offered in Horkheimer's programmatic essay "Traditional and Critical Theory." Dussel emphasizes a number of points of methodological convergence between Horkheimer's vision of critical theory and his own: (1) both take as their point of departure the experience of the victim, (2) both aim at a critique of the prevailing system of domination (what the Frankfurters called a critique of the social totality), (3) both presuppose a conception of critical reason that is material and negative, (4) both understand the perspective of the victims not as something to be taken at face value but rather as part of a process of critical articulation (though in different ways), (5) both are addressed to a specific social-historical subject, (6) both reject progressive philosophies of history, and (7) both incorporate a significant material moment into their ethical views (the early Frankfurt School through its acceptance of Freudian drive theory).[15]

Of all these points of convergence, the one that receives the most sustained and developed discussion is the philosophy of history. In this section of the text, Dussel offers a close reading of Walter Benjamin's *Theses on the Philosophy of History*. Elaborating on Benjamin's famous distinction between empty, homogeneous historical time and the revolutionary messianic time that explodes the continuum of history, Dussel emphasizes that "historical time" for Benjamin is "the time characteristic of the prevailing system" within which "arises 'progress,' whose mystification has been promoted not just by the bourgeoisie but by social democrats (and even common Marxists)."[16] The critical edge of Benjamin's philosophy of history consists in his denial of the prevailing system—and its conceptualization of time—from the standpoint of the victims. This enables him to offer what Dussel calls "a complete reinterpretation of history."[17] At the center of this reinterpretation is Benjamin's notion of messianic time (the *Jetztzeit* or now-time), a discontinuous eruption into the empty, homogeneous continuum of historical time that is generated by the victim's becoming conscious of her status as a victim. This explosion of the continuum of history constitutes what Dussel calls a "struggle against the prevailing order" that he interprets in terms of "messianic time as something new, as 'development.'"[18] However, he worries that Benjamin never clarifies "exactly how 'messianic time' becomes transformed into 'historical time' of the messianic community or movement itself'" and whether this is "impossible or contradictory."[19]

For what it is worth, my own sense is that what Dussel calls the transformation of messianic time into historical time is, for Benjamin, if not impossible, then at the very least deeply paradoxical. As I read him, Benjamin's philosophy of history entails a much more radical and complete rejection of the notion of progress, precisely because he rejects the very conception of time that makes such a concept comprehensible. This would mean that to talk of messianic time as the starting point of a new "development," as Dussel does here, would be misleading. Insofar as Dussel wants to draw on Benjamin's critique of progress while still holding on to some ethical notion of development—about which more in a moment—I think that Dussel's position is actually more reminiscent of Adorno's than of Benjamin's. Although Adorno endorsed Benjamin's rejection of the idea that history could or should be read as a story of progress, viewing it instead as an ever-growing pile of catastrophes, he, unlike Benjamin, thought it was crucial to hold on to the possibility of progress in the future. As he put it, "Too little that is good has power in the world for the world to be said to have achieved progress, but there can be no good, not even a trace of it, without progress."[20] Much like Adorno, and for similar reasons, Dussel insists that any view that maintains that change for the better is impossible is conservative—even, he says, necrophiliac, or death-loving—and therefore unacceptable. As Dussel puts it, "For the victims, the future is the time of hope; struggle is necessary in order to improve their state of being, because the present is dominated by the negation that they suffer and that makes it impossible for them to live."[21] Thus although I completely agree with Dussel's defense of *Dialectic of Enlightenment* in this chapter—both his defense of the text's quasi-tragic vision and his critique of Habermas's extremely one-sided interpretation of it[22]—I think that Adorno's philosophy of history offers underexplored resources for the positive conception of development that Dussel wants to retain even in the wake of his radical critique of reading history as progress. As Dussel argues at the end of chapter 4, the ethics of liberation embraces "an ethical principle of 'qualitative progress' defined by new criteria, which differ from those of Modernity, being not purely

173

technological or quantitative but instead referring to the sustainability of norms, actions, institutions, and systems of ethics that are capable of permitting and developing human life—and the life of other species."[23]

2. THE ETHICS OF PROGRESS

With this invocation of the idea of qualitative progress defined by the new criteria of the development of life, we come to the second aspect of Dussel's conception of progress, what I called earlier the ethics of progress. The importance of both positive and negative aspects of the material moment of ethics, its reference to both the dignity and the embodied and corporeal suffering of the victims of the modern world-system, is crucial for Dussel's critical engagement with the Frankfurt School. For although he references here his earlier criticisms of Habermas's defense of modernity, Dussel's main critique of Habermas in the *Ethics of Liberation* turns on the formalism of discourse ethics. Because of this formalism, Habermas is unable to affirm the "*universality* of the material principle,"[24] and as a result, his "discourse ethics is not critical."[25] An ethics that incorporates a materialist moment is, to that extent, an ethics of content, not merely of form. By saying farewell to the possibility of such an ethics, "Habermas said a definitive farewell to the *critical* thought of the first Frankfurt school."[26]

The ethics of liberation, by contrast, combines the formal conception of intersubjective validity claims established by discourse ethics with the view that the primary material origin of all possible ethical claims is "the pain of the corporeality or bodily reality of the victims."[27] This negative material moment is recognized and given its due by the first Frankfurt School, but Dussel reads that moment mainly through the early Frankfurt School's reception of Freud's theory of the death drive. As such, he finds the account of the material moment in the first Frankfurt School to be overly negative. What the first Frankfurt School fails to realize is an insight that Dussel finds in the work of Marx and Levinas—namely, that "'negativity' emerges, presents itself, is discovered . . . from 'positivity' as the point of departure";[28] that is, it rests on a prior affirmation or recognition of the dignity of the

Other/victim as a living human being.[29] This affirmation of the dignity of the Other is the positive condition of the possibility of critique; critique's negative condition of possibility stems from the recognition of the victim *as a victim*, whose bodily life is made impossible by the current world-system.[30]

175

So Dussel's ethics of liberation seeks to combine both positive and negative material moments: positively, the affirmation of the dignity of the living human subject and the bodily basis for the reproduction of her life; negatively, the recognition of the embodied suffering of the victims of the world-system. Mirroring this dialectic, his conception of progress likewise contains both negative and positive moments: a negative critique of the developmentalist fallacy and a positive conception of development or qualitative progress. But what exactly does Dussel mean by development or qualitative progress? His discussion of Ernst Bloch's principle of hope provides some clues. Following Bloch, Dussel argues that the ethics of liberation is moved by the drive for hope "toward the *positive future* content, the project of liberation or the possible utopia. The future utopia is the 'possible' *development* of the life of every single subject in community (phylogenetically speaking as well)."[31] In other words, development is a future-oriented concept, a concept that projects a possible future utopia of liberation. As Dussel reads Bloch's principle of hope, however, the positive content of this utopia is defined by an act of negation: the negation of the existing negativity of the suffering of the victim. As Dussel puts it, "A nonexistent scenario has to be created whose constitutive determinations are positively defined in terms of the negation of the negativity of the victim—if there is hunger, food; if there is homelessness, home; if there is illiteracy, education; if there is nonsymmetrical political representation, real democracy; and so on."[32]

Thus for Dussel, critical-discursive reason too has both negative and positive tasks or moments. The negative task is the critique of the current ethical norm, institution, or system; the positive task is the "creative pro-jection by means of critical utopian-constructive reason."[33] For Dussel, anyone who aims to critique and transform a given ethical system should be able to imaginatively construct or propose possible alternatives. But "negativity is the source of the positive alternatives. It is to the positive as a mold is to a sculpture."[34] The relationship between negative and positive moments in Dussel's conception of critique is thus highly complex. Although at the level of critical-discursive reason, Dussel argues that negativity is the source of all critique of existing ethical systems or institutions and also, indirectly, of our positive-utopian projections—precisely insofar as the latter consist of determinate negations of the existing negativity of the victims—he also maintains, at the level of the material moment of the foundations of ethics, that the affirmation of the status of the dignity and bodily needs of all human beings is the precondition for recognizing the victim as a victim. Thus it seems to me that it is an open question whether and in what sense Dussel's ethics might be considered a negative moral philosophy along Adornian lines, as Eduardo Mendieta has suggested.[35] Although Adorno too places embodied suffering at the center of his moral philosophy—as he famously put it in *Negative Dialectics*, "The physical moment tells our knowledge that suffering ought not to be, that things should be different. Woe speaks: 'Go'"[36]—it seems to me that his negativism may be more thoroughgoing than Dussel's.[37]

In the final chapter of the *Ethics of Liberation*, through his articulation of his feasibility criterion, Dussel argues that the aim of this ethics is neither mere reform of the existing ethical system nor a revolution if this is construed narrowly in political terms. Rather, the aim is the radical, revolutionary transformation of every norm, action, institution, and structure that make up the current world-ethical system. Such a process of transformation would produce what Dussel calls "the moment of development," a moment that enhances and supports the production and reproduction of the life of every human subject.[38] Dussel defines the moment of qualitative development—as distinct from quantitative developmentalism or progressive philosophies of history—as "the creative moment that opens up the 'reproduction' of human life of all ethical subjects, and of their communities, to a qualitative moment of overcoming, enrichment, evolution."[39] Thus on his view, the critique of "quantitative modern 'progress,'" defined in terms of technical mastery and the efficient deployment of instrumental reason, goes hand in hand with the affirmation of a future-oriented "ethics of the life of human subjects and their symmetric discursiveness."[40] As

Dussel explains, "I then deny . . . modern quantitative 'performative *progress*' that is independent from the possibility of the life of each subject; however, I affirm the need for qualitative 'efficient *development*' (performativity or critical-ethical feasibility) in favor of life, as the material content and co-responsibility of discursively participant moral subjects."[41]

Dussel readily acknowledges that the utopian aspirations that inspire our attempts to achieve progress or development in this future-oriented sense will, as a matter of principle, never be fully or completely realized. "If the 'good' is finite," he writes, "if it is impossible to achieve a perfect work, then ethics teaches us to be attentively critical and in permanent struggle. Those who 'install' themselves in the power of the 'good' are already evil, and the prevailing good has already become transformed into that which is 'not-good.'"[42] Still, the obligation to attempt to achieve qualitative progress in the future is crucial to his liberation principle, which articulates an ethical obligation to liberate the victim by means of a feasible transformation of the existing ethical system that produces the material negativity and/or formal exclusion of the victims and the construction of new ethical systems that would support the life and full participation of the victims. To attempt to live up to this principle is to fight for "a 'qualitative historical advance' or development."[43]

Once again, I think there is a striking yet underexplored concordance between Dussel's account of qualitative progress—and its relation to quantitative progress—and Adorno's philosophy of history. Like Dussel, Adorno is highly critical of the assumption that the history of the progressive technical mastery of nature through the growth of instrumental rationality—what Dussel calls quantitative progress, but with "progress" usually in scare quotes—deserves to be called progress. Thus he says, "We can find nothing in reality that might help to redeem the promise inherent in the word 'progress.'"[44] And yet there is a sense in which this quantitative development creates the conditions of possibility for the realization of genuine progress. As Adorno puts it, "Our progress from the slingshot to the megaton bomb may well provoke satanic mockery, but . . . the age of the bomb is the first in which we can envisage a condition from which violence has disappeared."[45] In other words, the technological development of the forces of production, though it is predicated upon a domination of inner and outer nature that is currently running amok, having driven humanity to the brink of self-annihilation, has also created the capacity to eliminate material want: "Thanks to the current state of the technical forces of production," Adorno notes, "no one should need to suffer privation any longer."[46] Thus progress, understood as the elimination of material want and scarcity, the meeting of the bodily, material needs of all human beings, is possible for us, even if up to now it has not been actual. Moreover, the means for achieving qualitative progress can be wrested from the very technology that has been the driver of the problematic notion of quantitative "progress"; as such, "the progress in mastering nature . . . is not entirely without hope."[47]

But what would qualitative progress in the future consist in for Adorno? He offers a few formulations, none of which are developed in any detail. The one that resonates most with Dussel's notion of qualitative progress or development is found in the following passage: "No progress may be supposed that implies that humanity already existed and could therefore be assumed to continue to progress. Rather, progress would be the establishment of humanity in the first place, the prospect of which opens up in the face of its extinction."[48] Adorno says little about what he means by claiming that we may not suppose a conception of progress that assumed that humanity already exists. To be sure, for all his sober critique of the limits of the Enlightenment and its entanglement with systems of domination, he remains frustratingly and virtually completely blind to the role of colonialism, racism, and Eurocentrism in constituting both the Enlightenment and the relations of domination with which the Enlightenment is dialectically entangled. And yet here we might productively read the broader and more trenchant critique of progress found in Dussel's decolonial theory back into Adorno's recognition of the fact that humanity as such cannot be assumed to exist. Humanity has not existed up to now *not only* because of the ways in which bourgeois capitalist societies are grounded in the domination of inner nature, thus simultaneously cutting us off from nature and deforming our nature, but also, and perhaps even more fundamentally, because the formation and continued global dominance of those societies depend materially and ideologically on the denial of the humanity of those that Dussel calls the victims of the world-system. Reading Dussel back into Adorno, then, would generate a much more expansive conception of the establishment of universal humanity than Adorno himself seems to presuppose. On this view, the establishment of universal humanity would have to consist not only of a genuine reconciliation of human beings with nature but also of the radical transformation of the racialized, ongoing legacies and forms of colonialism and imperialism.[49]

3. CONCLUSION

In this chapter, I hope to have accomplished the following three things: first, an articulation of Dussel's complex reception of and engagement with the Frankfurt School in his ethics of liberation, showing how that engagement sheds light on some of his core ethical and political commitments; second, a reconstruction of Dussel's complex and ambivalent conception of progress; and third, a mapping of some points of convergence between Dussel's and Adorno's philosophy of history. In closing, I'd like to suggest that we might productively read Adorno's dialectical insistence that "progress occurs where it comes to an end"[50] as a way of connecting the politics and the ethics of progress in Dussel's work. In Dusselian terms, this phrase might become something like the following: progress understood as the possibility of liberation occurs where the developmentalist fallacy of modernity and its ongoing and devastating legacy come to an end.

NOTES

1. I am grateful to Linda Martín Alcoff for pointing out these connections to me in her insightful and incisive comment on my work. See Alcoff, "Critical Theory's Colonial Unconscious: Comments on the *End of Progress*," *Berlin Journal of Critical Theory* 2, no. 2 (April 2018): 149–63.
2. Enrique Dussel, *Ethics of Liberation: In the Age of Globalization and Exclusion*, trans. Eduardo Mendieta, Camilo Pérez Bustillo, Yolanda Angulo, and Nelson

Maldonado-Torres, ed. Alejandro A. Vallega (Durham, N.C.: Duke University Press, 2013), 121.

3. Ibid., 234.

4. Ibid., 235.

5. Ibid., xxii.

6. Ibid., 24.

7. Ibid., 25.

8. Ibid.

9. Ibid., 29.

10. Ibid., 26.

11. See ibid., 34.

12. Ibid., 38; emphasis in the original. Enrique Dussel develops this critique of Habermas's work more fully in Dussel, "Eurocentrism and Modernity (Introduction to the Frankfurt Lectures)," *boundary 2* 20, no. 3 (1993): 65–76.

13. Dussel, *Ethics of Liberation*, 38. For a helpful discussion of this point, see Linda Martín Alcoff, "The Hegel of Coyoacán," *boundary 2* 45, no. 4 (2018): 183–201.

14. Dussel, *Ethics of Liberation*, 218.

15. See ibid., 236–49.

16. Ibid., 242.

17. Ibid.

18. Ibid., 243.

19. Ibid.

20. Theodor Adorno, *History and Freedom: Lectures, 1964–1965*, ed. Rolf Tiedemann, trans. Rodney Livingstone (Cambridge: Polity, 2006), 149.

21. Dussel, *Ethics of Liberation*, 287. Compare Adorno's critique of the fallacious claim that "because there has been no progress up to now, there will be none in the future." By "elevating historical despair into a norm that must be adhered to," such a view "sides with everything that is dreadful"; Adorno, *History and Freedom*, 158–59.

22. See Dussel, *Ethics of Liberation*, 247 and 578–79n277.

23. Ibid., 290.

24. Ibid., 139.

25. Ibid., 140.

26. Ibid.

27. Ibid., 210.

28. Ibid., 280.

29. Ibid., 281.

30. For a compelling defense of Dussel's use of the term *victim*, see Alcoff, "Hegel of Coyoacán."

31. Dussel, *Ethics of Liberation*, 341.

32. Ibid., 338.

33. Ibid., 350.

34. Ibid., 352.

35. Eduardo Mendieta, "Macondo Time: On Alejandro Vallega's *Latin American Philosophy: From Identity to Radical Exteriority*," *Inter-American Journal of Philosophy* 8, no. 2 (Fall 2017): 24–32, at 28.

36. Theodor Adorno, *Negative Dialectics*, trans. E. B. Ashton (London: Continuum, 1973), 203.

37. To be sure whether or not this is a good thing depends on one's assessment of the prospects for negativism. The best available reconstruction and defense of Adorno's negativism is Fabian Freyenhagen, *Adorno's Practical Philosophy: Living Less Wrongly* (Cambridge: Cambridge University Press, 2013).

38. Dussel, *Ethics of Liberation*, 396–97.

39. Ibid., 644n232.

40. Ibid., 397.

41. Ibid.

42. Ibid., 427.

43. Ibid., 420.

44. Adorno, *History and Freedom*, 143.

45. Ibid., 159.

46. Ibid., 144.

47. Ibid., 160.

48. Ibid., 146.

49. Something similar could be said about reading Adorno's conception of progress alongside Achille Mbembe's call for a new universalism in the wake of what he refers to as the becoming Black of the world. See Mbembe, *The Critique of Black Reason* (Durham, N.C.: Duke University Press, 2017). For a brief discussion of Mbembe in relation to Adorno, see Amy Allen, "Progress, Normativity, and Universality: Reply to Rainer Forst," in *Justice and Emancipation: The Critical Theory of Rainer Forst*, ed. Amy Allen and Eduardo Mendieta (University Park: Penn State University Press, 2019), 145–56.

50. Adorno, *History and Freedom*, 152.

CHAPTER 10

Epilogue

Enrique Dussel[1]

1. EDUCATION (UNTIL 1969)

The work of an author remains relatively determined by the author's formative experiences. In my case, my birth in a small town with unpaved roads (La Paz, Mendoza, Argentina), inhabited by simple folk, in some cases Indigenous members of the original people of America, allowed the future philosopher that I would become to place myself close to the poverty of the peasant people while being the son of the community's doctor. Coming from a family of four generations of German immigrants (on my father's side) and Italians (on my mother's side), I spent my youth next to vineyards, orchards, and horses and traveling to the provincial capital (Mendoza) by means of English trains (in the 1930s) and by means of a highway only recently paved. The dry, almost desert-like surroundings that were fertile because of irrigation canals that brought water from the distant mountains of the Andes, on their Argentinean slopes, allowed me to experience landscapes similar to those of the Spanish plateau or the Arab desert that would later become Israel. This will later become source of a philosophical reflection that will drink from telluric and mountainous experiences.

My physician father's immigration to the great capital city of Buenos Aires in 1940 allowed me to undergo urban and political influences while still a young child as well as experience the revolution that would give rise to the long legacy of Peronism that began in 1944, and with it all the characteristics of a popular movement that would last until the twenty-first century.

The study of fine arts from age thirteen onward and later the study of philosophy at the National University of Cuyo (in Mendoza, until 1957), within a classical Eurocentric, Aristotelian-Thomistic training with a strong Greek and Latin influence, together with a political university student militancy allowed me to earn a scholarship to pursue a doctorate in the Complutense University of Madrid. It was an incredible first experience: crossing the Atlantic by boat, journeying from Latin America to Europe, and beginning a ten-year academic stay in a part of Eurasia (Europe and the Middle East).

Having earned my Ph.D. in philosophy in Spain and following the intellectual project of launching a critique of the Eurocentrism that I had experienced during my university life, I lived in Israel for two years (1959–61), studying Hebrew and the Semitic cultures while also living as a simple carpenter in Nazareth (Israel) and becoming a member of the Ginosar Kibbutz (in Tiberias). All of this was to obtain materials with which to evade the Hellenocentric culture of my previous studies.

Once I returned to Europe (four years in Paris, France, and two years in Mainz, Germany), I took in the phenomenological thinking of the time, especially the teachings of Paul Ricoeur. I deepened my knowledge of Latin American history by exploring the subject of the genocide of the conquest of native peoples, especially in the sixteenth century. After earning two doctorates (in philosophy in Madrid and in history at the Sorbonne), in addition to a bachelor's degree in theology, I was nevertheless eager to return to Latin America.

I delivered my first university course, Hypothesis for a Study of Latin America in Universal History, at the National University of Resistencia (Chaco, Argentina). When in Mendoza, I had already begun to think about how to sketch a critique of Hegelian Eurocentrism, and since I was a regular guest at the Quito Institute (Ecuador), I was able to take numerous trips throughout Latin America, the Caribbean, and the United States, making note of the philosophical situation on the continent and the political situation of the critical social movements throughout.

2. THE PHILOSOPHY OF LIBERATION: ORIGINS AND DEVELOPMENT (UNTIL 1980)

184   On my boat trip to Europe (in 1957), I discovered Latin America (as I passed through Montevideo, Santos, Rio de Janeiro), and I began to discover Africa (as I landed in Dakar, Senegal) and the Muslim world (Casablanca, Morocco). Since the Cuban revolution in 1959, the youth of the Latin American continent protested loudly in all the countries. Thus in 1970 J. C. Scannone and I organized, in the midst of the military dictatorship, the Latin American Forum (Semanas) at the University of San Salvador in San Miguel (Buenos Aires), where the thought movement that would later become the philosophy of liberation was first articulated. In 1973, by the time of the third forum, there were already eight hundred participants (many of them university philosophy professors in Argentina). Among some of the participants were the Mexican Leopoldo Zea, the Peruvian Augusto Salazar Bondy, and many of their other Latin American colleagues.[2] The aforementioned movement of the philosophy of liberation had begun earlier through informal meetings that took place in Cordoba (Calamuchita, Argentina) and had made itself public in the Second Argentine Congress of Philosophy (March of 1971).[3] I wrote a declaration in the manner of a manifesto for the philosophy of liberation stating that "a new style of philosophical thinking has been born in Latin America. . . . The philosophy of liberation intends to think from the exteriority of the other, from beyond the imperious *machista* system, of the dominating pedagogical system, of the oppressing political system."[4]

The new philosophical school had emerged in the context of the research of scholars of Latin American thinking and from within the context of the Hegelian and Heideggerian horizon, which took into account the Levinasian critique—the French philosopher with whom we developed a friendship—and erupted critically in chapter 3 of *Para una ética de la liberación Latinoamericana* (Toward an ethics of Latin American liberation), which I began to publish in 1973.[5] This work was the fruit of all the generational experiences in the face of the antipopular dictatorships that had taken over power in Latin America. Beyond the ruling totality of the political and economic systems that the theory of dependency had been denouncing (since 1968), it was necessary to discover the exteriority already enunciated by the Semitic king Hammurabi ("I have done justice by the widow, the orphan, and the poor") in the Code of Hammurabi, promulgated in Babylonia in the seventeenth century B.C.E., and by Bartolomé de las Casas, critic of modernity and capitalism at the beginning of the sixteenth century in conquered Mexico and thus defender of the Indigenous peoples of our American continent.

This was a fruitful time for writings[6] and filled with experiences from the numerous trips, conferences, and seminars in Latin America and the Caribbean and among the "Latinos" in the United States. During this time, I published several works on Latin American history: *El humanismo semita*, *El humanismo helénico*, *El dualismo en la antropología de la Cristiandad*, *Para una de-strucción de la historia de la ética*, and *Método para una Filosofía de la Liberación*, among others.[7] My critical commitments during this time became dangerous for me and my family, which culminated when a bombing attempt was made on my own home (October 2, 1973). I was also then fired from the university (in March of 1975). So began my exile from my small fatherland (Argentina) in order to leave for another small fatherland (Mexico) within the large fatherland: Latin America. Barely arrived in Mexico, I had to write the synthesis of what I could not articulate in Argentina, now that I had changed geographical and historical contexts. Thus I published a small work on what we had accomplished up to that point, opening a horizon for future works: *Philosophy of Liberation* (1977). This was when I set out to clarify the theme of populism and make good on the many other commitments that I had made in my new fatherland and finally write the works on Latin American history that I promised.

3. THE MATERIAL SPHERE OF ETHICS AND POLITICS:
THE DISCOVERY OF MARX (UNTIL 1989)

There were three main reasons that I had to undertake a task that I did not at first suspect would be so long, meticulous, and demanding—the rereading of Karl Marx's magnum opus, *Capital*:[8] first, in order to understand more in depth the theme of the "poor," which is central to the philosophy of liberation; second, in order to be in tune and up to date on the Mexican debates concerning Marxism and its economic-political significance, which were in fashion at the time; and third, in order to personally verify the validity of the Latin American dependency theory, so superficially dismissed by many. What I originally thought would be a brief reading became a decade-long one, with more than sixteen semesters of a seminar in which I undertook a passionate reading with a large community of students at the National Autonomous University of Mexico (UNAM).

Immediately, a Marx that belongs within the Semitic tradition was revealed (because of his always implicit anthropological and metaphysical vocabulary and categories) as a Hegelian that surpasses Hegel himself in a very different way than that presented by the standard or Soviet Marxist ideology. I thus wrote five volumes of commentaries, line by line, on the works written by Marx in German while also consulting the unpublished manuscripts in the Marx archives in Berlin and Amsterdam. In this way a new Marx began to appear over the course of semesters, thanks to a genealogical consideration of the thinking displayed in volume 1 of *Capital* that emerged from its five successive redactions (from 1857 until the end of Marx's life), including numerous unpublished manuscripts of volumes 2 and 3 of *Capital*. From out of a metaphysics of life, the essence (*Wesen*), the being, and the foundation (*Grund*) of capital are described as the "accumulation of value that valorizes itself," as "a creation out of nothing" (*creatio ex nihilo*): accumulation of surplus value (as unpaid work) that the "living labor" of the wage earner has that is its originating *source*. This seemed to me and my students like an unknown philosophical novelty.

I will be brief, as I want to clarify some aspects in the spirit of a dialogue and mutual learning. After what I just noted, I want first of all to thank Mario Sáenz Rovner for having concerned himself with my work, and I will attempt to explain my opposition to the background of his critique. First, I think he was inspired by only some of my writings, which is why the critique remains partial, given that there are other works not referred to that would give grounds for a broader interpretation of the theme of "living labor," a theme that I have dealt with in some of these other texts.[9] Second, it would seem that he applied an a priori Levinasian interpretation to Marx, whereas I began my close reading of Marx without interpretative hypotheses at the beginning of my research, and for that reason, the possible coincidence of Marx's thinking with that of Levinas only becomes clear to me a posteriori. I articulated in a very precise text the discovery of a new interpretation of Marx: "Which would not be my astonishment when I read the lines that I immediately copied. I had never thought them until this moment here in Oaxtepec in December of 1983."[10] This concerns the very beginning of the logic or systematic categorical order that Marx had begun to develop in 1857, where it is indicated that (1) negatively, living labor was, on the one hand, "absolute poverty" (*Absolute Armut*),[11] inasmuch as it is the "owner of the work," and because he comes from the agricultural and farmers' world, the worker can only rely on his immediate "corporeality" (*Leiblichkeit*), without any other means to survive (no dwelling, no work instruments, no raw materials to produce anything, no food, nothing). But on the other hand, (2) positively, it was the "living *source* of value" (*lebendige Quelle des Wertes*). In this way, the poor farmer who arrives in the city causes a confrontation between the "owner of labor" and the "owner of money" (not yet a capitalist). This is already an unequal relationship wherein the wealthy dominate the poor. Once the owner of money buys and uses for some time the living subject of work (living labor), he subsumes him (technically, it is an *Aufhebung*, *subsumption*, or incorporation of living labor that in the circulation of commodities was still an *exteriority* or *alterity* to capital) in the process of labor that when it creates value transforms,[12] for the first time, original money into capital.

However, it is here that I discovered how Marx had been inspired by Friedrich Wilhelm Joseph von Schelling's theses, around 1841, and specifically with reference to Schelling's famous unpublished philosophy of revelation (*Offenbarung*). In other words, Schelling paved the way for Marx's critique of Hegel. It was thus that before 1970 (during the year that the second centenary of Hegel's birth was being celebrated), I dove deep into Hegel's thought (publishing my first book, *Hegel's Dialectics*, in that same year). Studying the post-Hegelian tradition (Feuerbach, Kierkegaard, Marx, etc.), I came to discover in Schelling the mentor of that generation. Advancing on this path during the 1980s and deepening my knowledge of Marx's thought using his texts in German, holding in my hand still-unpublished manuscripts being cataloged in Berlin and Amsterdam, I began to find Marx's formulations that were inspired by Schelling's critique of Hegel.[13] The coincidence with Levinasian categories is *posterior* and *unexpected*. It was in this way that I began to become aware of the logical development of the categories that Marx had fashioned patiently and that we in many seminar sessions read and commented on in a chronological and strict fashion, directly reading from Marx's work when that work had not yet been fully edited. The whole of the second section of the *Marx-Engels-Gesamtausgabe* (*MEGA*) on Capital, which presently has fourteen volumes, was not known in their entirety during the 1980s.

For Marx, at the most abstract level of economic science, one has to deal with the "*critique of the economic categories* or, 'if you like' [in English in the original], present critically the system of the bourgeois economy" (*Kritik der ökonomischen Kategorien* oder, if you like, das System der bürgerlichen Ökonomie kritisch dargestellt).[14] It is a matter not of situating oneself at either a concrete empirical or historical level of investigation but rather of being able to discover and constitute the *critical system of categories* needed in order to understand the essence (*Wesen*) of capital. The debate is abstract, categorical, and methodological. It concerns the "theoretical framework" of a *critical* political economy.[15]

In the first category (or determination, *Bestimmung*), in the constitution and description of the *essence* of capital in Marx's definitive writings (including the 1873 second edition of *Capital* and subsequent manuscripts) that he analyzed explicitly and *precisely*, he frequently refers to the "creative source of value out of nothing" (schöpferische Quelle des Wertes aus Nichts). "From nothing" indicates that there is no participation on the part of capital when living labor creates surplus value, since the laborer does not receive any salary as payment in the surplus time of their surplus work; this is to say, from out of her own creative subjectivity, she gratuitously introduces new value. For Marx (in opposition to Hegel), the creative "source" (*Quelle*) is not "Being"

(*Sein*). In the Hegelian terminology, this *source* is the "labor force," as the form of appearance of "living labor" (*lebendige Arbeit*), which for Marx is the "not-capital" (*Nicht-Kapital*) or "not-Being" (*Nichtsein*),[16] which nonetheless operates as the "substance"[17] of creation (*Schöpfung*) of surplus value (*Mehrwert*). Marx writes, "In order to be able to extract value from the consumption of a commodity, our friend, Moneybags, must be so lucky as to find, within the sphere of circulation, in the market, a commodity, whose use-value possesses the peculiar property of being a source of value (*Quelle von Werth*), whose actual consumption, therefore, is itself an embodiment of labour, and, consequently, a creation of value (*Wertschöpfung*)."[18] Once living labor is acquired in the sphere of circulation, in the exteriority and anteriority of the existence of productive capital, the capitalist *enters* (this means that they are outside) into the hell of Dante's *Divine Comedy*, but this changes the wording over the gates, where now we read, "No admittance except on business": "He, who before was the money-owner, now strides in front as capitalist; the possessor of labour-power follows as his labourer."[19] The overcoming of Hegel or the transformation of the order of categories (its logic) consists in Marx's opposition of Hegel precisely in this very moment. For Hegel, the system begins with "indeterminate being": "Pure being (*reine Sein*) makes the beginning (Anfang), because it is pure thinking of the indeterminate (*unbestimmte*), what is simply unmediated."[20] For Marx, the system of categories starts with Non-being, with the No-capital, with "living labor." As with Schelling, the beginning (*Anfang*) is the "creative source" (*schoepferische Quelle*). However, in Schelling's theodicy, that beginning is divinity, although he was opposed to the tradition for which the divinity (God) is the Being. Schelling calls the absolute a priori "the creative *source* of being"; put differently, it is the "Lord of Being"[21] and not Being. Marx, who uses Schelling's formulation by secularizing theodicy and applying this expression to political economy, replaces creative divinity (that for Hegel is Being) with human subjectivity as living labor. This is about the material *corporeality* of the worker (*Leiblichkeit*).[22] "Living labor" is the "creative source of *surplus value*" (and is neither only nor strictly of mere *value*), surplus value that is the "Being" of capital or the consequence of the creative act of said labor: it is labor, then, the source of

189

"the value that valorizes" (Verwertung des Wertes), the fruit of accumulated surplus value.

It is, then, in the section of *Capital* dealing with the "transformation of money into capital" (*Die Verwandlung von Geld in Kapital*)[23] that Marx *overcomes and inverts Hegel*.[24] Hegel began his entire ontology (his *Logic*) with Being. Marx does it from Non-being, with "living labor" proceeding from the *exteriority* to circulation, from whence it is subsumed in "the labor process" of the *totality* of productive capital that only thus becomes money in capital by the *creation* of surplus by living labor. Now in the *interior* of capital, living labor is situated in the productive structure itself of capital but preserves a transcendental activity (as internal *alterity*) as the subjectivity of labor that is the creative source of surplus. Living labor has been in-corporated (subsumed: *Auf-gehoben* in German or as an act of *subsumption* in Latin). What *was the Other* (*Autrui*) of productive capital is now part, an essential determination and internal mediation of the creation of surplus: the person (living labor) has become a thing (mediation for the acquisition of surplus), and the thing has become a person (capital that claims to be the creator of surplus). This is the fetishistic inversion. Nothing of this is Hegelian, and it is strangely convergent with Levinasian thought on an ethical-phenomenological level.

To summarize, Marx inverts or overcomes the very root of Hegelian ontology following Schelling's path and thus coincides with Levinas in the thesis of a metaphysical overcoming of the ontology. Levinas titled his famous second book *Autrement qu'etre ou au-delà de l'essence* (*Otherwise Than Being, or Beyond Essence*). This is an anti-Hegelian title that coincides with the critical anti-Hegelian position of Marx. "Otherwise than being" precisely indicates the transcendence or the *alterity* of the *creative source* (*Quelle*) of Being, this being its effect. "Beyond essence" (as I have indicated, essence is for Hegel the reflection of Being and at the same time the *ground* [*Grund*] of the entity) once again indicates the same: the *creative source* is beyond the essence of the entity (*Dasein*). Hegelian noncreationism is inspired by Spinoza, but Marx departs from Schelling, instead, against the opinion of many Spinozist Marxists.[25]

The *pauper ante festum*, a term that originates from the medieval peasant class (or the colonial Indigenous peoples, such as the Aztecs or Incas in the silver mines of sixteenth-century Latin America), had a communitarian relationship among themselves before their exodus to the cities. From this *exteriority* to capital (in its beginning, money was not yet capital), the poor will be alienated by legalized domination through the labor contract, producing the subsumption of living labor *within* the totality of capital. This negation of the indicated exteriority inaugurates the fact that living labor becomes a mediation of the creation of surplus value. And here enters a new and clear distinction that will remain hidden to traditional Marxism. Marx indicates *explicitly* that in the "socially necessary time," the worker accomplishes the "reproduction" (*Reproduktion*) of the value of the salary, but in the surplus time (*Surpluszeit*) of the surplus work (*Surplusarbeit*)—during which capital pays no salary whatsoever to the worker—living labor brings about a "creation" (*Schöpfung*) of value from out of the nothing of capital. This is a strange use of the medieval thesis of *creatio ex nihilo*,[26] as has already been underscored in this epilogue: "What in the time of *living labor* (*lebendige Arbeit*) produces extra is not *reproduction* (*Reproduktion*), but rather a *new creation* (*neue Wertschöpfung*), and precisely a *new creation of values* (*neu Wertschöpfung*), given that the new time of work becomes objective in a use value."[27] And then, Marx continues, "The creation (*Schöpfung*) of value . . . is not seen as a *source* (*Quelle*) of surplus value. [Capital], since it cannot *create something out of nothing* (*nicht aus Nichts schaffen*), should find its objective conditions before it."[28] "Living labor" is situated in three moments: (1) as what is *prior* to capital and as *pauper ante festum* (Latin expression used by Marx), which is living labor as exteriority (coming from circulation, of feudalism or other systems, originally); (2) as what is *present* in the interior of the labor process or in the totality of capital as its essential "determination" (which we could indicate as the *pauper in festum*); and (3) as what happens in third place, *afterward*, the exteriority of the labor of the unemployed expelled by capital: the *lumpen* masses of the unemployed or underclass (*pauper post festum*), who today become agents among the people with social classes and within the numerous new social movements.

As I have explained these themes at length in my works, here I will not be able to reply to each one of the objections to my work that Mario Sáenz Rovner articulates. I am simply referring to the central thesis. I do not want to forgo indicating once again that the coincidence of Marx with Levinas is evident in the Semitic sources of the thinking of both, which is little known and little studied in the case of Marx—to which I have referred in my book *Las metáforas teológicas de Marx* (The theological metaphors of Marx)[29]—and which is more disconcerting than what I have said thus far against the *traditional* interpretations of Marx's work. I thus suggest new aspects that situate the debate on an interpretative horizon that remains to be explored.

4. ON CONSENSUAL VALIDITY AS THE EXPANSION OF THE ETHICS OF LIBERATION (UNTIL 1998)

In the very year that I finished definitively incorporating (up to the present) Marx's anthropological materialism into the philosophy of liberation, there began a new and passionate stage of this philosophical "school," thanks to the dialogue that I held during the following years with Karl-Otto Apel's precise and creative discourse ethics. It all began two weeks after the "fall of the Berlin Wall" in November of 1989, and it took place at the University of Freiburg (Germany) thanks to the initiative of a north-south dialogue that was organized by Raúl Fornet-Betancourt, a Cuban professor at the University of Bremen and editor of the journal *Concordia*. The dialogue that took place, in weekly seminars held alternating between Germany and Latin America, lasted until 2005.[30] Apel aimed to situate the ethics of liberation as complementary to discourse ethics. This slowly led to our defining more precisely the question to be elucidated. From the perspective of the philosophy of liberation, the grounding of a neo-Kantian consensual morality, as proposed and accepted by discourse ethics, was nonetheless insufficient in order to justify fully the ethical character (*eticidad*) of a decision or an act that should be not only formally valid but also just or good because of its content. Thanks to the advancement made before through the discovery of the material level in Marx, the community of communication, which reached the symmetrical participation of those affected through rational argumentation with a communitarian validity (quotidian, political or philosophical), according to our interpretation, also needed to integrate the *content* of the discussion under the vigilance of a normative principle, which for discourse ethics fell outside the horizon of morality and only in the hands of experts. It was thus that we discovered a second normative principle of ethics, but now *material* or of content, that grounds the obligation to affirm and make possible the growth of human life in community and ultimately of all of humanity (and not of the ethical values of particular cultures that are grounded in human life and nature) that determines the *formal* principle of consensus and that in turn was determined by it.

193

In addition, at a critical level, the ethics of liberation included the theme of the inevitable exteriority of those affected by the discussion that were not invited to the dialogue due to the ignorance of their existence or because of domination or exclusion that in fact denied their existence.

All of this and many other aspects were argued in response to Apel's objections to the philosophy of liberation in my 1998 work *Ethics of Liberation: In the Age of Globalization and Exclusion.*[31]

Thus the philosophy of liberation not only has been able to set out from the ontological phenomenology of Heidegger, criticized by Levinas and in addition by us in the Global South, but also has now subsumed the formalist analytical thinking in Apel's pragmatist neo-Kantian development. This allowed the philosophy of liberation to elaborate not only a morality but also a critical material ethics from the perspective of the oppressed, socially and geopolitically speaking. The assimilation of a formalist neo-Kantianism from the perspective of a *reinterpreted* Marxism of the oppressed was a fundamental step forward.

5. THE POLITICS OF LIBERATION (UNTIL 2018)

The new stage consisted in dealing with a politics of liberation for two decades, which was fundamentally possible thanks to the sufficient development of an ethics of liberation, which in turn assumed an anthropology, an ontology, an analytical logic, a philosophy of history, and many other novel aspects.

194   The normative principles, praxis, and ethical institutions with a universality claim were subsumed in the political sphere, which meant that the determination of the abstract ethical categories was now articulated on a more concrete horizon: that of politics. The relationship between ethics and politics does not simply result in morality giving ethical principles to politics (since politics does not have, as such, its own normative principles but instead borrows from ethics) or political ethics being a philosophical discipline juxtaposed to politics. It is a matter of diverse relationships. Morality, as the quotidian practical life in the life-world, transforms into ethics when it criticizes said morality in the name of its victims (such is Marx's conception in which ethics is the practical critique of the ruling morality). However, the indicated ethics deals, as a theoretical philosophical discipline, with universal and abstract problems such as the ethical praxis, institutions, and ethical principles properly said. Since there are practical spheres (such as spheres of the economy, family, gender, the political, etc.), these subsume the ethical principles and transform them into distinct normative principles in each sphere. Here "normative" replaces the word "ethical," although it retains the whole content of the obligating practical principle but now is determined by a conceptual content typical of the sphere. An ethical duty such as "thou shall not kill" in the political sphere becomes the normative principle that belongs to this sphere in the form of "thou shall not kill the political opponent," which is no longer abstract but concrete. In this way the whole question of *political* praxis, *political* institutions, and so on can be analyzed.[32] All of this has resulted in several publications, but the *Politics of Liberation* should be especially cited.[33]

Politics necessarily transverses through three *constellations*:

1. The first, dialectically *positive*, in the words of Max Horkheimer, orders the ruling political order, which can be described as the Global South taking into account political praxis, institutions, or normative principles that rule them, be they material, formal, or of feasibility. It is the biopolitical moment of the given system.

2. The second, dialectically critical-*negative*, is exercised when the first constellation has been fetishized (thus constituting itself into a necropolitical order of domination, such as the modern colonial system), a moment that Walter Benjamin thought about intensely. This concerns the deconstructive or de-structive stage, whether it is merely transformative or revolutionary. Heroes, who fulfill the materialist messianic normativity of the previously mentioned Benjamin, from the exteriority of the dominated and excluded, bring about a rupture within the ruling system and sometimes even produce a revolution (such as Cromwell's bourgeois revolution of the seventeenth century, the Leninist one of 1917, or the Cuban one of 1959). This is the de-struction of necropolitics, thus expanding upon Achille Mbembe's ideas. Some, however, stop at this constellation and deny the essential importance of political institutions (especially the state) as being intrinsically dominating. This is, for instance, the position of the extreme or anarchist left. It is here where Marx and Lenin opposed Bakunin.

3. The third, once the rupture has taken place, deals with the politics that evolves into a creative-*positive* constellation of the new institutions of the *new* state in biopolitics proper (not the Foucauldian version). This is the true political moment, the most complex and ambiguous, and it never achieves perfection. That is to say, since there is neither a perfect order nor a way we can anticipate it, failures are inevitable, and we must learn through the march toward the construction of a more just order (if the leadership-people symbiosis operates within what is possible, feasible, with extreme creativity in the face of Machiavelli's unforeseeable *fortuna*). This is a politics of liberation, an affirmation of the communitarian life—that is to say, of a biopolitics in its essential structural moments—departing from normative principles (the ethical principles subsumed in the political sphere) of the praxis and the institutions of liberation, beginning with the "*new type* of state" in the hands of the sovereign people previously dominated and excluded, as Lenin had already written in 1917.

6. EPISTEMOLOGICAL DECOLONIZATION AND ECOLOGICAL TRANSMODERNITY: BEYOND THE CAPITALOCENE

196 At the end of the 1960s—that is to say, sixty years ago—we discovered the need to undertake the practice of a philosophy rooted in the Global South. Against the majority opinion of the Eurocentric philosophical community (that exercises its profession in the south, in Latin America), it was customary to say that there was no original philosophy on our Latin American continent. That is to say, the philosophy of liberation originates in the proposal of a counterhypothesis. Not only has there been philosophy in that region from the beginning of the sixteenth century, but it is the home of modern philosophy in general. *The first debates of modern philosophy took place* in the Caribbean, dealing with several essential themes: Are the inhabitants of the American continent, its original peoples, human? Are the wars of conquest just, and is there a right to dominate the new territories, peoples, cultures, and states (such as those of the Aztecs, Mayas, or Incas) recently invaded? These questions are neglected by the so-called modern philosophy that allegedly began with only René Descartes in 1637 (with the *Discourse on Method*, taken as the beginning itself of modern philosophy and today still dominant in Eurocentrism), denying status and staking strict *philosophical* claim to the anthropological, ontological, ethical, and political dimensions of these questions. A head-on critique of the Eurocentric colonial system (at the same time that mercantile capitalism began, so did the racism of "whiteness," the *machista* gender domination of relationships with Indigenous women, and the annihilating contempt of cultures external to Europe, not only American but also Chinese, Hindustani, Muslim, and Bantu) began in 1511, with the preaching of Antonio de Montesinos in Santo Domingo, or in 1514, with Bartolomé de las Casas's conversion in Cuba, thus launching the struggle for the liberation of the original peoples of America (the Abya Yala); with those critiques, there began in general a critique of *modernity*.[34]

Years before the postmodern proposal (with Jean-François Lyotard in 1979) and the important discovery of *Orientalism* by Edward Said, the philosophy of liberation (at the end of the 1960s) had started, as I noted earlier, to critique modernity. For this philosophical school, modernity began in 1492, when Europe overcame the Ottoman-Muslim blockage of the Mediterranean, dominating oceanic navigation and accumulating the wealth being generated primarily in Latin America, allowing for the expansive presence of Spain and Portugal. That is to say, modernity began almost three centuries before the continental occupation of India and other countries in Asia and the subsequent Berlin Conference (at the end of the nineteenth century) in which the metropolises of Northern Europe distributed Africa among themselves.

"Epistemological decolonization," a movement that was so recently named (although it has many precedents, as we have shown: dependency theory, the philosophy of liberation, and Immanuel Wallerstein's theory of the world system), expands with the contribution of the contemporary Caribbean Marxism that demonstrates the importance of race in the process of global domination that was planetary at the time. When the Peruvian Aníbal Quijano takes up the discovery of the theme of slavery by Caribbean Marxism and of racism against the American Indigenous peoples as a criterion of social classification and domination, the hypothesis of "the coloniality of power" is thus born, which is then taken up by a whole team, among which we find many thinkers, such as Ramón Grosfoguel or Agustín Lao Montes.

The philosophy of liberation, in addition to being one of the pillars of this hypothesis for more than a half a century of work on the theme and as a critique of the latest creative stage of modernity (postmodernity), proposes to sketch the exhaustion of said capitalism; antiecological, with its particular machismo; racist; and so on modernity and imagines a new age of the world,[35] beyond modernity, which for the moment I have denominated with a negative connotation: *trans-modernity*.[36] This is a period in which the individualist limitations of liberalism, the exploitation of work by capitalism, and the de-struction of the conditions of possibility for the ecological survival of humanity will have to be overcome. This would be not to overcome capitalism so that modernity can actualize the goals that such an economic system made impossible but rather to understand modernity and capitalism as mutually codetermining, where the second is the economic system of the culture and way of living of the first.

In view of cultural diversity and the claim of Western culture of being global, which defines itself as superior thanks to universal homogenization, the philosophy of liberation proposes an intercultural dialogue in which each culture, by contributing its different experiences, can thus establish a dialogue that presupposes the effort to translate the wisdom of each one in order to be able to mutually enrich themselves on equal footing. The task of translation and the dialogue of mutual understanding will elaborate a pluriversal (not universal) culture enriched, as we indicated, by the disclosing of the millennial creation of each culture that instead of being impoverished in univocity (in identity/difference) will sustain an open, common similarity in an enriched distinction.

Lastly, the philosophy of liberation has been insisting on the radicality of life on planet earth (*Gaia*) and of human life, understanding it as the culmination and glory of life as such. When the human being, like no other living being, destroys the very conditions of the reproduction and increase of life in general, there begins an entropic process that instead of growing the quality and quantity of life, decreases the possibility of survival (of evolving its vitality). The entropic process that the human species, *Homo sapiens*, accomplished inevitably, which was done very slowly during the beginning of modernity (1492) but accelerated after the Industrial Revolution of the eighteenth century and exponentially in the last decades, unleashed a collective suicidal logic that will lead in the short term to the extinction of the *Homo sapiens* species and together with it a large number of other living beings of the flora and fauna and the very conditions that life itself produced on the planet earth so that life could exist and evolve. If we name geologically the Anthropocene as the age that began two thousand years ago, during which human beings transformed the earth's surface, its atmosphere, and the other conditions that make life possible, we term the *capitalocene* as the last five hundred years of modernity under capitalist rationality, which multiplies incrementally global entropy through the irrational use of technology (which is not how we will show the ultimate ground of the ecological catastrophe), accelerating the process of the extinction of life. A simple argument can be formulated in the following way.

Since the capitalist market is the place where commodities offered by different industries compete, in which the capitals that offer the cheapest commodities (less value) are the successful ones in this competition, this better price is achieved thanks to the better technology that decreases the portion of the salary of the worker that goes into the price of the commodity. Said reduction in the price of the commodity is achieved because of the better technology—that is to say, by the technology that produces the same commodity with less use of time and raw material. Since the rationality of capital is grounded in the increase of the rate of profit of the process of the selling of commodities, it is necessary to develop better technology than that of the other competitors in the market. But the *better* technology in capitalism is measured by the reduction in the price of the production of commodities and not by how it contributes to the preservation of the conditions of the reproduction of life on earth. If, however, the goal were to aim at an ecological technology, a long time would be needed, a time in which meanwhile the other competitor destroyed the capitalist that sought to use technology with ecological criteria. In conclusion, the adoption of technology that allows the increase in the rate of profit for capital must be incorporated by the logic of capital in the productive process, even if it is antiecological and against the affirmation and increase of life. This is to say, the ecological danger is not found primarily in technology but rather in the criteria by means of which technology is introduced in the production of capital. In a sentence, capital is, in its essence, what opposes the existence of life on earth itself!

Translated by Eduardo Mendieta

NOTES

1. My works can be found at http://www.enriquedussel.com. My selected works have been published by the Editorial Docencia, Buenos Aires. Thirty volumes of my works are available in the philosophy section of the website.
2. The annual *Semanas* were published in the journal *Stromata* (Buenos Aires).
3. See Enrique Dussel, "Metafísica del sujeto y liberación," in *Temas de filosofía latinoamericana* (Buenos Aires: Sudamericana, 1971), 27–32.

4. Enrique Dussel, "A Manera de Manifiesto," in *Hacia una filosofía latinoamericana de la liberación* (Buenos Aires: Editorial Bonum, 1973), on the book's back cover. See also the chapter "La filosofía de la liberación," in Enrique Dussel, Eduardo Mendieta, and Carmen Bohórquez, eds., *El pensamiento filosófico latinoamericano, del Caribe y "Latino" (1300–2000)* (Mexico City: Siglo XXI, 2011), 399–412.

5. Enrique Dussel, *Para una ética de la liberación Latinoamericana*, vols. 1–2 (Buenos Aires: Siglo XXI, 1973). On the website, the five volumes are listed as book 21 (1973), book 22 (1973), book 27 (1977), book 33 (1979), and book 34 (1980), all of them written between 1970 and 1975, before the exile in Mexico.

6. See the works from this period at https://www.enriquedussel.com/Libros_O Selectas.html.

7. On the website, these works are listed as book 4 (1969), book 26 (1975), book 23 (1974), book 17 (1972), and book 18 (1972).

8. On the website, see the related materials.

9. See, e.g., the following chapters: 9 ("Marx contra Hegel") and 10 ("El hegelianismo de Marx") in Enrique Dussel, *El último Marx (1863–1882)* (Mexico City: Siglo XXI, 1990), 334–450; Enrique Dussel, "The Exteriority in Marx's Thought," in *Toward an Unknown Marx* (London: Routledge, 2001); and so on.

10. See Enrique Dussel, *La producción teórica de Marx: Un comentario a los "Grundrisse"* (Mexico City: Siglo XXI, 1985), 138.

11. This text can be found in Karl Marx, *Grundrisse*, vol. 3 (Berlin: Dietz Verlag, 1974), 203.

12. This is the "transformation of money into capital" (*Die Verwandlung von Geld in Kapital*), the second section of chapter 1 of volume 1 of Karl Marx, *Das Kapital: Kritik der politischen Ökonomie*, vol. 2, part 6 of *MEGA* (Berlin: Dietz Verlag, 1987), as we will see.

13. I explained all of this in the five volumes already cited that were devoted to an unusual interpretation of Marx that would seem to misrecognize the author of the critique of my interpretation.

14. Friedrich Engels and Karl Marx, *Marx-Engels-Werke*, vol. 29 (Berlin: Dietz Verlag, 1978), 550.

15. See Dussel, *El último Marx*, chap. 10, sec. 3.

16. This is a frequent expression in Marx. For example, "Labor posits itself objectively but posits this objectivity as its own nonbeing (*Nichtsein*), or as the being of its nonbeing—of capital" (Sie setzt sich objektiv, aber sie setzt diese ihre Objektivität als ihr eignes Nichtsein oder als das Sein ihres Nichtseins—des Kapitals); Marx, *Grundrisse*, part 4, the chapter on the "Reproduction and Accumulation of Capital," 358. My translation.

17. For Hegel, "substance" is the thing inasmuch as it is the cause of an effect; see G. W. F. Hegel, *Enzyklopädie der philosophischen Wissenschaften*, *Werke*, vol. 8 (Frankfurt am Main: Suhrkamp Verlag, 1970), sec. 153 and following.

18. Marx, *Kapital*, vol. 1, chap. 4, sec. 3, 183. The translation is by Samuel Moore and Edward Aveling and edited by Frederick Engels and can be found at https://www.marxists.org/archive/marx/works/1867-c1/ch06.htm. The original passage reads, "Um aus dem Verbrauch einer Waare Weth herauszuziehn, müßten unser Geldbesitzer so glücklich sein innerhalb der Circulationssphäre, aus dem Markt, einer Waare zu entdecken, deren Gebrauchswerth selbst die eingthümliche

Beschaffenheit besäße, Quelle von Werth zu sein, deren wirklicher Verbrauch also selbt Vergegenständlichung vor Arbiet ware, daher Wertschöpfung."

19. Marx, *Kapital*, vol. 1, chap. 4, 191. The original passage reads, "Der ehemalige Geldbesitzer schreitet voran als Kapitalist, der Arbeitskraft-Besitzer folgt ihm nach las sein Arbeiter." The worker is metaphorically presented as the sacrificial lamb: "The one with an air of importance, smirking, intent on business; the other, timid and holding back, like the one who is bringing his own hide to the market and has nothing to expect but—a hiding" (der Eine bedeutungsvoll schmunzelnd und geschäftseinfrig, der Andre scheu, widerstresbsam, wie Jemand, der seine eigne Haut zu Mark getragen und nicht Andres zu erwarten hat als die–Gerberei); ibid., 192. Even metaphorically, the ship is introduced from *outside* (*exteriority of the Other*) the *inside* of the factory, of capital.

20. Hegel, *Enzyklopädie*, sec. 86, 182; my translation. The passage reads, "Das *reine Sein* macht den Anfang, weil so es sowohl reiner Gedanke als das unbestimmte, einchfache Unmittelbare ist."

21. This formulation is not traditional, given that for it, and for Hegel, divinity was being. Schelling writes that the divine (God) is the "free original cause"; Friedrich Wilhelm Joseph von Schelling, *Philosophie der Offenbarung (1841–1842)*, lecture 12 (Frankfurt am Main: Suhrkamp Verlag, 1977), 305. And "In the universal doctrine of creation [*Schöpfung*], it is said that something was created out of nothing"; ibid., 179–89.

22. This is a question that Marx formulated a few lines later, after the text from *Kapital* we cited.

23. This is part 2 of vol. 1 of *Kapital*.

24. This is not the simplistic opposition of Marx's materialism to Hegel's idealism.

25. Hegel writes, "The ground (*Grundlage*) of every determination is the negation (*omnis determinatio est negatio*, as Spinoza says)"; Hegel, *Enzyklopädie*, sec. 91, Zusatz, 196. Even the entity (*Dasein*) originates in the first determination of Being; there is no creation but the negation of the source itself (Being) by itself: Spinoza. At the very least on this thesis, Marx coincides with Levinas and not with Hegel.

26. See chapters 8 and 9 of Dussel, *El último Marx*. The texts are clear: "The only use value that can constitute itself as opposed term to capital [the totality] is [living] labor, and precisely the labor that *creates value (wertschaffende)*"; Marx, *Grundrisse*, vol. 2, 183.

27. Marx, *Grundrisse*, vol. 3, 264–65.

28. Ibid., vol. 4, 354. Since it does not find these objective conditions, it attempts, according to Marx's interpretation, to attribute to itself surplus (as its ground) and gain (as its superficial phenomenon) from out of nothing, which is reproached as a fallacy.

29. Enrique Dussel, *Las metáforas teológicas de Marx* (Estella, Navarra: Editorial Verbo Divino, 1993).

30. See https://www.enriquedussel.com/Libros_OSelectas.html, book 55 (2005).

31. See book 50, in English and Spanish.

32. See Enrique Dussel, *14 tesis de ética: Hacia la esencia del pensamiento crítico* (Madrid: Editorial Trotta, 2016).

33. On my website, see book 56, *Twenty Thesis of Politics* (2006); book 58, *Politics of Liberation*, vol. 1 (2007); book 61, *Politics of Liberation*, vol. 2 (2009); and in 2020, *Politics of Liberation*, vol. 3, will be published.

34. See my recent works on my website: *The Anti-Cartesian Meditations and Transmodernity*, book 69 (2019); and *Filosofías del Sur, Descolonización y Transmodernidad*, book 67 (2015).
35. See *Filosofía de la cultura y la Liberación*, book 57 (2006).
36. See Linda Martín Alcoff, "Enrique Dussel's Transmodernism," *TRANSMODERNITY: Journal of Peripheral Cultural Production of the Luso-Hispanic World* 1, no. 3 (Spring 2012): 60–68, https://escholarship.org/uc/item/58k9k17t.

CONTRIBUTORS

LINDA MARTÍN ALCOFF is professor of philosophy at Hunter College and the Graduate Center, CUNY. She is a former president of the American Philosophical Association, Eastern Division. Her recent books include *Rape and Resistance: Understanding the Complexities of Sexual Violation* (Polity, 2018); *The Future of Whiteness* (Polity, 2015); and *Visible Identities: Race, Gender and the Self* (Oxford, 2006), which won the Frantz Fanon Award in 2009. For more information, go to www.alcoff.com.

AMY ALLEN is liberal arts professor of philosophy and women's, gender, and sexuality studies and head of the Philosophy Department at Penn State. Her recent books include *The End of Progress: Decolonizing the Normative Foundations of Critical Theory* (Columbia University Press, 2016); *Critical Theory Between Klein and Lacan: A Dialogue*, coauthored with Mari Ruti (Bloomsbury, 2019); and *Critique on the Couch: Why Critical Theory Needs Psychoanalysis* (Columbia University Press, forthcoming). She has also coedited, with Eduardo Mendieta, *From Alienation to Forms of Life: The Critical Theory of Rahel Jaeggi* (Penn State University Press, 2018); *The Cambridge Habermas Lexicon* (Cambridge University Press, 2019); and *Justification and Emancipation: The Critical Theory of Rainer Forst* (Penn State University Press, 2019).

DON THOMAS DEERE is adjunct professor of philosophy at Fordham University. He received his Ph.D. with distinction in philosophy from DePaul University and previously taught as visiting assistant professor of philosophy at Loyola Marymount University. His work on Latinx and Latin American philosophy, decolonial theory, and continental philosophy has been published or is forthcoming in venues such as *Inter-American Journal of Philosophy*, *Journal of World Philosophies*, *Oxford Bibliographies in Latino Studies*, and *The Cambridge Foucault Lexicon*. He is the cotranslator of Santiago Castro-Gómez's *Zero-Point*

Hubris: Science, Race, and Enlightenment in New Granada (Rowman & Littlefield International, forthcoming). Presently Deere is completing his book manuscript, *The Invention of Order: Modernity, the Américas,* 204 *and the Coloniality of Space.*

ENRIQUE DUSSEL is emeritus professor of the Metropolitan Autonomous University in Mexico and distinguished chair in the Faculty of Philosophy and Letters (UNAM). He is one of the founders of the Latin American philosophy and theology of liberation and a major figure in the development of world philosophies. He has been a guest professor at Harvard, Duke, Johns Hopkins, Rutgers, University of South Africa, University of Cologne, Goethe University in Frankfurt, University of Vienna, the Catholic University of Louvain, and Korea University (Seoul), among many others. He is the author of more than fifty books, among which are *Philosophy of Liberation* (Orbis Books, 1985); *Ethics and Community* (Orbis Books, 1988); *The Invention of the Americas: Eclipse of "the Other" and the Myth of Modernity* (Continuum, 1995); *The Underside of Modernity: Apel, Ricoeur, Rorty, Taylor, and the Philosophy of Liberation* (Humanities Press, 1996); *Politics of Liberation: A Critical World History* (SCM, 2011); *Ethics of Liberation: In the Age of Globalization and Exclusion* (Duke University Press, 2013); and *Filosofías del Sur: Descolonización y Transmodernidad* (Akal, 2015).

OSCAR GUARDIOLA-RIVERA is professor of political philosophy and human rights at the University of London, Birkbeck College. His *What If Latin America Ruled the World?* (Bloomsbury, 2010) won the 2010 Frantz Fanon Award and *Story of a Death Foretold* (Bloomsbury, 2013) was short-listed for the 2014 Bread and Roses Award. Both were selected among the best nonfiction books of the year for 2010 and 2015 by the *Financial Times* and the *Observer*. In 2017 he cocurated the Global Art Forum, which premiered his play *Funk!* He has appeared in major literary festivals around the world, including Hay, Jaipur, London Literature Festival, Beyond Borders, and Edinburgh, and curates the yearly Focus of the Funk art and thought event in London. He is a fellow of the Royal Society for the Advancement of the Arts. His most recent publication is

A Defence of Armed Art/Struggle (Universidad de Bogotá Jorge Tadeo Lozano, 2019).

EDUARDO MENDIETA is professor of philosophy and affiliated faculty at the School of International Affairs and the Bioethics Program at Penn State University. He is the author of *The Adventures of Transcendental Philosophy* (Rowman & Littlefield, 2002) and *Global Fragments: Globalizations, Latinamericanisms, and Critical Theory* (SUNY Press, 2007). He is also coeditor with Jonathan VanAntwerpen of *The Power of Religion in the Public Sphere* (Columbia University Press, 2011), with Craig Calhoun and Jonathan VanAntwerpen of *Habermas and Religion* (Polity, 2013), and with Stuart Elden of *Reading Kant's Geography* (SUNY Press, 2011). Most recently, he coedited with Amy Allen *From Alienation to Forms of Life: The Critical Theory of Rahel Jaeggi* (Penn State University Press, 2018), *The Cambridge Habermas Lexicon* (Cambridge University Press, 2019), and *Justification and Emancipation: The Critical Theory of Rainer Forst* (Penn State University Press, 2019). He is the 2017 recipient of the Frantz Fanon Outstanding Achievements Award.

MARIO SÁENZ ROVNER is professor of philosophy at Le Moyne College. His research interests include dialectics and critical social theory, which encompasses the various generations of the Frankfurt School but also the Latin American philosophy of liberation. He is the author of *The Identity of Liberation in Latin American Thought: Latin American Historicism and the Phenomenology of Leopoldo Zea* (Lexington, 1999); editor of *Latin American Perspectives on Globalization: Ethics, Politics, Alternative Visions* (Rowman & Littlefield, 2002); and author of articles on Latin American philosophy and critical theory.

ALEJANDRO A. VALLEGA is professor of philosophy at the University of Oregon. His work focuses on the philosophy of liberation, decolonial philosophy, Latin American popular and Indigenous thought, continental philosophy, and aesthetics. Professor Vallega is editor of the World Philosophies Series, published by Indiana University Press, and U.S. coordinator of the Sociedad de Filosofía y Liberación (FyL).

206

He is the author of *Heidegger and the Question of Space: Thinking on Exilic Grounds* (Penn State University Press, 1999); *Sense and Finitude: Encounters at the Limit of Language, Art, and the Political* (SUNY Press, 2009–10); *Latin American Philosophy: From Identity to Radical Exteriority* (Indiana University Press, 2014); and *Tiempo y Liberación* (Time and liberation; Editorial AKAL, 2020). He is also the editor of the English edition of Enrique Dussel's *Ethics of Liberation* (Duke University Press, 2013) and coeditor of *Anti-Cartesian Meditations and Transmodernity: From the Perspective of Philosophy of Liberation* (AMRIT, Decolonizing the Mind Series, 2018).

JORGE ZÚÑIGA M. is currently professor in the Faculty of Philosophy and Literature (UNAM), where he teaches contemporary practical philosophy, Latin American philosophy, and contemporary critiques of neoliberalism. He received his Ph.D. from the Goethe University in Frankfurt am Main, Germany (2011–16), participating primarily in research colloquia with Matthias Lutz-Bachmann (2011–16) and Axel Honneth (2013–16). From 2011 to 2015, he was the recipient of a scholarship from the German Academic Exchange Service (DAAD). With Enrique Dussel, from 2017 to 2019, he coordinated and taught the postgraduate seminar Critical Political Philosophy: Criticism and Deconstruction of the Political Order. He has published various articles and chapters on practical philosophy in both Spanish and English and delivered various conferences in Spanish, German, and English in forums and international seminars as well.

INDEX

Page numbers with an *f* refer to a figure or a caption; *n* refers to an endnote.